Marine Molluscan Remains
from
Franchthi Cave

Excavations at Franchthi Cave, Greece

T. W. Jacobsen, General Editor

FASCICLE 4

Marine Molluscan Remains
from
Franchthi Cave

JUDITH C. SHACKLETON

With a Report on the Oxygen Isotope Analyses of Marine Molluscs from Franchthi Cave by

M. R. Deith and
N. J. Shackleton

INDIANA UNIVERSITY PRESS
Bloomington & Indianapolis

Manufactured in the United States of America

Library of Congress Cataloging-in-Publication Data

Shackleton, Judith C.
Marine molluscan remains from Franchthi Cave.

(Excavations at Franchthi Cave, Greece; fasc. 4)
Bibliography: p.
1. Franchthi Cave Site (Greece). 2. Animal remains
(Archaeology)—Greece—Franchthi Cave Site. 3. Mollusks—
Greece—Franchthi Cave Site. 4. Greece—Antiquities.
I. Shackleton, N. J. II. Deith, M. R. (Margaret R.). Oxygen
isotope analyses of marine molluscs from Franchthi Cave. 1988.
III. Title. IV. Title: Oxygen isotope analyses of marine
molluscs from Franchthi Cave. V. Series.
GN816.F73S52 1988   938   87-45115
ISBN 0-253-31976-5 (pbk.)

CONTENTS

FIGURES

TEXT

APPENDIXES

TABLES

TEXT

APPENDIXES

PLATES

ACKNOWLEDGMENTS

During the time when, as conditions allowed, this study was undertaken, many people helped me and contributed to my interest in and understanding of the marine molluscan remains from Franchthi Cave. It is clear, however, that the first acknowledgment must be to Professor T. W. Jacobsen who not only entrusted the Franchthi marine molluscs to me for study, but who has been most generous in allowing me to publish aspects of my work before the final publication of the excavation results has appeared. I am indeed grateful to him for all aspects of his continuing support and have also, like many others, benefited from the atmosphere in the group he assembled to work on the site and on its finds.

Secondly, I should like to thank Dr. Nicholas J. Shackleton for his guidance and for the pleasure of three earlier field seasons' work, and for opening his bottom drawer to give me his available records. I trust that when reading this account he will think that they have been put to good use. I should also like to thank Professor Tj. H. van Andel to whom I spoke of my dream to produce a map which would show where specific types of shellfish could have been collected by the prehistoric inhabitants of Franchthi. I am grateful for his interest and collaboration in turning this into the reality of the maps presented here.

In the field in 1979, I was for a short time assisted by Kate Clark and Edith Wilson and for a longer period in 1981 by Janet Douglas. I am grateful for their assistance.

The staff of the mollusc section of the British Museum (Natural History) has been most helpful. In particular, Mrs. Morris and Ms. Way have borne the brunt of my descents and have always made me welcome. To them I offer my thanks, as well as to Dr. Evans for the identifications he has provided. I am also grateful for the help I received from the Smithsonian Institution in Washington, D.C.

In Cambridge, I have received editorial assistance from Ann Johnston and have benefited from the help of Dr. John Cherry, Mr. Sebastian Payne, and especially Dr. Margaret Deith. Apart from discussing problems of seasonality, she has taught me much about molluscan studies in general. Sadly far less accessible for geographic reasons have been Drs. K. D. Vitelli and C. Perlès. Despite this drawback, I have found them generous and stimulating colleagues and have received much support from them. I should like to thank both my colleagues on the Franchthi Project and Drs. C. Sancetta and S. Karl for running the factor analysis computations. I should also like to acknowledge the support I have received through grants made to Professor Jacobsen by the National Science Foundation, the National Endowment for the Humanities, and the Indiana University Foundation. The final acknowledgment is due to Dr. Betty Meehan whose work on the shellfish-gathering habits of the Anbara in Northern Australia has proved such a stimulus to studies of molluscan remains on prehistoric sites.

This manuscript was initially prepared in December, 1982, and subsequently revised and submitted in March, 1985. Since then I have made no substantive changes in the text.

JUDITH C. SHACKLETON

FOREWORD

This is the last of the four fascicles that comprise the initial installment of the Level One series of publications on the Indiana University excavations at Franchthi Cave. Like its immediate predecessor (Fascicle 3:Perlès 1987), it is a presentation and analysis of a substantial body of excavated material. In this case, however, the remains are bioarchaeological rather than artifactual, and their distribution is therefore described in terms of biostratigraphic *zones* rather than ethnostratigraphic *phases* (cf. Fascicle 1:Jacobsen and Farrand 1987).

The corpus of material that makes up the sample reported here is the largest of its kind yet excavated in Greece. This study thus becomes not only the fullest treatment of marine molluscan remains from an archaeological context in Greece, but it is also the first volume devoted exclusively to the publication of such remains from the whole of the eastern Mediterranean region. As such, it represents an important beginning in the reporting of this long-neglected category of archaeological material.

The role of shellfish and shellfish collecting is of potentially great significance in arriving at an understanding of past subsistence practices, seasonal adaptations, and environmental conditions, all issues of primary concern to our project. Yet, in order to deal fully with those problems, this report can not stand alone. It must be taken into consideration along with other studies in this series of publications. Examples of the latter are van Andel's reconstruction of the regional landscape through time (Fascicle 2:van Andel and Sutton 1987) and the forthcoming studies of Hansen on the carbonized plant remains, Payne on the mammalian fauna, Rose on the fish bones, and, not least, Whitney-Desautels on the land snails.

Marine shells were also an important source of raw material for other, non-dietary, purposes. This dimension of their role at prehistoric Franchthi is only partially touched upon in this volume (see Chapter 7 and Appendixes D and E), but more can be expected on this subject in subsequent fascicles.

The reader will note that this fascicle actually consists of two reports. That of Judith Shackleton makes up the bulk of the volume (Chapters 1-8 and Appendixes A-E), while the isotopic analyses of Margaret Deith and Nicholas Shackleton appear in a final chapter (9) and Appendix F. Though written independently and not conceived as integrated parts of a whole, they have been united here for obvious reasons. In accordance with the wishes of the authors, the general editor has largely maintained their organizational structure and autonomy. The reader should be alert to this independence, especially as it is reflected by differences in sampling procedures and chronological framework employed in the two reports. As regards chronology, the relative sequence followed here is site specific and generally coincides with that of our preliminary publications (e.g., Jacobsen 1976) — with the exception of a "Final Mesolithic" phase in addition to an "Upper Mesolithic" (for more on which see Perlès, forthcoming). In any case, as with all fascicles in this level of the final publication series, the most precise indicators of chronological comparability throughout the site are the individual excavation unit numbers. The two manuscripts essentially attained their present form by August, 1986, and have not been revised by the authors since that time.

Finally, the general editor once again wishes to express his gratitude to those who had a major hand in the preparation of this manuscript for publication: Ms. Frances Huber, Mr. Jeffrey Harlig, and Ms. Mary Ann Weddle of the Program in Classical Archaeology at Indiana University and Mr. John Gallman and his staff at the Indiana University Press. All photographs in Plates 1-3 were taken and printed by Professor Reginald Heron, with the exception of Plate 3c which was done by Mr. Dennis Blackburn. Much of this work was again made possible by generous funding from the National Science Foundation, the National Endowment for the Humanities, and the Indiana University Foundation (Edward A. Schrader Endowment).

T. W. JACOBSEN

PART I

Judith C. Shackleton

CHAPTER ONE

Introduction
The Site and the Methodology

Though bioarchaeological studies are not new (e.g., Clark 1954), their impact, in some areas, has taken a long time to be felt. In Greece, with its long history of exploration of Classical and Bronze Age sites (and reliance on Classical authors), it is perhaps less surprising that only recently have workers begun to incorporate biological studies in the general attempt to interpret excavated sites. In particular, few attempts have been made to utilize marine molluscan remains. The most influential exception has proved to be N. J. Shackleton's (1968) study of the marine shell found at Saliagos, which has become a primary reference for all subsequent studies of Greek molluscan material. Generally speaking, however, such studies as have hitherto been published have tended to be of the checklist type (e.g., Gejvall 1969; Reese 1978). An approach such as that is less likely to throw light on past human activity than more integrated studies. In part this situation has arisen from archaeologists' reluctance or inability to involve their colleagues from other fields in the pursuit of archaeologically interesting problems. As a result, an increasing number of archaeologists themselves are working directly with faunal and botanical remains, and more integrated studies are now appearing. It is the intention of this report to use the marine molluscan remains found at Franchthi Cave as a medium through which to monitor human activity in the prehistoric past.

Marine shell usually preserves well and so has a high archaeological "visibility." As studies of marine shell proceeded, it was noted that vast quantities of shellfish were needed to provide the nutritional requirements of even a small group of people (Bailey 1975). Similarly, it was recognized that the presence of a few larger fish vertebrae from species such as tunny, or the odd seal bone, though inconspicuous, if not invisible, amongst heaps of shell, could indeed represent the major dietary contribution at a particular site. Consequently, the presence of a certain quantity of marine shell at a given site should not necessarily be seen as representing a quantitatively significant part of the prehistoric diet, nor does it readily contribute to an understanding of man's past foraging strategies.

Recent studies have turned away from attempting straightforward estimates of the number of calories contributed by marine molluscs to the total diet. More effort has been devoted to lines of research such as determining the season at which shellfish were collected (N. J. Shackleton 1973; Deith 1983a). It is now recognized that, though shellfish may not play a substantial role in terms of the total diet of a group over a whole year, they may have had considerable importance in a particular season and so may have enabled the group to follow a specific living pattern or at least to do so with much greater security (Rowley-Conwy 1981). There is an increasing interest in understanding the reasons that underlie behavioral patterns, as perceived through the archaeological record. It is in such a framework that this study of the Franchthi marine shell has proceeded.

Since it very rapidly became apparent that none of the marine shell excavated at Franchthi Cave represented deposits which could be termed "middens" and that there was a relatively small quantity of shell (about 64,000 were analyzed for this study), the main emphasis of the study has been to note changes in the molluscan assemblage through the history of the occupation of the cave and adjacent areas and to attempt to account for the patterns observed.

The method adopted here has been to reconstruct the shorelines for different points in time, together with information about coastal environments and molluscan habitats. This provides the baseline for establishing what was environmentally available if one wished to collect shellfish. With this anchor it is possible to compare the sequence of shell species actually found at the site with what might have been readily available from the adjacent coasts, and so monitor the extent to which selective gathering of shellfish can be observed. It then emerges that rarely did the inhabitants of Franchthi simply collect what was there to be picked up and eaten. This approach of shoreline reconstruction and comparison of postulated environmentally available options in relation to shellfish actually selected allows one to monitor selectivity in shellfish gathering and to put forward hypotheses to account for the observed gathering patterns.

One of the exciting dimensions of the excavation of Franchthi Cave has been the number of specialists working on a very wide range of materials, both artifactual and non-artifactual. Publication policy demands that the various studies be presented at this level, as this one is, in isolation from each other and from the interpretation of the site as a whole (cf. Jacobsen and Farrand 1987). That decision has affected the direction and scope of the ensuing report. Since the patterns of shellfish collecting cannot be put into the context of the use of the site as a whole, the material will be presented here as a discrete entity.

THE SITE

Franchthi Cave is located in the southern Argolid, Greece (Figure 1). The cave itself is at the end of a rocky headland (maximum elevation 176 m) at the entrance to Kiladha Bay on the Gulf of Argos, where the sea meets a steep, rocky shore just outside the entrance to the cave. However, for much of the occupation of the cave, the sea was some distance away from the site owing to a major lowering of sea level during the last glaciation. The cave is directly opposite the village of Kiladha and about five kilometers north-northwest of Kranidhi.

The cave itself is in Mesozoic limestone and is oriented northwest-southeast. It is more than 150 m in length and has a width at the mouth of about 30 m. The mouth of the cave is about 12.5 m above present sea level. At the very back of the cave is a small pool of brackish water. There are, and always have been throughout the occupation of the site, fresh water springs in the area, some of them below present sea level. During the history of the cave there have been several rockfalls, some of them severely affecting its configuration. The most impressive of these formed a "window" in the roof of the cave near its center. There was also a series of brow collapses during the prehistoric occupation of the cave, at least one of which seems to have occurred in the Neolithic.

Excavations were carried out at the site between 1967 and 1976 by T. W. Jacobsen of Indiana University (Jacobsen 1969, 1973, 1976, 1979, 1984). As part of the work on these excavations the marine molluscs from the site were studied in six seasons over a period of 13 years, first by Nicholas J. Shackleton with my assistance in 1968, 1969, and 1973, and subsequently in 1979, 1980, and 1981 by me alone. Dr. Shackleton has generously made all his data available to me for the present study, but both the approach adopted and the

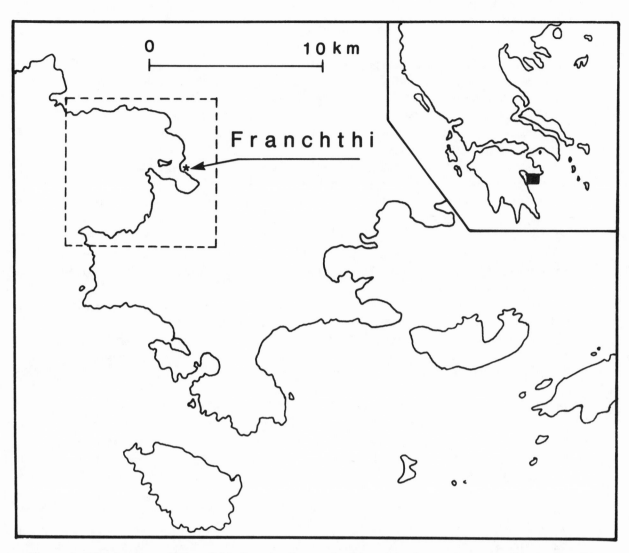

Figure 1. The location of Franchthi Cave in Greece (*inset*) and in the southern Argolid. Dashed line marks the area shown in Figures 8-13.

interpretation put forward here are mine alone and no doubt have taken a turn different from the one he might have followed. In the initial season the molluscs were studied at the dig house in Porto Kheli, and in the following two seasons in Kiladha. Recently (1979-1981) the material was more favorably housed in Kranidhi and studied there. In 1983 the marine molluscan collection was transferred to the Nafplion Museum where it is now securely housed in rather cramped conditions.[1]

A sketch plan of the site (Figure 2) illustrates the position of the main trenches inside the cave and outside on the shore, the "Paralia." [For detailed plans of the site and the excavated areas, see Jacobsen and Farrand 1987.—EDITOR] The trenches selected for study inside the cave were those offering the longest sequences of marine shell, while outside those likely to provide the most informative material were chosen. The selection was also influenced by two other factors: whether at the time of the initial analyses the trench was thought to have a secure, undisturbed stratigraphy; and secondly, whether the material had been water-sieved.

As work progressed the significance of this second factor became increasingly clear. While the general importance of this method of handling excavated material has been discussed elsewhere (Payne 1972; Diamant 1979), Appendix A cites an example to illustrate the particular relevance of this method to the study of marine molluscs. The selected trenches were: H1A, H1B, FAS, and FAN, all inside the cave, and L5, O5, Q5S, Q5N, and QR5 outside the cave. It did not prove practical, for various reasons, to look at every excavated unit from all trenches selected (see Appendix C).

The final point I should like to make here may appear self-evident, but it has crucial importance in limiting the scope of this study. Marine shell contains no direct chronological information. In other words, a limpet is a limpet and, outside its find context, it cannot be dated without recourse to geochemical techniques. In practice, this has meant that it is necessary to work with large suites of excavated units at least approximately in stratigraphic sequence before changes in shellfish patterns could be confidently distinguished from background "noise." Since the *stratigraphic* sequence for the trenches selected inside the cave is approximately the same as the *numerical* sequence of excavated units, there is no major problem for those trenches. This good sequence has been used to establish the zonation of shell assemblages and their change with time. Unfortunately, the assemblages themselves cannot be used independently to establish stratigraphic sequences. At the time of analysis of the molluscan remains from the Paralia trenches, no adequate independent stratigraphy had been determined to enable the detailed work on molluscan assemblages to proceed. This part of the study must wait until such a stratigraphic sequencing of the excavation units has been established (cf. Jacobsen and Farrand 1987; Wilkinson and Duhon, forthcoming). The data are presented in numerical order of excavation units in Appendix C.

METHODOLOGY

It is perhaps opportune to state at this point that it has been a guiding principle during my studies to consider the nature and quality of the information likely to be retrieved before deciding what parts of the excavated sequence should be studied and at what level. Since the minimum size of the identifiable and countable fragments of shell is both species-dependent and often quite small (ca. 5 mm), the emphasis has mainly been on obtaining sequences of shell from those trenches where the material had been water-sieved. Most effort has been invested in those species which had obviously been intentionally and frequently collected for food or for some other utilitarian purpose.

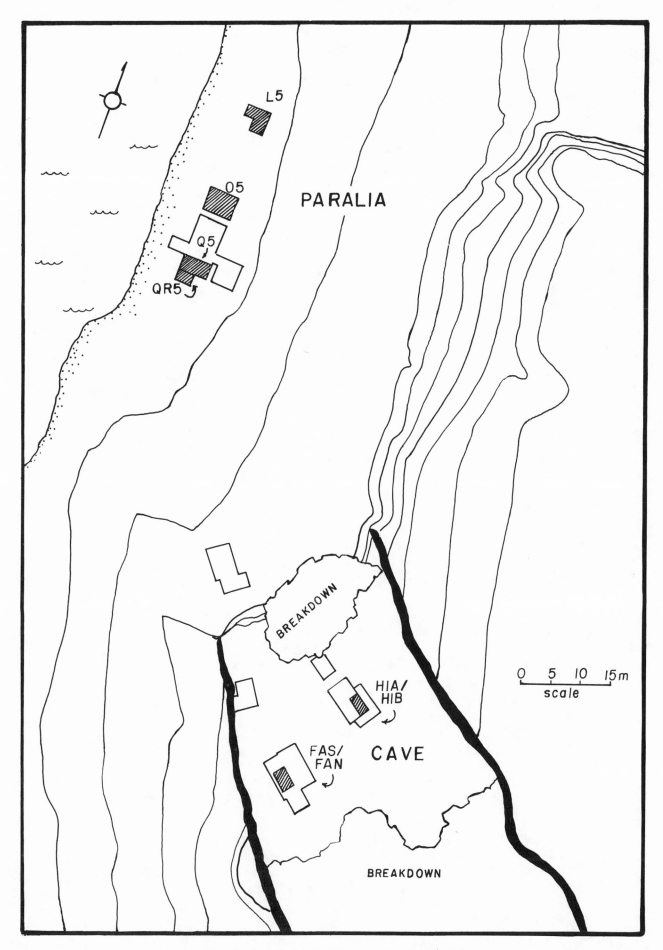

Figure 2. Sketch plan of site showing trenches discussed in the text.

The primary data have been acquired by identifying and counting the marine molluscs present in the excavated deposits from Franchthi Cave. Though specialist studies have been undertaken by others, such as [18]0 analysis to determine seasonality by Deith and N. J. Shackleton (Chapter 9), the presentation here rests on straightforward work carried out in the field. The primary counts were made in Greece; subsequent identifications and analysis have been conducted mainly in England.

In Greece, bags of marine shell were first examined to determine what fragments could be identified to species or genus level, and from those what could be termed "countable." Whole shells obviously did not present the latter problem. Both whole shells and countable fragments were then recorded in order to build the profiles presented in this account.[2]

"Countable" fragments were defined according to whether the species was a bivalve or a gastropod. This approach can only give a basic minimum number for each species present. Gastropods are quite straightforward. The tip, or *apex,* of the individual has been considered the countable part of the shell. For bivalves the situation is more complex. With these, the area of the hinge, the *umbo,* was the portion counted. This part of the shell, even in thin-shelled species, seems relatively resistant to fracture. It does mean, however, that one umbo is counted per valve so that a *single bivalve individual* would theoretically yield a count of two. Throughout this study counts of bivalves are given in terms of *single valves.* In other words, in order to obtain an estimate of the minimum number of specimens (MNI) the counts should be halved. Koike (1979), however, has shown some of the pitfalls of this method. In a study of a closed deposit she had the very unusual opportunity of working with a bivalve species where it was possible (because of surface patterning and umbo shape) to match *individual pairs of valves,* given enough time and determination. The excavated material came from a small midden inside a house which had been meticulously excavated and recorded. Even with all these positive conditions, Koike showed that only 68.7% of the original shells were present in this deposit. In the light of this work and the various difficulties and uncertainties involved, I have followed the usual convention of presenting the marine shell by giving counts in which each bivalve valve counts as *one.* I have not attempted to give an estimated figure for MNI. Since the same method has been used throughout the Franchthi sequence, there is comparability between gastropods and bivalves in that one can monitor changes in relationship between species present without worrying about how to estimate absolute quantities.

It was found that the method of retrieval during excavation not merely alters the total numbers found, but it also affects some species more directly than others. Appendix A demonstrates this in more detail, but it is necessary to stress again the importance of water sieving for this study. Two sieved fractions were relevant to the study of marine molluscs: >10 mm and 5-10 mm. Material collected from those screens increased very considerably the total numbers of identifiable shells recorded and so provides greater confidence in the zonation described. In addition, it was seen that, because of differing patterns of breakage in the species of molluscs involved, some species consistently fragmented into smaller countable pieces than others. Retrieving material down to 5 mm in size helped eradicate problems of differential recovery of species.

LEVEL OF IDENTIFICATION

A list of consulted sources can be found in the appropriate section of the bibliography, but it is not intended to be a comprehensive listing of the taxonomic literature. Illustrations in the literature are rarely adequate, especially for bivalves, and much work had to be done using the collections at the British Museum (Natural History).

Archaeological marine shell presents problems of identification: the molluscs no longer contain the soft parts; much of the surface color and pattern may have vanished; the outermost edge of the shell is frequently damaged; the pallial line may not be clearly visible, and so on. I have in all cases tried to arrive at an absolute identification; but, since my prime interest has been in man's past activities, I have taken into account the type and quality of the archaeological information to be gained in proportion to the time involved in achieving a given level of confidence. The most important practical result has been the grouping of certain species (such as those of the difficult genus *Patella*) where the habitats, and consequently the type of gathering activity involved, are sufficiently alike for the loss of detail resulting from such "lumping" to be offset by the gain in time. In many instances, in any case, only a generic name is possible because of the condition of the shell or existing uncertainties of species definition, as with Mediterranean limpets. Analogous identification problems exist with *Monodonta* and *Gibbula.* As with *Patella,* the relevant species of those two genera are presented together as a single unit. Two other species have been grouped: *Donax trunculus* L. and *Donacilla cornea* (Poli). The work of the initial seasons did not distinguish between them. A later sampling of excavated units showed that *Donacilla cornea* was much the more common, though *Donax trunculus* was present in small numbers in some of the most recent deposits. Both species have similar habitats (see Chapter 3), and since it was not practical to restudy all the material involved, the two species have been presented together.

It is also relevant to note here that the approach to studying the marine molluscan fauna from Franchthi rests on the Linnean system of classification, the divisions and subdivisions stemming from his perception of order in the natural world. There is no a priori reason to assume that prehistoric people divided and subdivided life forms as post-Renaissance man does. Indeed, present day taxonomy relies on characteristics such as the radulae (teeth) when observed under very high magnification. The analysis that follows, presented in terms of our present perception of distinctions between shellfish, should be moderated by the understanding that this is a mere convenience of communication and is unlikely to be a reflection of the natural order as perceived by the original collectors of the material.

NOMENCLATURE

My report is that of an archaeologist writing for colleagues in that field, most of whom are unfamiliar with the Latin species names of Mediterranean molluscs. There are, however, only a few common names, in English at least, for the species found at Franchthi. I have thus consistently used Latin species names throughout, giving the full name when first used, but frequently using a shorter form thereafter: e.g., *Cyclope neritea* (L.), and then *C. neritea.* The only exception to this is for the names of the various zones based on molluscan assemblages, where the genus name has been preferred, e.g., the *Patella* zone. Taxonomic nomenclature is always in a state of flux. Though I have tried to use the current names for species, e.g., *Mytilus galloprovincialis* Lamarck for the Mediterranean mussel, this report has not been used to argue questions of nomenclature.

CHAPTER TWO

The Marine Shell Record from Franchthi Cave

Approximately 64,000 shells examined during the course of fieldwork form the basis for the profiles used here. This data base comprises the marine molluscs retrieved from the main trenches excavated inside and outside the cave. These trenches were selected for study for the reasons given in the previous chapter. This chapter will only present material from the trenches within the cave. As indicated above, a detailed stratigraphic framework for the Paralia is not yet available. The resolving power of the molluscan zones is low and not such that it can be used to sort out stratigraphic difficulties of the Paralia trenches. Fortunately, it is clear that Zones I-III (see below) are not represented in the Paralia, where the molluscan remains are consistent only with Zone IV.

Inside the cave, the two main trenches—in terms of depth of excavation, amount of water-sieved material, and importance of finds—were H1 and FA. Each was further sub-divided, and so four sequences will be presented: H1A and H1B, FAS and FAN.

The marine shell is presented in accordance with the project's approach, i.e., it has been ordered relative to its own clear internal patterning (Jacobsen and Farrand 1987). A brief discussion, however, is presented at the end of this chapter regarding the relation of the molluscan zones to sequences achieved in other categories of material and to conventional archaeological periods.

One of the main interests of the Franchthi marine molluscan fauna lies in the long span of time it covers, a span unparalleled at any other site in Greece. In order to monitor changes occurring within this span from the end of the Upper Palaeolithic to the end of the Neolithic, several species (or groups of species) of shellfish have been selected as indexes by which to measure change. The species selected were those most commonly found throughout the site, in terms of horizontal and vertical distribution (Plates 1-3). Nine categories were selected, most of which are likely to represent food refuse.

ZONATION

Table 1 shows the general species variation at Franchthi Cave. Zone 0 has been defined by the virtual absence of all molluscs of dimensions substantial enough to represent food refuse. It is also positively defined by the very small marine molluscs detected through sampling of the finest grades of water-sieved material, those of 2.8-5 mm and <2.8 mm. There are no quantitative data for this zone (see Appendix B), and most of the species have not been identified. Additionally, and most importantly, there is no evidence that the majority were carried in by man. The presence of very small marine molluscs in Zone 0

TABLE 1

GENERAL SPECIES VARIATION THROUGH TIME
IN FRANCHTHI MARINE MOLLUSCS

Chronology[a] and Molluscan Zones	Most Abundant Species	Infrequent Species
ca. 5,000 BP		
IV	Mixed assemblage characterized by several bivalves, e.g., *Cerastoderma glaucum,* *Tapes decussatus, Donax trunculus,* and *Donacilla cornea*	Generally 3-10%
ca. 6,900 BP		
III	*Cerithium vulgatum* dominant, 60-80% of assemblage	Generally <5%
ca. 8,500 BP		
II	*Cyclope neritea* dominant, 40-80% of assemblage; remainder mainly *Cerithium vulgatum,* with *Cerastoderma glaucum* in lower part	Generally <5%
ca. 9,400 BP		
I	*Patella* spp., *Monodonta* spp., and *Gibbula* spp., together with other species of gastropods, form 60-80% of the assemblage	Generally <5%
ca. 11,000 BP		
0	Dominated by species of small molluscs, e.g., *Bittium* spp.[b]	
ca. 26,000 BP		

[a]Dates, though based on C-14 determinations (Libby half-life), are only approximate because they were not always available at zone boundaries.

[b]No quantitative data (see Appendix B) and no evidence that they were introduced by man into the cave. Zone 0 is likely to be purely natural.

was probably brought about by natural factors rather than by human agents. This zone will not be discussed further here since information is sparse and the zone does not seem to relate directly to the human use of the cave, the main concern of this study.

Because of the lack of quantitative data for Zone 0, the graphs published here (Figures 3-6) start at or near the base of Zone I. The species shown in Table 1 and in Figures 3-6 are those used for establishing the zonation. All other species together normally represent less than 5% of the total shell for trenches in the cave, and the numbers are too low to rely on. (See Appendix C for the numbers of specimens from given units.)

A single graph per trench is used here to show shell zonation. The practice for other types of data in this publication series, such as lithics and ceramics, is to plot variables against the vertical sequence of units at each of the four corners of a trench. This type of presentation has not been followed here because it has disadvantages in the present context. In addition to requiring the reader to compare multiple sets of graphs simultaneously for each trench, such graphs can result in a significant reduction in the number of units represented in each graph. Consequently, since shell-zone definitions are statistical in nature, they are less clearly documented and may appear sharper than the data set warrants. Therefore, for the purpose of discussing the marine shell sequence, excavated units have been plotted in numerical order in Figures 3-6.

Marine shell representing food refuse first appears in the deposits at Franchthi around 11,000 B.P., as can be seen from the radiocarbon dates at the base of the graphs for FAS and H1A (Figures 3 and 6). I define "first appearance" not literally as the first marine shell found in the deposits, but rather as the first consistent appearance in some number, albeit low, of marine species of a size considered edible or usable. From about 11,000 B.P. onwards marine shell which must have been brought into the cave by man is found consistently in the cave deposits.

Trench FAS (Figure 3) has the longest and most complete sequence of marine shell, even though it is thought to contain possibly as many as three hiatuses. From the sequence in this trench it is clear that there are four main phases or zones. They will be designated here by their shell composition. Following Zone 0 (already dismissed), the earliest is called the *Patella* zone, composed almost exclusively of *Patella* spp., *Gibbula* spp., and *Monodonta* spp. The second is the *Cyclope* zone, composed largely of the small gastropod *Cyclope neritea* (L.). That is followed by Zone III, also dominated by a single species, the gastropod *Cerithium vulgatum* Bruguière. Zone IV, the last, has a mixed assemblage, but it consists predominantly of bivalves. For subsequent discussion, the sequence will be referred to as the *Patella, Cyclope, Cerithium,* and bivalve zones or, as convenience terms, Zones I to IV.

There are fine-scale fluctuations within each zone, but with the very small area excavated, it is not possible to filter out horizontal variation resulting from differential use of the cave interior. It is also not always possible to reconstruct from field notebooks the precise point at which the material was excavated within a specific unit or part of the trench. At this stage of reporting, it appears futile to attempt to resolve a stratigraphy finer than the zonation presented here.

Although the definition of the various molluscan zones is clear (in view of the small number of highly dominant species), an attempt has nevertheless been made to test the validity of the zonation by statistical means. For this purpose, the entire data matrix (excavation units versus species counts) has been subjected to Q-mode factor analysis (Davis 1973; Imbrie and van Andel 1964), a technique designed to resolve the variance within such a matrix in terms of a rigorously defined number of end members. The analysis involved the computation of varimax end members (Klovan and Imbrie 1971), first separately for each trench, then for appropriate pairs (e.g., FAS and FAN), and finally for clusters, such as

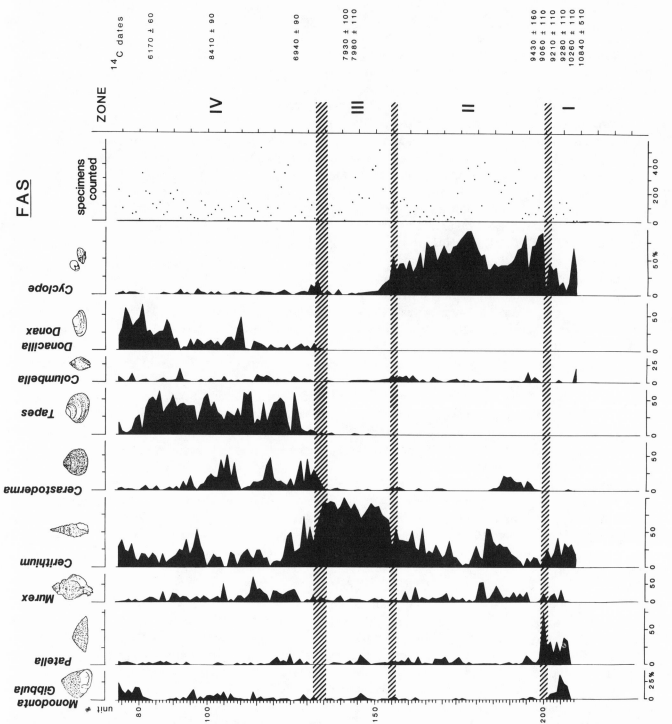

Figure 3. Marine molluscan zonation of Trench FAS. Shaded bands indicate transitions between molluscan zones. Dates are in radiocarbon years (BP).

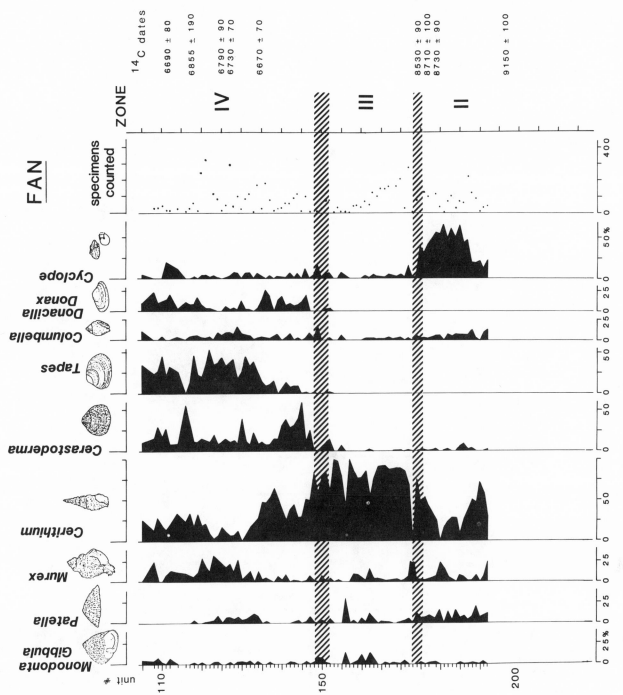

Figure 4. Marine molluscan zonation of Trench FAN. Shaded bands indicate transitions between molluscan zones. Dates are in radiocarbon years (BP).

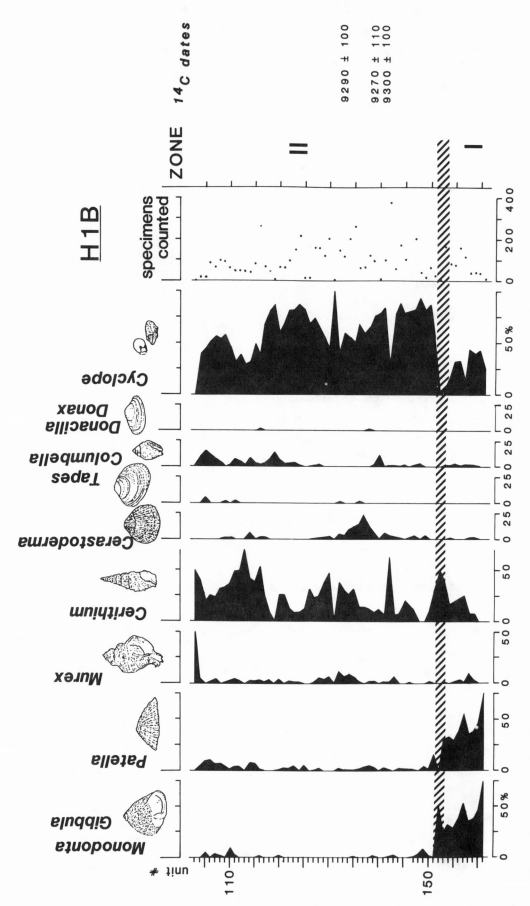

Figure 5. Marine molluscan zonation of Trench H1B. Shaded band indicates transition between molluscan zones. Dates are in radiocarbon years (BP).

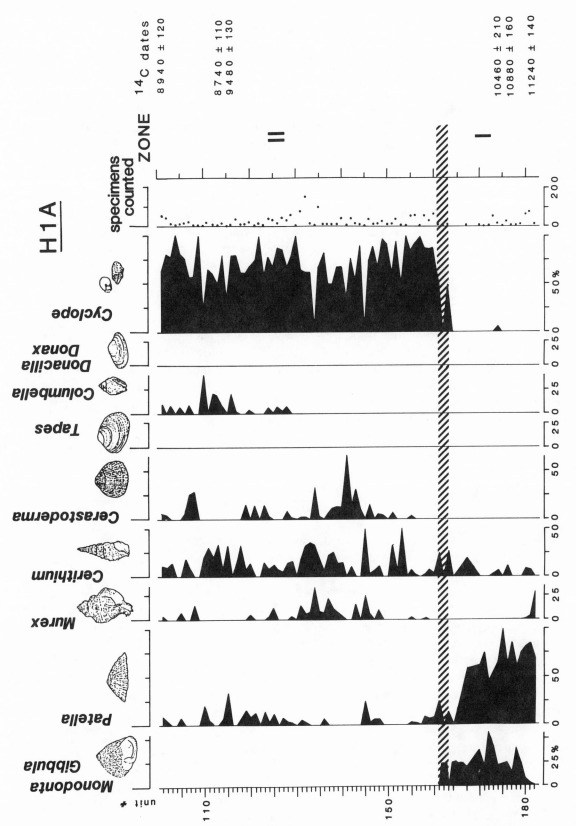

Figure 6. Marine molluscan zonation of Trench H1A. Shaded band indicates transition between molluscan zones. Dates are in radiocarbon years (BP).

all trenches within the cave or Paralia. To test for the influence of units with low shell counts, separate computations were made for data sets containing more than 100 and more than 50 specimens per unit, as well as for sets containing counts of all shells present.

Not surprisingly, given the simple structure of the data matrix, four factors (which correspond in shell composition to Zones I-IV) in general sufficed to account for more than 90% (often more than 95%) of the entire variance, the values being higher for obvious reasons in single trench matrixes than in clusters. In no case did four varimax factors account for less than 85%. Correlations between factor loadings and percentages of variables indicate that the four varimax end members are identical with the zone assemblages identified above. Extraction of additional factors did not provide (with one exception towards the end of Zone IV in FAS) greater resolution of the system, so that the fine-scale variation referred to above evidently falls into the category of system noise devoid of information in terms of the available data.

Each excavated area will now be discussed with reference to the most salient features of its marine shell assemblage. The zones are shown in Figures 3-6, using percentages of species as indexes of change (see Appendix C for details). Available C-14 dates (Libby half-life) are shown along the right side of each graph. Each zone boundary is indicated with a shaded band including a number of excavated units such as 153-151 in H1B (Figure 5), since none of the zone transitions are sharp. This is to be expected given the nature of the excavation, the type of human activity recorded (food preparation and refuse disposal), and post-depositional factors such as "kick-ups." Nor would a transition from one mode of shell collecting to another be expected to be sharp.

ASSEMBLAGES BY TRENCH

The Cave

FAS (Figure 3). As indicated above, this trench shows the most complete sequence of water-sieved marine shell from the site and so should be discussed first.[3] From the base of the graph to Units 201-199 is Zone I, the *Patella* zone. Here various gastropods, viz., *Patella* spp. and *Monodonta* spp., together with *Murex trunculus* (L.) and *Cerithium vulgatum* Bruguière, form 60-80% of the assemblage. After Zone I *Monodonta* and *Gibbula* are virtually totally absent. Zone II is defined by *Cyclope neritea* (L.), forming 40-80% of the assemblage. The rest of the shell assemblage in this zone consists mainly of *C. vulgatum*, together with *Cerastoderma glaucum* Bruguière in the early part of the zone. In FAS this zone is present by Unit 199 and gives way to Zone III in Units 156-154. Zone III is characterized by the dominance of *Cerithium vulgatum,* which forms 40-80% of the assemblage. This zone lasts through Units 135-132. By Unit 132, the final zone (IV) appears and is characterized by the presence of several species of bivalves. Though the range of percentage values for the dominant species defining Zones II and III may seem wide, inspection of the figure and comparison with the figures for the other trenches show that each zone is quite distinct.

FAN (Figure 4). This trench was not excavated to the same depth as FAS. In addition, time constraints did not allow the basal part of the trench to be studied (for details, see Appendix C). It should be noted that the top part of FAN is not included because that material was not water-sieved. Zones II to IV are present. It is interesting to note that in both FAS (cf. Figure 3) and FAN the transition between Zones III and IV is partly defined by the presence, in small numbers, of *Donacilla cornea* and *Tapes decussatus* (L.), i.e., in Unit 135 in FAS and Unit 153 in FAN.

It is also worth noting that, in terms of the stratigraphy of these adjacent trenches, zone changes II to III and III to IV occur simultaneously in both trenches. FAS:156-154 are approximately equivalent to FAN:176-173, and FAS:136-132 to FAN:150-148.

It is possible that the uppermost part of the FAS sequence (Units 90-74, Figure 3) shows a sub-phase of Zone IV. This is characterized by an increased percentage of two very similar bivalves, *Donacilla cornea* and *Donax trunculus*. These two species were mainly retrieved from the water-sieved part of the sample, and direct comparison is not possible with the uppermost part of FAN (not shown) which was not so treated (see Appendix C for details).

H1B (Figure 5). The top part of this trench was not studied because, at the time that the main body of shell was being analyzed, it was thought that much of the upper part was stratigraphically disturbed. Units 161 to 103 are shown on the graph and represent Zones I and II. The available C-14 dates show that these zones fit in well with the sequence in FAS.

H1A (Figure 6). Time constraints meant that, though the lower part of the trench had been water-sieved, it was possible to look only at non-water-sieved material. However, for the portion illustrated, Zones I and II can be clearly seen. The C-14 dates similarly fit, as shown by a comparison of Figures 5 and 6. The date at the top of the sequence would suggest, by comparison with Figure 4 (FAN), that it might be near the transition from Zone II to Zone III.

The only problem with the material from these adjacent trenches, H1B and H1A, is that the change between Zones I and II does not appear to be synchronous. Units H1B:153-151 are stratigraphically equivalent to Units H1A:173-169 (cf. Jacobsen and Farrand 1987: Plate 13). Conversely, Units H1A:163-161 are roughly equivalent to Units H1B:147-145 (*ibid.*). The more pronounced variations seen throughout the sequence in H1A can be accounted for by the lack of water-sieved material. Therefore it is quite possible that the discrepancy in the change from Zones I to II in these trenches is more apparent than real.

In view of the evidence just outlined for the four trenches it is possible to say that, for the deposits within the cave, the same phenomena are observed, with only minor fluctuations, for the marine shellfish gathered and brought to the site for the period approximately 11,000 B.P. to 5,000 B.P. The changes appear to be synchronous (on the time scale that is possible to use) from trench to trench, with the one possible exception noted. If for much of the discussion in subsequent chapters only one trench (FAS) is cited, it is because it contains the longest and most complete sequence of marine shell of any trench at the site. It is also clear that the sequence shown in this trench is representative of the other three trenches analyzed within the cave.

Paralia

Material from six excavated areas was studied, much of which has not been water-sieved. Percentage counts of the main species present can be found in Appendix C. Unlike the material studied from inside the cave, which came from reasonably straightforward stratigraphic sequences, the Paralia trenches do not offer such a context. From the analyses already carried out, it is quite clear that Zones 0 to III are *not* represented in the marine shells from the Paralia trenches; the assemblages present are consistent with Zone IV from the cave. At the time of writing, the majority of the samples could not be ordered stratigraphically by criteria other than the marine shell, and it is not yet possible to refine this zone into subzones. Since the largest collections of shells in Zone IV are found in Paralia trenches and since it is here that the *total* count of shell is usually 5-10% higher than that of the main species used as indexes of change, I have not attempted a subdivision using cave material alone.

DISCUSSION OF ZONATION

So far, the molluscan zonation has been discussed entirely on the basis of the distribution of the shells themselves. However, a few points can be made here about the relation of the marine shell zonation to other bodies of material. Not all information about other categories of data is at present available. Despite this limitation, it is not premature to draw attention to two problem areas, the first of which concerns the initial appearance of marine shell in the cave, and the second the transition from the Mesolithic to the Neolithic. As already indicated, we are concerned here with the first appearance of marine molluscs of a size range such as to suggest that they represent edible species, and that this first appearance occurs around 11,000 B.P.

The earliest excavated cave deposits date to before 22,330 B.P., perhaps to as early as 30,000 B.P. (W. R. Farrand, personal communication; see also Perlès 1987). At that time, a period of maximum lowering of sea level, it is not surprising to find no direct evidence in the cave of marine exploitation (see Chapter 4). There appears to have been a long hiatus in the occupation of the cave, ca. 20,000-13,000 B.P. (C. Perlès, personal communication). After this point there is good evidence for continuous occupation beginning around 13,000 B.P. Yet the deposits do not begin to contain marine molluscs of any size and quantity until about 11,000 B.P., when they appear approximately coincident with Lithic Phase V (C. Perlès, personal communication; see also Perlès 1987) and Phase C of the animal bone sequence (Payne 1975). It is not yet possible to suggest whether the changes observed in these other remains reflect a change in hunting and gathering strategies which is also documented in the appearance of shellfish at the site, or whether another factor independently accounts for the appearance of marine shell. The environmental evidence for shellfish collecting at this time will be discussed later (Chapter 6).

So far, the marine molluscan assemblages have only been described according to their own zonation and without reference to conventional archaeological terminology at Franchthi. In broad terms, Zone 0 covers much of the Upper Palaeolithic to the late Upper Palaeolithic, which is represented by Zone I, the *Patella* zone. Zone II includes the Lower Mesolithic and much of the Upper Mesolithic. Zone III, the *Cerithium* zone, is very interesting in that it covers the very end of the Upper Mesolithic, the Final Mesolithic and the "Aceramic Neolithic." Zone IV, the bivalve zone, covers the ceramic Neolithic.

At this stage, the choice of terminology used here—Upper, Late or Final Mesolithic—is not important. What is significant is that the marked change seen in material such as animal bones and botanical remains (Payne 1975; Hansen 1980) signaling the transition from Mesolithic to Neolithic is *not* observed in the marine molluscan sequence, where the major shift to Zone IV occurs at the start of the ceramic Neolithic. I have no explanation to offer here other than to say that I find it difficult to conceive of an intrusive Neolithic, at least in terms of a significant population change, while the existing habits and pattern of selectivity in gathering shellfish continued without any visible change.[4] I would further add that I find it interesting that the transition to Zone IV, contemporary with FAS:131 and FAN:147, corresponds with the first appearance of pottery in the cave (though a very few pieces have been found below these units; K. D. Vitelli, personal communication).

These remarks merely hint at areas to be explored when a synthesis of the various bodies of data is attempted. Attention will now return to the marine molluscan remains in their own context by examining shellfish-collecting patterns through time.

CHAPTER THREE

Habitats of the Principal Franchthi Molluscs

This chapter is a brief discussion of the habitats of the main molluscan species found in the deposits at Franchthi Cave that have been used to establish the zonation of the assemblages. A discussion of habitats is relevant not only for the information it can provide about skills and equipment necessary for successful gathering but is also an essential component of the data base used in the environmental reconstructions that follow.

SOURCES

This section is intentionally brief, and the information used in it is mainly from the following publications: d'Angelo and Gargiullo (1978); F.A.O., Species Identification Sheets for Fisheries Purposes, Area 37 (Fischer 1973); Locard (1892); Montero (1971); Riedl (1963); and Sakellariou (1957). The second part of the bibliography at the end of this volume lists works consulted in the pursuit of mollusc identifications and habitat requirements.

One of the main difficulties in trying to tabulate information about molluscan habitats is that not only do different workers use differing environmental terminology but frequently such terminology is not precisely defined. An additional problem with many sources, apart from the F.A.O. sheets, is that the data are not presented consistently. It is therefore not always clear whether the absence of a certain category of data implies a negative statement or is merely an omission.

Sakellariou (1957) is the only relatively detailed source known to me for the molluscs of Greece and, unfortunately, itself presents difficulties. Firstly, she records an area distant from the southern Argolid and one clearly with a different maritime regime at present, particularly in terms of freshwater inflow and nutrient supply. Secondly, her depth information in particular can be at variance with other sources. I have therefore had recourse to other regional studies which seemed reliable, notably Montero (1971) and Locard (1892).

Obviously, more detailed information for Greece, let alone for the southern Argolid itself, would be most welcome. What is needed is not only information about average conditions for species but also a knowledge of what conditions are optimal, as well as an understanding of those factors restricting or inhibiting molluscan growth and colonization. Neither my own collections in the southern Argolid and elsewhere in Greece nor a three-day dredging campaign in 1981 in the area of the southern Argolid have added detailed information. Figure 7 shows the areas included in the collecting trips and the dredging campaign.

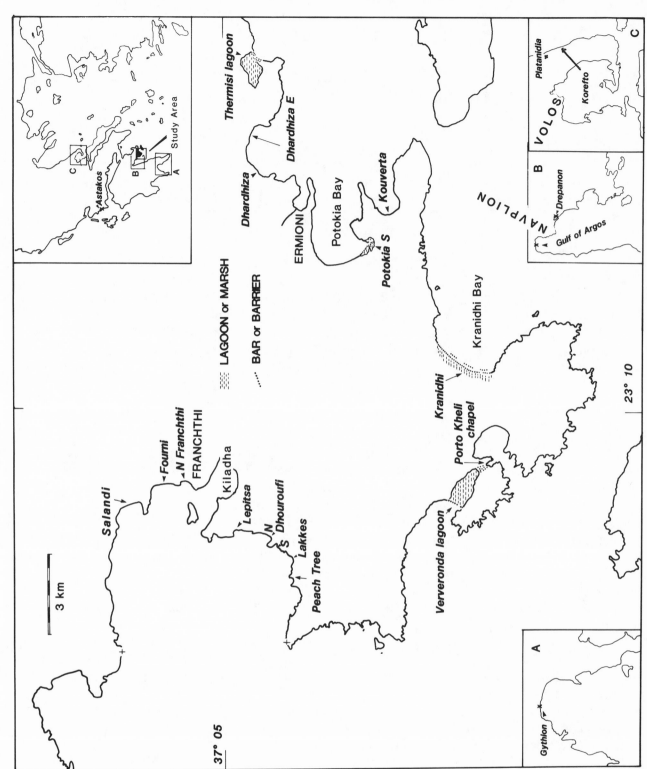

Figure 7. Present shores and beach-collection areas where data on modern marine shell have been obtained. Insets show other collecting areas in Greece from which data are reported in the text.

HABITATS OF MAIN MARINE MOLLUSCAN SPECIES FOUND AT FRANCHTHI CAVE

Summary information only is presented here, but major discrepancies among sources are noted, as is other useful information from my own collecting expeditions.

Monodonta and Gibbula

Monodonta turbinata (Born); *Monodonta articulata* Lamarck; *Gibbula divaricata* (L.); *Gibbula rarilineata* (Michaud)

M. turbinata and *G. divaricata* seem to be more common than the other two species. All share the same habitat, though there is the suggestion that *G. divaricata* is to be found among algae. Likewise, there is the suggestion that *M. turbinata* is to be found higher on the shore than the other three species. It is possible that *M. turbinata* would be easiest and quickest to gather, but on the data available I would not think that there would be much bias towards any one species over another.

Sizes:[5]

M. turbinata: ca. 20-25 mm (ave. height)

M. articulata: ca. 20-25 mm (ave. height)

G. divaricata: ca. 16-18 mm (ave. height)

G. rarilineata: ca. 13 mm (ave. diameter)

Patella

Patella caerulea L.; *Patella aspera* Lamarck; *Patella lusitanica* Gmelin

P. aspera seems less readily found than the other two limpet species and not so frequently associated with algae. *P. lusitanica* is occasionally to be found higher up the shore than the other two species, whereas *P. caerulea* (d'Angelo and Gargiullo 1978) can be found in deeper water, up to 8-10 m in depth. This information would suggest that, though there may be local variation on any beach in the ease with which different *Patella* species could be gathered, the differences are probably not significant.

Sizes (ave. length):

P. caerulea: ca. 45-60 mm

P. aspera: ca. 40-50 mm

P. lusitanica: ca. 25 mm

Murex trunculus (L.)

The consensus is that this species lives on hard bottoms. The F.A.O. sheet states "sandy mud" which, however, can be hard enough to allow for movement without miring. The depth information given in Sakellariou is 0-60 m, and the F.A.O. sheet indicates 5-30 m. It seems clear that this species can be found in shallow water as well as at greater depths.

Size: ca. 40-130 mm (ave. height)

Cerithium vulgatum Bruguière

The consensus is that this species tolerates both sandy and hard substrates, though Riedl notes only hard substrates in the Adriatic. As with all such discrepancies, it is not clear whether one is dealing with regional differences or with inequalities and inaccuracies in the primary data used to compile the source volumes. One also notes here that packed fine sand can often be a hard substrate. Sakellariou states that she found *C. vulgatum* in river mouths and lagoons, with the implication that it is tolerant of lower salinity values.

Size: ca. 50 mm (ave. height)

Cerastoderma glaucum Bruguière

Information compiled for this species indicates that it has a preference for areas with either low or fluctuating salinity. Similarly, it seems to prefer to burrow in muddy bottoms, though d'Angelo and Gargiullo suggest that, if found in the open sea (as opposed to lagoons and estuaries), it lives in sand. From my own observations, the valves of this species living in a closed lagoon, viz., Thermisi lagoon (Figure 7), were quite thin and looked stressed in comparison with valves collected on open beaches along the southern Argolid peninsula or in open marsh conditions as at Potokia Bay (Figure 7), where the shells were much thicker.

Size: ca. 50 mm (ave. length)

Tapes decussatus (L.)

It is disconcerting that the F.A.O. sheet indicates that this species is not to be found in the eastern Mediterranean. The specimens that I have contradict this statement, as do other sources. Available habitat information for *T. decussatus* describes it as living in sandy and muddy conditions. Depth information suggests somewhat deeper water than *C. glaucum.*

Size: ca. 50 mm (ave. length)

Donax trunculus L.

The information about this species is consistent except for depth data. Sakellariou claims depths from 0-45 m, while the F.A.O. sheet suggests "upper infralittoral" which would be far less than 45 m. It is also in this region, near the high tide line, that I have found specimens in the southern Argolid today. Indeed, it is highly likely that Sakellariou dredged non-recent examples from greater depths.

Size: ca. 25 mm (ave. length)

Donacilla cornea (Poli)

This species has a habitat similar to that of *D. trunculus.* The only difference recorded (and this may be an accident of the available information) is that *D. trunculus* lives in very dense colonies. I would suggest that both species can be found in sand, fairly high up on the shore and, from my experience at Lepitsa (Figure 7), can be quite easily collected in large numbers at the water's edge.

Size: ca. 20 mm (ave. length)

Columbella rustica (L.)

This species appears to be common on rocky shores. Unlike the other principal species from the Franchthi excavations, it is not postulated as a source of food. I believe that it was only collected dead on the shore.

Size: ca. 20 mm (ave. height)

Cyclope neritea (L.)

There is no disagreement among the sources here. This species, as Sakellariou reports, "flourishes close to river mouths," and she found it in large numbers there. In the three areas in Greece where I have gathered live examples of this species (at the head of the Gulf of Argos, in Akarnania, and at the head of the Gulf of Lakonia) the locations were subject to at least a seasonal influx of freshwater from rivers emptying nearby. In addition, at least in the Gulf of Argos, *C. neritea* appears to be able to withstand considerable daily fluctuations of temperature.

Size: ca. 15 mm (ave. diameter)

CHAPTER FOUR

Reconstructions of Past Shore Environments and the Implications for Shellfish Gathering

The initial description of the present situation at Franchthi Cave in the introduction concluded by noting that "the sea meets a steep, rocky, shore just outside the entrance to the cave." It is difficult, when visiting the site today, to see the cave as being anything other than marine oriented. That, however, is a false image. The purpose of this section is to examine the changes in sea level that occurred during the prehistoric occupation of the cave and to suggest some of the implications that different stands of the sea would have had on the inhabitants, if they wished to procure shellfish to supplement their diet.

Five points in time have been chosen for which to present a reconstruction of the shoreline. The importance of these reconstructions is not merely to draw attention to the fact that the positions of the shore are not fixed through time, nor just to indicate how accessible the coast would have been from the cave. Instead, the main thrust of these reconstructions is to suggest the *shore environments* that would have been present and consequently the types of molluscs that could be expected to have lived there. The reconstructions postulate marine molluscan habitats likely to have been present in the general area around Franchthi Cave and the environmental options available for collecting shellfish. This is not an environmentally deterministic position, but merely one that attempts to place some limits on the choices available to past cave inhabitants.

Figure 8 illustrates the present coastlines around Franchthi. When compared with Figures 9-13, it shows that simple and direct backward extrapolation from present conditions is at best hazardous and very often grossly misleading. Obviously, it is necessary to reconstruct past shore conditions with a different approach. The method adopted here is straightforward in principle, though intricate in practice, since data with the right degree of chronological and topographic resolution are difficult to obtain.[6]

SHORELINE RECONSTRUCTIONS

During the last 18,000 years, the shore moved from a depth of about −120 m (van Andel and Lianos 1983) to its present position as the continental ice caps melted and water was returned to the ocean. Ancient submerged shorelines of this age have been identified and dated in many parts of the world. Global sea level rise (or fall) as a result of the melting or growth of ice caps is a complicated subject because the shifts in load from ice on the

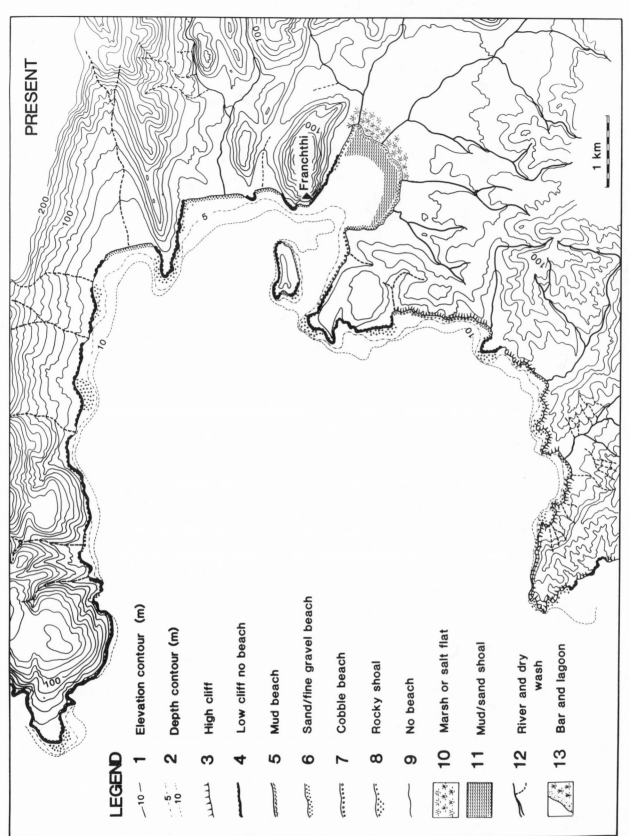

PRESENT

LEGEND

1 Elevation contour (m)
2 Depth contour (m)
3 High cliff
4 Low cliff no beach
5 Mud beach
6 Sand/fine gravel beach
7 Cobble beach
8 Rocky shoal
9 No beach
10 Marsh or salt flat
11 Mud/sand shoal
12 River and dry wash
13 Bar and lagoon

1 km

Figure 8. Present shore environments of the Franchthi embayment. The 20 m contours on land and the 5 m and 10 m isobaths are taken from Greek topographic maps at scales of 1:50,000 and 1:5,000. This legend also applies to Figures 9-13.

continent to water in the ocean, or vice versa, depress or cause to rise different areas of the earth's crust. Thus, the post-glacial melt added water to the sea, but the resulting rise in sea level was reduced as the added load caused the ocean floor to sink. In addition, geological processes unrelated to glaciation and deglaciation may cause the sea floor to rise or the land to sink. The whole subject (including discussion of tectonic movements) has been dealt with in more detail elsewhere (van Andel and J. C. Shackleton 1982; van Andel and Sutton 1987).

The maps of the prehistoric shores in the Franchthi area (Figures 9-13) are based on two converging lines of analysis: that of the position of the shore for certain chosen dates and that of the nature of the shore and immediate offshore region at those dates. Various strands of evidence have been used to prepare the reconstructions. For the maps presented here, an average sea-level-rise curve was used (van Andel and Lianos 1984), with an allowance for possible local long-term subsidence not in excess of 1 m/1,000 yr (Flemming 1968). This curve has, of course, only limited accuracy, and one is faced with two possible ways of using the information. One may choose to depict the shore for a precise instant in time and must then accept an uncertainty in the depth of the corresponding sea level. That, in turn, will yield an uncertainty in the geographic position of the shore. Conversely, if one chooses to depict the shore in a precise position, as is more convenient because the geo-physical data provide such positions (van Andel and Lianos 1984), then the map will represent an age-range rather than a narrowly defined instant in time. This latter is the strategy that has been adopted here.

The position and configuration of the shore are obtained from geophysical and bathymetric information and are thus affected by the density of the observation network. In addition, any sediment deposited subsequently must be discounted. In the Franchthi area, this correction is small because the thickness of the Holocene sediment cover is usually less than one to two meters. For depth information, use was made of Greek topographic charts at 1:50,000, British Admiralty charts and manuscripts in British Admiralty archives, and a dozen bathy-metric traverses obtained in 1981 and 1982. Because the ancient shores used are clearly identifiable on fifteen seismic reflection traverses (van Andel and Lianos 1983:Figure 1), the horizontal error, even where they have to be interpolated, is less than 100 m. If one adopts a fixed shore position as here, the uncertainty of its age is about 500 years for the 11,000 B.P. shore, and about 300 years for the later ones (van Andel and Lianos 1984: Figure 8). The late glacial low stand of the sea lasted from at least 25,000 B.P. to about 15,000 B.P. and therefore represents the most mature shore in the area. The configuration shown for each shore depends on the density of data; all are shown smoother than they really were, but, because they were either depositional or the product of simple erosion factors, the smoothing effect is not large.

The nature of shore and foreshore is determined by different means and is less amenable to quantitative evaluation of its confidence limits than the geographic position. The difference between rocky erosional shores and depositional ones can be ascertained from sidescan sonar data, seismic reflection records, and bottom samples. Micro-morphology and seismic reflection traverses, and comparison with the present coastal environments of the area, aided by theoretical considerations, help resolve the nature of the shore environments. Leaving a discussion of the precise methodology for elsewhere (J. C. Shackleton and van Andel 1986), I shall here make only general use of the information of the maps, considering them an acceptable image of past conditions. The periods chosen for reconstruction are 18,000, 11,000, 9,500, 8,000, and 5,000 B.P.

DISCUSSION OF MAPS

The 18,000 B.P. shore (Figure 9) marks the height of the last glaciation at the lowest stand of the sea; this map is valid for an interval from before 25,000 B.P. to perhaps 15,000 B.P. Such a long period of stability leads to a well-developed, largely depositional shore as the map shows. At this time it would not have been possible to stand at the entrance of the cave and view the shore, since it was six to seven kilometers distant along the shortest route. It should be noted that the interval represented by this map coincides in part with a hiatus in the sedimentary record of the cave.

Around 15,000 B.P. or perhaps a little later (van Andel and Sutton 1987) there followed a rapid rise of the sea during which the shore remained at any given position for only a short time. Such ephemeral shores, especially in a region of low sediment supply as here, tend to be poorly developed with low, erosion-cut cliffs, and thin beach and nearshore mud deposits. Mudflats or lagoons are unlikely to have been present. Under such conditions, even the smoother portions of the 11,000 B.P. coast (Figure 10) probably had less sand and mud and much more exposed hard substrate than more mature coasts.

During the last part of the rapid rise of the sea, the shore reoccupied an older coastal zone formed at a time of lower sea level between approximately 45,000 B.P. and 30,000 B.P. This shore lasted long enough to be well developed; the shore between approximately 10,000 and 8,000 B.P. was superimposed on its deposits, inherited some of the characteristics of this relict Middle Palaeolithic coast, and so possesses greater maturity and thicker sands and muds than it would otherwise have acquired. The rather level seafloor produced a flat coast and extensive mud shoals offshore, at least in the vicinity of Franchthi Cave, with considerable repercussions for molluscan habitats. A comparable situation exists today in the northern Gulf of Argos where one can wade a few hundred meters offshore, as I have done, without getting wet much above the waistline. Thus one may reasonably postulate that the shores from 10,000 to 8,000 B.P. furnished suitable habitats for burrowing bivalves and those other molluscan species which prefer sandy and fine-grained substrates.

I should now like to point out some salient features of the maps. The reasons for including the 18,000 B.P. map have already been given. The first shellfish representing food refuse appear in the cave around 11,000 B.P. It is not surprising that marine molluscs of reasonable size and in reasonable numbers are not found in the earlier deposits, but this does not suggest that such resources were not used. Given the distance from cave to shore, any shellfish collected are more likely to have been consumed near the sea than to have been carried back over more than an hour's walk.

The map most nearly contemporaneous with the first finds of edible marine molluscs is that for 11,000 B.P. (Figure 10). This reconstruction still shows a distance between coast and cave of about 4 km. The shore itself most probably consisted of fairly sheltered shingle or sandy beaches, with a gentle slope, lying in front of low, wave-cut scarps. The −5 m contour suggests a moderately shallow offshore environment. Moreover, a rocky limestone shore was present on the northern side of the bay throughout the rise from the low stand at 18,000 B.P. This zone would have provided suitable habitats for rock-dwelling species, as would part of the lengthening rocky shore farther to the south. On the other hand, the thin sediments and the shingle or gravel beaches were not conducive to an abundance of burrowing bivalves.

Figure 11 represents the 9,500 B.P. stand and illustrates shore types which are quite different in distribution and kind. The type that dominates the area near the cave consists of very shallow, muddy, or silty beaches which would have favored species very different

Figure 9. Shores of the Franchthi embayment at 18,000 BP during the last glacial maximum. The shore was at −118 m, and elevations are in meters above sea level *at that time.*

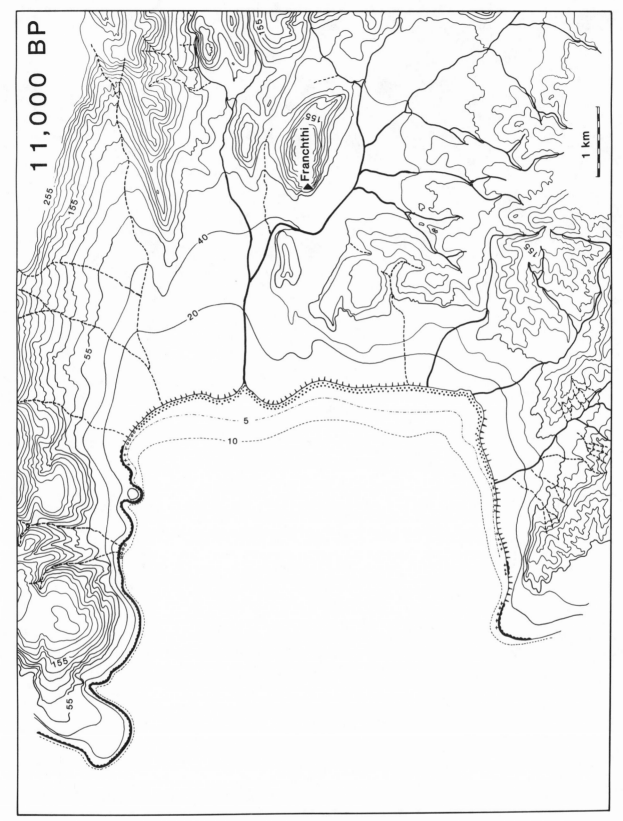

Figure 10. Shores of the Franchthi embayment at 11,000 BP, when sea level was at −54 m. Elevations are in meters above sea level at that time.

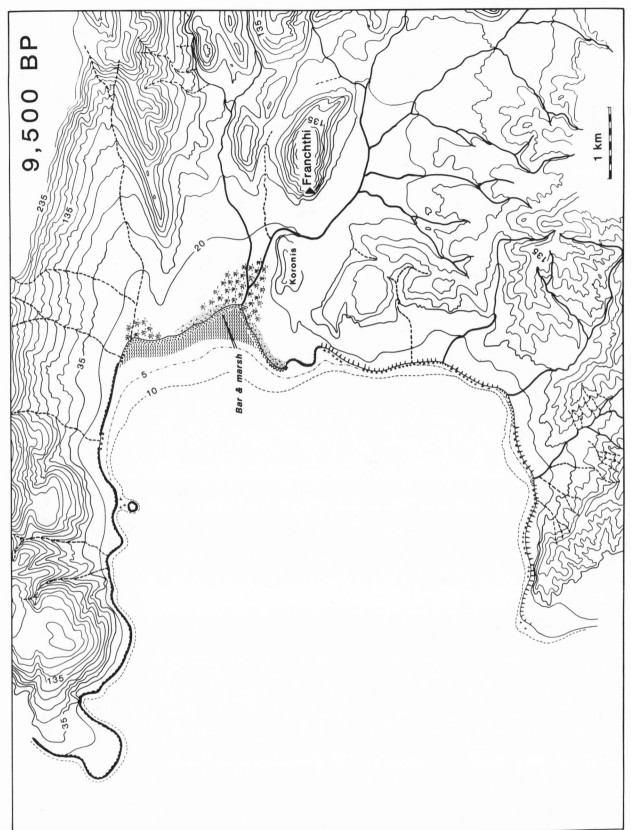

9,500 BP

Franchthi

Koronis

Bar & marsh

1 km

Figure 11. Shores of the Franchthi embayment at 9,500 BP, when sea level was at −37 m. Elevations are in meters above sea level *at that time.*

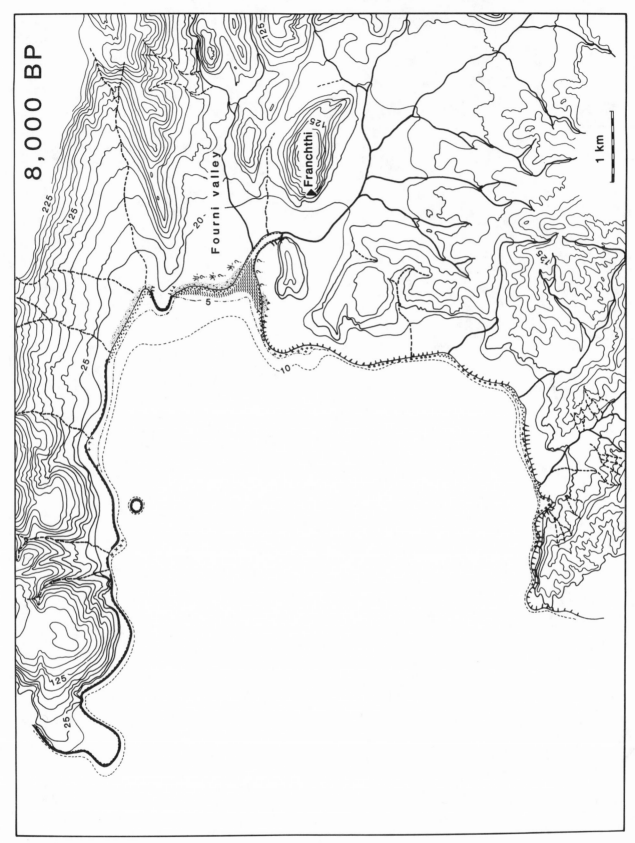

8,000 BP

Fourni valley

▲ Franchthi

1 km

Figure 12. Shores of the Franchthi embayment at 8,000 BP, when sea level was at −27 m. Elevations are in meters above sea level *at that time.*

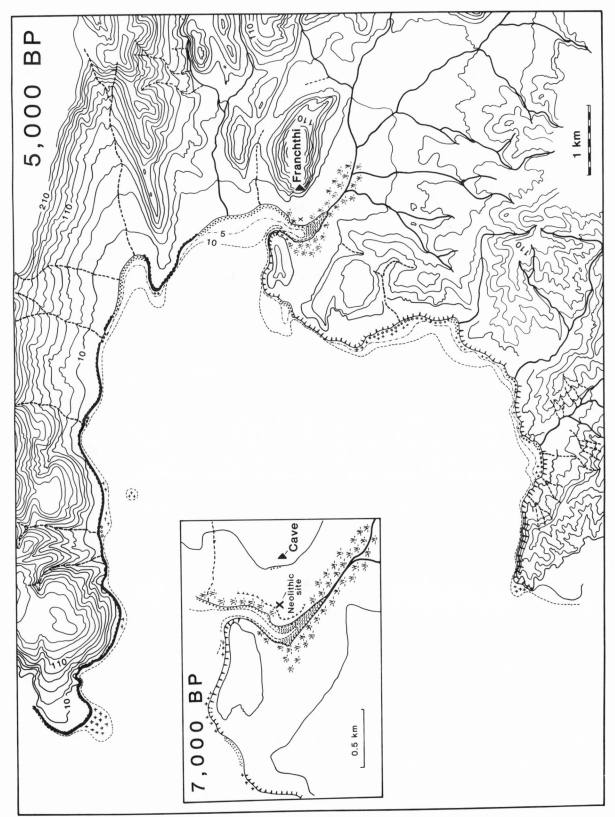

Figure 13. Shores of the Franchthi embayment at 5,000 BP, when sea level was at −10 m. Elevations are in meters above sea level *at that time*. Inset shows setting of cave and presumed offshore site at 7,000 BP, with sea level at −16 m.

from those of the preceding reconstruction. Marshes or mudflats existed behind the shallow nearshore waters. In the south, the shoreline was composed of a mixture of sandy and locally rocky beaches. To the northwest, long low limestone cliffs, little interrupted by coarse gravel beaches, persisted. The presence of the extensive sandy beaches and open mudflats or marshes off Franchthi is probably mainly the result of the sediment reservoir left behind by the Middle Palaeolithic shore. Kutzbach (1981) has reasoned on both theoretical and empirical grounds that around this time monsoonal activity was more intense and extended from the western Indian Ocean farther into the Middle and Near East and possibly the eastern Mediterranean than is true today. This might have yielded occasional heavy summer rains likely to bring abnormal sediment supplies and high sedimentation rates in shallow, sheltered portions of the coastal zone. A reduced salinity during part of the year could also have been a consequence.

Turning to the fourth map (Figure 12), that for 8,000 B.P., there is a decrease in the area of the very shallow marine environments just described, while to the south and southwest, rocky shores and unstable very coarse gravel beaches have come to dominate. Otherwise, the shoreline is not greatly different from that presented in the previous maps, and so requires little additional comment.

The final map given here (Figure 13) reveals a rather different coastline. Instead of the fairly smooth configuration of previous periods, the shore was now much indented with several small bays. In addition, a large incursion of the sea near the cave had produced an embryonic Kiladha Bay. This change had already begun by about 7,000 B.P., and its effect (whether after 7,000 B.P. or a little later) was not only that the cave acquired an essentially marine aspect, but also that, though on a small scale, all of the previously described molluscan habitats now occurred very close to the cave itself. On the 7,000 B.P. map (inset, Figure 13) one also notes the site of a possible Neolithic open air settlement on the broad level bank between the cave and the shore of the inlet (Gifford 1983).

CHAPTER FIVE

The Relationship between Franchthi Shell Assemblages and the Shoreline Reconstructions

The previous chapter drew attention to the more prominent features of the shoreline reconstructions. This section returns to the marine molluscan assemblages from the excavations at Franchthi Cave, beginning with a brief resumé of the main zones in relation to the environmental maps.

MOLLUSCAN ZONATION AND SHORELINE RECONSTRUCTION

Zone I is composed of species of the genera *Patella, Monodonta,* and *Gibbula,* all inhabitants of rocky shores. Although Figure 10, the map for ca. 11,000 B.P., shows that gravel and sand beaches occur nearest to the cave, a long sequence of rocky shores can be reached by following the northern bank of the river.

Zone II, the *Cyclope* zone, probably begins around 9,400 B.P. *C. neritea* flourishes in shallow water and even marshy conditions, which were present at the time near the cave (Figure 11). The rest of the coast on the 9,500 B.P. map provided habitats for both rock-dwelling and sand- or gravel-loving molluscs.

By 8,000 B.P., the assemblage of the *Cerithium* zone (III) is found in the deposits at Franchthi. *C. vulgatum* appears able to cope with a large variety of habitats, and such a variety indeed occurs on Figure 12. The area of silty/muddy shallow water that appeared on the previous map is now at least halved in extent, and a more broken pattern of sand and rock beaches has taken its place.

Zone IV, the mixed bivalve zone, starts around 6,800 B.P. The corresponding map (Figure 13) shows the coast at the end of this phase, around 5,000 B.P., and indicates that much of the shore was rocky as it is today. The area immediately adjacent to the cave and just to the north of the site, however, provided the soft substrate necessary for the main species of Zone IV.

DISCUSSION

This outline shows that, in broad terms, the main zones of the shellfish assemblages are consistent with what was environmentally available. There have been considerable fluctuations from one zone to the next, however, in the proportions of the different species of marine molluscs collected. Even more noticeable are the omissions—the species not selected, those that fail to appear in the molluscan assemblages of the site either in a particular zone or altogether. The following discussion examines some of these aspects in more detail. Several hypotheses are put forward to account for past gathering strategies, the results of which are now represented by the shells found at the site.

Basic and obviously reasonable is the hypothesis that, in order to survive, one must acquire at least as many calories as are expended in the food quest. Therefore, all things being equal, people will collect shellfish from nearby beaches rather than those more distant to minimize the energy used in traveling to gathering areas. Ethnographic evidence (e.g., Meehan 1977, 1982) makes it quite clear that all things are not equal, and I see no reason to assume a different reaction in the prehistoric past because many factors come into play as people decide on "strategies" for their food quest.

If one looks at the species first seen in the deposits at Franchthi, it is apparent that this least-cost principle already seems to have been violated. As Figure 10 shows, the nearest beaches during the period around 11,000 B.P. were shingle/sandy ones on which bivalves and gastropods such as *C. vulgatum* ought to have provided an adequate supply of shellfish resources for people frequenting the cave. It is only at a distance of about five to six kilometers from the cave that a continuous rocky shore begins on the north side of the river. Yet the species actually seen in the deposits from this period are all rock-dwellers (*Patella* spp., *Monodonta* spp., and *Gibbula* spp.).

Several possible explanations can be put forward for the fact that only rock-dwellers were collected. One might argue that, since there had been several millennia of very rapid shore advance (the sea rising at 10-20 m and the shore migrating at 500 m per millennium), species not dependent on deep, soft substrates might be more likely to colonize the new shores rapidly. Alternatively, the sand and gravel beaches of the central part of the rapidly migrating shore, dominated by small-scale erosion of the edge of the coastal plain, might have offered only a very thin veneer of new deposits over the hard erosion surface, a setting not conducive to producing large numbers of burrowing organisms. Finally, it is quite likely that, in the main, the central, sedimentary portion of the shore, rather than being covered with sand (and mud offshore), actually consisted of mobile shingle and gravel, again not the best environment for bivalves. However, certainly after about 10,000 B.P., when the shore moved onto the more gentle upper slope with its thick wedge of relict Middle Palaeolithic coastal deposits and the rise gradually began to slow, none of these explanations for the absence of sand- and mud-dwelling species seems valid.

One might then suggest that the inhabitants of Franchthi were unaware that the sandy beaches then becoming prevalent concealed edible molluscs a few centimeters beneath their surfaces, and so they turned to the visible resource of rocks and boulders. This hypothesis does not credit the users of the cave at that time with much perception. Alternatively, a common feature of the *Patella* species and those of the genera *Monodonta* and *Gibbula* found at the site is that all are molluscs which can be easily seen and collected with minimal equipment from the very edge of the water. In no case would it be necessary to get one's feet wet and the prey would be easily visible—both of which might be attractive characteristics. A further possibility is that bivalves were actually collected but processed, cooked or consumed elsewhere, perhaps near the shore, rather than in the cave. Of course, there may also have been a social avoidance mechanism for certain species. The last hypothesis offered here is that a route taken in pursuit of some other activity would pass a shore area supplying rock-dwelling species and that, not infrequently on returning to the cave, people would pause and gather a few shellfish to take with them. I offer no "final solution" but suggest that this type of reconstruction allows one to attempt a more detailed monitoring of past use of resources than has commonly been attempted up to now.

The second topic I wish to discuss here is that of the presence in the deposits of quite large numbers of the small gastropod *C. neritea* (Zone II), a small gregarious carnivore able to tolerate conditions of low salinity and considerable temperature fluctuations. At approximately 9,400 B.P. the molluscan assemblage at the site drastically changed to one dominated by, if not composed exclusively of, this gastropod. The obvious collecting area was close to the cave (Figure 11). The interest in the presence of this species lies in the question of why such a small mollusc was so heavily used and why such a large number of the discarded shells have holes in them. The holes, man-made, are worked from the inside, so they cannot have been intended to ease the extraction of flesh from the shell. (For about 30% of the shells examined it is possible to say unequivocally that they had been intentionally holed, and only about 25% show no such alteration.) It is obvious that the pierced shells could have decorative value. The question is the extent to which *C. neritea* represents an activity, in terms of shellfish gathering, similar to that of the other main recorded species, that of a food supply. It seems most economical to suggest that, since the reconstruction (Figure 11) clearly shows an area near the cave where these gastropods could have been collected (they can be fished for with bait: Morton 1960), they were collected alive and the flesh was eaten. This could have been done either by turning the molluscs into a soup or by eating them winkle-fashion by picking the flesh out with a pin or similar implement. In the latter case they might represent more of a social than a subsistence activity. It is interesting also that the habitat in which this species flourishes existed near the cave in substantial area only for a short period. It is during this time span that the species dominated the shell assemblage at Franchthi.

There is another problem associated with the dominance of *C. neritea* in Zone II. There is no reason to suppose that it was the only species living in the area. Today, for example, *Mactra corallina* (L.) is found only a few meters away from the *Cyclope* habitat in the Gulf of Argos. This introduces a consideration of "negative evidence." From my observations of the molluscan variety in the area and in similar areas elsewhere in Greece today, and from my general knowledge, it would seem that, given the conditions of past shore environments, other molluscan species must have been present which should also have offered good food to gatherers of shellfish based at Franchthi Cave. The fact that several of the species one might reasonably expect to find among the food at the site (sporadically or throughout the sequence) are absent may be taken as negative evidence to support the contention that shellfish collecting by the users of Franchthi Cave was quite selective. Therefore, though the only incontrovertible evidence for the existence of a species in the area in the past has so far come from its presence in the archaeological record, it is reasonable to postulate, from the evidence available, a range of species that most likely were also represented in the coastal zone of Franchthi. Even though detailed information on past conditions, such as seasonal temperature ranges or local salinity fluctuations, is lacking, it is possible with present data to make informed guesses about what species the environments might have favored during the time-span under consideration.

The species presented in Table 2 are some of those commonly found in the Mediterranean. In particular, I have selected those whose shells I have found on beaches in the southern Argolid today. All are species that one can reasonably call edible, even tempting. The table divides them according to habitat preference: rock-dwellers; those which require soft substrates and, among the latter, those which will tolerate muddy or sandy bottoms; and those which are tolerant of brackish conditions. Finally, suggested water depths are given at which each species might easily be found. The water depth at which a species lives is of obvious relevance

TABLE 2

HABITATS OF MEDITERRANEAN MOLLUSCAN SPECIES
FROM FRANCHTHI CAVE

Rock-dwellers	*Species Associated with Soft Substrate*	*S*	*M*
	Depth of ca. 1-2 m[a]		
Patella caerulea L.[b]	*Mactra corallina* (L.)	+	+
Patella aspera Lamarck[b]	*Donax trunculus* L.[b]	+	
Patella lusitanica Gmelin[b]	*Donacilla cornea* (Poli)[b]	+	
Monodonta turbinata (Born)[b]	*Cerastoderma glaucum* Bruguière[b,d]	+	+
Gibbula divaricata (L.)[b]	*Solen vagina* L.	+	+
Gibbula rarilineata (Michaud)[b]	*Ensis ensis* (L.)	+	+
	Depth of ca. 2-5 m[a]		
Mytilus galloprovincialis Lamarck	*Tapes decussatus* (L.)[b]	+	+
Modiolus barbatus (L.)	*Venerupis aurea* (Gmelin)[b]	+	+
Arca noae L.[b]	*Venus verrucosa* L.	+	+
Arca barbata (L.)	*Chlamys varia* (L.)	+	
Murex trunculus (L.)[b]	*Cerithium vulgatum* Bruguière[b]	+	
Cerithium vulgatum Bruguière[b]			
Columbella rustica (L.)[b]			
Ostrea edulis L.[b]			
	Depth of ca. 5 m or more[a]		
Spondylus gaederopus L.[c]	*Pinna nobilis* L.[c]	+	
	Glycimeris glycimeris (L.)	+	+
	Glycimeris bimaculata (Poli)	+	+

[a] Depths based on contemporary data and do not imply strict limits of range.

[b] One of main species of molluscs at Franchthi.

[c] Found in small but consistent numbers at certain levels at Franchthi.

[d] Tolerates low salinity.

S = sandy substrate; M = muddy substrate.

in terms of ease of collection, especially in a sea with as small a tidal range as the Aegean. The type of substrate and the salinity tolerance are important in order to make correlations with the reconstructions of past coastal environments.

An examination of Table 2 shows that the main species of gastropods found in the area today and common in the Mediterranean (genera *Patella, Monodonta, Gibbula,* together with *C. vulgatum* and *M. trunculus*) are also seen as the dominant species in the archaeological record. However, when one turns to the bivalves, it is clear that a much wider range of equally edible species must have been available than the few selected by the occupants of the site. Practical matters could have influenced the ease of collection, such as the depth at which a species lived, whether it lived in colonies, or how easy it was to prepare the flesh for eating. Yet it is difficult to imagine that serious problems would have been encountered in locating, collecting, and processing molluscs such as *Mytilus galloprovincialis* or *Mactra corallina.* In the case of the latter, I have rapidly collected many individuals in the Gulf of Argos simply by feeling for them with my feet in the very shallow, muddy water as the molluscs rested, hinge uppermost, lightly dug into the fine silt at the bottom of the bay. Yet there are less than 50 specimens of this species at Franchthi, and *M. galloprovincialis* is represented at the site by no more than a dozen or so fragments, most of which show signs of working.

It is unlikely that the variation observed would have resulted from major fluctuations in the availability of molluscs in areas adjacent to the site. Were one able to monitor shellfish-gathering activities on a yearly basis, fluctuations between bivalve species might be found to have been due to natural causes such as disease, predators wiping out a particular year's spatfall or population, or heavy winter storms. Factors such as these cannot be seen with the temporal resolution available at Franchthi where the rate of change of shellfish-gathering habits can, at best, be measured in generations. As a result, the record is averaged out and such factors cannot account for the obvious lack of some species and evident preference for others.

I suggest that the most likely explanation for selective exploitation of bivalves, at least during the last zone (Zone IV), is what might best be termed *perceived edibility.* I am using this term to refer, not to those physical qualities inherent in a foodstuff, such as the presence or absence of toxins causing damage to humans, but rather to emphasize qualities attributed by a people to a food which are seen to enhance or detract from its desirability. It is clear even within our own society that a factor which can influence food choice, apart from an urge for dietary variety, is this *perceived edibility,* or ranking, that is given a food in terms of its attractiveness. Davidson (1972) comments on an example of the non-economic, non-logical factors affecting our perceptions of food. He notes that the "coral" of a scallop is not eaten in the U.S.A., but it is considered a delicacy in Britain. He concludes that the phenomenon "does not arise from any differences between the species of scallops but reflects different levels of gastronomic development within the human species."

CHAPTER SIX

Shellfish Gathering and the Role of Marine Molluscs in the Diet

There has been a curious absence of discussion in the literature of what might have been involved in the collection of species of shellfish found at archaeological sites. One of the few exceptions is the study by Elizabeth Voigt (1982) who considers, with the material from Stone Age sites at the Klasies River Mouth in South Africa, what parts of the shore were visited by gatherers. Since that region has a large tidal range, however, no direct comparisons can be made with the eastern Mediterranean.

Table 2 (Chapter 5) lists molluscan habitats, and a simplified tabulation for the main species of Franchthi is given now in Table 3 (sources: Riedl 1963; Fischer 1973; and d'Angelo and Gargiullo 1978). The categories selected are: those species living on hard substrates; those living on or in soft substrates; species capable of living in (or actually preferring) a brackish environment; and, finally, two categories dividing species into those inhabiting shallower or deeper water. Obviously, a single species may occur more than once. The tabulated categories, together with density of colonization, are those basic for determining collecting techniques and areas to be exploited.

All species of *Monodonta, Gibbula,* and *Patella* are to be found high on the shore and can be collected almost without getting one's feet wet. Being sufficiently exposed, they have a high visibility, even though they do not live in densely packed colonies. One can collect *Monodonta* and *Gibbula* spp. by just picking them up; the only necessary equipment is a container in which to take them back to the cave. Limpets (*Patella* spp.) require greater effort since they cling firmly to the rocks. On the other hand, because they are browsers, they can be collected more easily while they are feeding. An obvious aid in collecting is a sharp instrument to slip under a corner of the shell to prevent the limpet from clamping down onto the rock. This implement could have been made of stone, bone, wood, or even shell, but no such tool has (yet?) been identified among the artifactual types at Franchthi. It has been said that one can gather limpets by kicking them off the rocks with one's heel, but, given the relatively small size of the Mediterranean species, I think this might be a less likely means of collection.

I have no information about collecting *C. vulgatum*, but one would obviously be working in somewhat deeper water, perhaps up to a couple of meters. The same is true of *M. trunculus,* though I have a report (M. H. Jameson, personal communication) of this species being caught for bait by sticking a split-ended reed into the water and spearing individuals. Such a technique would not leave a trace in the artifactual record at the site.

TABLE 3

SIMPLIFIED HABITAT INFORMATION FOR MARINE MOLLUSCS TO SHOW EASE OF COLLECTION

Rocky	Sandy/Muddy	Brackish	Shallow	Deeper
Monodonta turbinata			Monodonta turbinata	
Monodonta articulata			Monodonta articulata	
Gibbula divaricata			Gibbula divaricata	
Gibbula rarilineata			Gibbula rarilineata	
Patella caerulea			Patella caerulea	
Patella aspera			Patella aspera	
Patella lusitanica			Patella lusitanica	
Murex trunculus	(Murex trunculus ? F.A.O.)		Murex trunculus	Murex trunculus
Cerithium vulgatum	Cerithium vulgatum	(Cerithium vulgatum ? Sakellariou)	Cerithium vulgatum	Cerithium vulgatum
	Cerastoderma glaucum	Cerastoderma glaucum	Cerastoderma glaucum	Cerastoderma glaucum
	Tapes decussatus		Tapes decussatus	Tapes decussatus
	Donax trunculus		Donax trunculus	(Donax trunculus ? d'Angelo and Gargiullo)
	Donacilla cornea		Donacilla cornea	
	Cyclope neritea	Cyclope neritea	Cyclope neritea	
Columbella rustica			Columbella rustica	

I do not consider the examples of *Columbella rustica* found at the site to represent food remains. This is mainly because of the small size of the mollusc, the number of examples with holes in them, and the fact that many of the holes are naturally made. I would therefore suggest that this species was most likely collected dead along the beaches or found while used by hermit crabs. It is quite easy to find them now, and one beach in particular (Kouverta, Figure 7) has a high concentration of these shells, together with *Conus mediterraneus* Bruguière.

Bivalves are most easily collected with a spade or some kind of rake. With such an implement one can turn over reasonable quantities of sand to the appropriate depth, though many can also be gathered by scrabbling with one's hands. From my experience, *Cerastoderma glaucum, Cyclope neritea, Donax trunculus,* and *Donacilla cornea,* all species living in colonies, can be found not only near the waterline but also sufficiently close to the surface of the sand or mud that their collection would be technically easy and quite fast if one knew where the colonies were. Morton (1960) describes catching the carnivore *C. neritea* in British waters by using bait (dead crabs) at low tide and watching the gastropods scurry to scavenge. I have collected both *D. trunculus* and *D. cornea* by digging with my hands in the sand at the water's edge. *Tapes decussatus,* though most likely collected by hand or with simple tools, was probably found in somewhat deeper water.

From this brief discussion it should be clear that for these species no very sophisticated equipment was needed to obtain enough shellfish for a meal. Yet other species may have required greater exertion, involving swimming, diving, the use of boats and possibly also nets. Species such as *Pinna nobilis* L. or *Spondylus gaederopus* L. (Table 2) are likely to be more typical of this second class of shellfish. Though neither appears in large numbers at Franchthi, they are consistently present during Zone IV.

P. nobilis grows attached to sandy or muddy bottoms by threads, its byssus. It favors areas of eel grass (*Posidonia*) in depths of 4-5 m.[7] Its flesh is said to be excellent, and it was also used to make ornaments at Franchthi. Since the shell is very brittle and fragile and rarely found intact on the shore, it must almost certainly have been collected alive from the sea floor. As it lives firmly anchored to the seabed, the most likely way to collect it would be by diving.

S. gaederopus is another species that lives on the sea floor, in this case firmly attached by its lower valve to hard substrates and rocks. Information about its preferred depth is discrepant, but a reasonable minimum estimate is about two to four meters. It is edible, its British name being "Spiny Oyster." The species is also regularly found in worked form throughout the Neolithic sequence at Franchthi. Because of its fairly massive structure it easily survives being washed ashore; some material found at the site clearly has been collected on the beach, but some was not. It is difficult to prise off the rocks (W. Phelps, personal communication), and quite considerable effort is likely to have been necessary in order to collect live specimens by diving.

Whatever technique or equipment was involved in gathering the different species of marine molluscs found at Franchthi Cave, it is clear that little evidence on this subject is likely to have survived from the archaeological deposits. The most important factor in successful shellfish gathering would have been "local knowledge": what beaches were favored by what species, what last year's spatfall had been like, where the colony was densest, where other people's collecting areas were, and so on. There is no reason to doubt that this knowledge and these skills would have been possessed by the prehistoric inhabitants of Franchthi Cave. This once again emphasizes the fact that, of the wide range of molluscs available, they selected at each time only certain species.

THE ROLE OF SHELLFISH IN THE DIET

Nutritional Contribution

It has been customary to give, at some stage in the publication of marine mollusca, an estimate of the caloric value contributed to the total diet by this category of faunal remains. Under most circumstances shell does not decay rapidly, and for that reason it often appears to represent a significant part of the food refuse at an archaeological site. In terms of caloric contribution to the annual needs of an individual group, this appearance is frequently illusory.

The problem has been extensively discussed and reviewed (e.g., Bailey 1975; Meehan 1982). Investigations such as these have concentrated on sites with a very much higher component of shell in the deposits than at Franchthi, usually actual shell midden sites. It therefore seems to me to be a meaningless, if not an actively misleading, exercise to attempt estimates of caloric value and dietary importance for the quantitatively rather unimportant shell remains found at Franchthi Cave. A moment's reflection will make this clear. If 100 grams of mussel (live weight) has 66 calories and 100 grams of chinook salmon 222 calories (values from G. R. Heath, personal communication), then people will clearly put their energy into acquiring a single 50 lb chinook and not 180 lbs of mussels. So the find of a single tunny vertebra or equid rib is likely to represent a far more important contribution to the nutritional needs of a group than that of a hundred shells.

The problem of estimating the dietary importance of different categories of faunal remains to the total nutritional needs of a group is further complicated by the fact that it is very difficult to estimate the role played in the diet by vegetable foodstuffs (e.g., Clarke 1976). Franchthi is no exception to this situation (Hansen 1978, 1980). Given these reasons, together with the current lack of information available about the other faunal remains, it seems to be pointless to attempt to quantify the contribution of marine molluscs to the diet, except to state that, overall, it cannot have been large. Unlike terrestrial molluscs, there is at no point in the excavated sequence any evidence for concentrations of marine shell. Though constantly present in the deposits after about 11,000 B.P., the quantities of marine molluscs are always small. To attempt to understand their importance for the people using the cave and the surrounding area, one must turn to other explanations.

Apart from providing necessary trace elements and apart from being gathered when other resources were temporarily meager, I would suggest that the main role shellfish may have had, at least in some periods, was that of adding "spice" to the diet (Meehan 1982). In other words, shellfish at Franchthi may have been eaten in order to relieve the monotony of the diet, to provide a relish, and not to act as a staple. While neither demonstrable nor quantifiable, this is reasonable and seems to me to accord a significant role to shellfish in the diet of the Franchthi people.

Seasonal Value of Shellfish

Though it is not possible to estimate reliably the importance of marine shellfish in the diet in terms of volume, there are some ways in which they may have had a considerable seasonal importance for the inhabitants of the site.

First, although shellfish may have contributed little in terms of the total annual food intake, it is possible that marine molluscs were not an insignificant resource during a particular season. That could either have been when certain other foodstuffs were not present or when they were not so easily or so reliably procured. Seasonality may be determined by counting the daily growth lines (Koike 1980) or by oxygen isotope analysis (Bailey et al. 1983). Such determinations may show a pattern that suggests regular gathering over a long period of time, or else clustering, suggesting that gathering took place during a very short period. One way such clustering has been interpreted (Rowley-Conwy 1981) is to suggest that the concentration of marine molluscs represents reliance on a stable and sessile food source at a time of shortage of other resources. Though such a food type may not be economic in itself, it can, under certain circumstances, be critical in reliably bridging a gap.

The interpretation of seasonal information about shellfish gathering must be carried out in the light of other data about the economy and the use of the site as a whole. Unfortunately, little faunal information is as yet available from Franchthi (Payne 1975). Yet it is possible that at some periods marine molluscs may have been acquired as a secondary activity when a primary activity such as herding or fishing took the group near the shore (see Deith 1983b). Studies of the seasonal pattern of collecting (Deith and N. J. Shackleton, this volume) suggest changes in the patterns of seasonal exploitation during the occupational sequence at the site.

A final point to emphasize about a seasonal role for shellfish is one that has not yet received much attention in the literature. It concerns seasonal variation in meat weight (e.g., Chambers and Milne 1979). Most shellfish are at their most nutritious and palatable either when their food supply is most plentiful or just prior to spawning. Seasonal analyses of shellfish collecting which show clustering for a particular season need imply neither that that season was a time of scarcity of other resources nor that it was the only time that people happened to visit the site. Rather, it is possible that it was the time when the particular mollusc species was in its prime and therefore most attractive to collect and eat.

PROCESSING AND COOKING OF SHELLFISH

Little other than speculation, unfortunately, can be recorded under this heading. In most instances it has not been possible to determine whether a particular species was cooked and, if so, in what manner. Nor can one detect signs on the shell itself to indicate what methods may have been used to extract the flesh. Essentially, all edible shellfish can be eaten either raw or cooked, although it may be easier to extract the flesh, from gastropods especially, if they are cooked. Likewise, as with fungi, practically all shellfish are edible in the sense that they are not poisonous; it is merely that certain species are considered "edible and very good" (Lange and Hora [1965] on fungi) by a particular social group, while others, perhaps prized by different groups, are not. One can only suggest, by virtue of the numerical presence and condition of the shells, what species appear to represent food refuse. Similarly, one can only suggest what practices might have been adopted in terms of food preparation. Here one is informed mostly by contemporary practice and taste, and by ethnographic parallels.

Bivalve species can either have the valves prised open and the flesh eaten raw (as we frequently do with oysters today) or they can be heated so that, when the animal dies, the muscles relax and the valve opens (as we tend to do with mussels). This heating can be done by putting the shellfish near a fire, by building a fire over them (Meehan 1982), or by placing them in hot liquid. Though there are few obvious signs of burning on bivalve shells from Franchthi, the degree of heat that is necessary to force the muscle to relax is low and one would not necessarily expect the shell to show signs of burning. Apart from the lack of a suitable field technique for assessing with reasonable certainty that the discoloration sometimes observed on valves was caused by burning and not by soil conditions, there is the additional problem that discarded shells might well have been dropped near a fire or had one built over them later.

Gastropods can be treated in the same culinary ways. Since it is obviously harder to extract the flesh from its protective casing with most gastropod species, there would seem to be a greater incentive to use heat to relax the muscles and facilitate the extraction of the flesh. Otherwise one would have to crush the shell and pick the pieces of shell off the meat, or spit them out like jagged grape pips. In the Franchthi deposits, one species of gastropod, *Cerithium vulgatum,* always tends to show the same breakage pattern. This may indeed be the result of the mollusc having been eaten raw and the flesh removed after crushing the lower half of the shell. If this explanation is reasonable, it would mean that the same pattern of dealing with this type of shellfish was in use over a considerable period of time.

Just as it has not yet proved possible to make any decision about methods of food preparation or cooking which might have been adopted at Franchthi,[8] so it has not been possible to detect any implements which might have been involved in food preparation. I have not seen a consistent pattern of damage to valves of shells such as *Cerastoderma glaucum* which could be ascribed to their having been prised open with an implement. This is either because the outer edge is no longer in good enough condition for one to detect the kind of chipping that would have resulted, or because there is no visible edge damage. This does not, however, preclude the use of, for example, a flint tool. In the same way, though one may be curious about the means used for conveying the shellfish back to the site, what containers, if any, were used in cooking, and whether any attempt was made to store the molluscs, all such questions remain unanswerable at present, relating as they do to a side of past human activity that is not easily recoverable.

CHAPTER SEVEN

Non-utilitarian Use of Marine Shell at Franchthi Cave

Though the bulk of the marine molluscan remains at Franchthi records past meals, not all marine shells are present because of past food-gathering expeditions. This chapter deals in outline with that small proportion of the total quantity of marine molluscs found at the site which does not represent food refuse but was put to some ornamental use. It is clear that from early on in the archaeological sequence some shells were brought into the cave for non-utilitarian purposes. The phrase "non-utilitarian purposes" is used since it is difficult to determine whether a shell which had been modified and changed from its natural state was intended to form part of a garment, bag or container, was used directly as jewelry worn on the person, was used for exchange, or was held to have some symbolic significance. All such possibilities (and no doubt others) are brought together here under the heading "non-utilitarian use of shell." I do not mean to imply, however, that all species or individual shells so categorized served the same purpose at the same time, let alone throughout the occupational history of the site.

The emphasis here is on the acquisition of marine shell as a resource to create non-utilitarian objects rather than on descriptive details of the artifacts themselves. The approach that I have found most useful was to begin by thinking in terms of the extent to which worked shell at the site originated from shells collected as live molluscs or from beach-collected material. Following on from that is an attempt to see what had been used unmodified, modified, or treated as raw material to be "mined." I therefore consider the term "utilized shell" less misleading than "worked shell." The names and object descriptions that appear here and in the catalogue (Appendix E), terms such as "spoon" or "pendant," are used for convenience only. We do not have adequate grounds for stating that all "pendants" or "beads," for example, were intended for use as jewelry, strung and worn in the manner we now associate with those terms. For the sake of expediency, I shall use the terms for familiar shapes without quotation marks and without implying a firm functional assignment.

Archaeologists have hitherto tended to be rather naive in their evaluation of shells with holes. It is necessary to recognize that there are many natural agents besides man capable of making a hole, even a very neat one, in a marine mollusc. Various carnivorous molluscs bore holes of different dimensions in other molluscs. Moreover, boring sponges modify shells, certain species of birds also prey on molluscs, and wave action on the beach may inflict shell damage. Natural agents such as these should be carefully considered and, only if all have been eliminated, is it wise to consider whether modifications are likely to have been man-made.

Appendix E contains a catalogue of the worked shell inventoried in the Nafplion Museum, with a brief description of each object and a species identification wherever possible.

Appendix D offers a brief description of the manufacture of beads from *Cerastoderma glaucum* found on Paralia.

This chapter concentrates on showing the manner in which certain species of molluscs were treated as *objets trouvés* and others were collected as primary raw material. The current absence of detailed chronological and stratigraphic information for the site makes difficult discussion of changes in the use of "ornamental" shell through time and space, except in the most general terms. This especially applies to the Neolithic remains from which most of the material is derived.[9] It is not yet possible to compare in detail finds from the deposits inside the cave with those from Paralia, where there is a heavy concentration of worked shell. Table 4 illustrates a general pattern of chronological distribution for the non-utilitarian use of shell at Franchthi.

Two collecting patterns are observable. First, there are those shells that were picked up on the beach and, because of their intrinsic shape or naturally occurring fractures or holes, were immediately usable. This is not to imply that these pieces were either incapable of receiving further modification or that they were always left unaltered. The other pattern is that in which the shell is seen as raw material from which a bead, pendant, or other article could be manufactured. These two patterns of shell utilization are distinct and recognizable, though they may not, of course, have been perceived as such by the users themselves.

The species of Mediterranean molluscs considered here are those most frequently represented among the shell artifacts at Franchthi. All (with the exception of *Dentalium* spp., *Luria lurida* (L.), and *Glycimeris* sp.) could theoretically have been obtained either by gathering on the beach or by collecting live molluscs in the sea prior to utilization of the shell. Given both the range of habitats and what, at least today, can be found washed up on beaches of the southern Argolid, it seems reasonable to suggest that the species most likely to have been collected as empty shells were *Dentalium* spp., *Columbella rustica, Conus mediterraneus,* and probably *Spondylus gaederopus.* This group would also include less frequently found species such as *Luria lurida* and *Glycimeris* sp.

Those species most likely to have been collected alive are *Pinna nobilis* and *Cerastoderma glaucum. Cyclope neritea* will be discussed separately. It is quite easy, in the right areas, to find plenty of dead *C. glaucum* and also perfectly possible to collect living *S. gaederopus.* Since substantial quantities of *C. glaucum* are present as food refuse, it is plausible that the source of shell for bead-making was the leftovers from meals. Conversely, though some specimens of *S. gaederopus* look very fresh, with clear pigmentation and unworn spines, many show little in the way of fresh spines and some are very obviously beach-rolled and worn. Because this species lives firmly anchored to rocks, shell workers may have found all they needed of this species on the beach without further effort.

Of all Mediterranean molluscs only the *Dentaliidae* grow in perfect bead shape. The common name for these species is "Tusk Shells," a name which accurately describes the shape of the thin, usually white, slightly curved cylindrical shell that surrounds the living organism. Several species of *Dentalium* are found in small numbers on many of the present-day beaches in the area, and a small sandy beach in the town of Porto Kheli (Figure 7) has a relatively large number of them, presumably concentrated there by prevailing winds and currents. From contemporary evidence there is no reason to suppose that in the past there would have been any difficulty in collecting sufficient numbers of *Dentalium* shells to use as beads.

When washed up, individual specimens of *Dentalium* spp. can be found either complete, in which case the curved tip needs to be snapped off so the remaining portion can be easily threaded, or this damage has already occurred. In this case one has a number of obvious beads, distinguished from each other only by the length and diameter of the shell and

TABLE 4

DISTRIBUTION PATTERN OF NON-UTILITARIAN USE OF SHELL AT FRANCHTHI CAVE

Zone	FAS 69[a]	FAS 7[a]	FAS other[a]	FAN 69	FAN 7	FAN other	H1A 69	H1A 7	H1A other	H1B 69	H1B 7	H1B other	Paralia 69	Paralia 7	Paralia other
IV	○	○	●	○	○	●	zone not present			zone not present				●	○
III	○	○	●	●			zone not present			zone not present			zone not present		
II	○		●	●		○	●		○	●	○		zone not present		
I	●			zone not present			●			●	○		zone not present		
0[b]	●			zone not present			●			●			zone not present		

[a]69 = *Dentalium* sp; 7 = *Cerastoderma glaucum*; other = other species, but for H1A and H1B this is only *Glycimeris* sp.

[b]Since the *Dentalium* shown in Zone 0 came from sampling a very fine-grained residue from water-sieving, it is not yet possible to be certain whether this material was intentionally brought into the cave by man or not.

○ species present   ● dominant species or group of species

characteristics of the species (smooth or ridged, white or faintly flushed with pink). Most of the *Dentalium* shells found at Franchthi show no obvious signs of having been manufactured into beads, though a few appear to have been smoothed at one or both ends. More interesting is the fact that a number appear to have had a red pigment rubbed over them. These are noted in the catalogue (Appendix E). For the most part, it seems that this genus provided Mesolithic and Palaeolithic man with ready-made beads. All that was needed was knowledge of the beaches in the area.

The problem species is *Cyclope neritea* which occurs predominantly in the Mesolithic deposits in the cave. Many of these shells have a hole poked through them. It is not known conclusively whether *C. neritea* was collected dead or alive. As suggested earlier (Chapter 5), I prefer the explanation of live collection and subsequent holing of the shells for decorative purposes.

After this use of *C. neritea,* from about 8,000 B.P., much more varied use of shell for ornamental and other non-utilitarian purposes can be seen at the site. Although there is still a reliance on shells which can be found as ready or almost ready-made beads, there is a greatly increased use of shell as raw material.

Two species which, after *Dentalium* spp., most nearly resemble beads in their natural form are *Columbella rustica* and *Conus mediterraneus.* Both are easily found on beaches in the southern Argolid today. My own collecting has shown me that Kouverta (Figure 7) has the highest concentrations of these two species washed up on the beach. Both have highly variable coloration, but local finds show *C. rustica* as pink, red, or red-brown on cream, while *C. mediterraneus* is less glossy. The normal size for both species, both at the site and on present beaches, is about 2 cm in length. Apart from their size and appearance, a major attraction of these species is that they frequently show signs of attack by boring molluscs. The latter tend to concentrate on the apex and leave a neat, round hole in the shell. Some specimens have additional damage, usually a rather rough-shaped hole on the dorsal surface. Though both species live in the littoral zone, it is likely that they were collected dead on the beach, with preference for those already holed at the apexes. They are also favored by hermit crabs, which may increase the likelihood of finding specimens in very shallow water. It is possible to pass a thread through this type of hole without further alteration to the shell, though it would be rather difficult to retrieve the end of a thread or sinew at the shell's base. Many examples of both species have therefore received further modification. Often the inner spiral (columella) has been removed, and quite frequently the shell has been ground down to make a hollow, more round, less elongated bead. This not only enhances the symmetry but considerably eases the stringing. An alternative or additional kind of working is a hole ground in the dorsal surface of the shell. Another species treated in this way is the cowrie, *Luria lurida.* The latter may also have had a groove or slit "filed" in the shell.

In other species of molluscs the original shell was seen primarily as raw material to be shaped, worked, and transformed. The shells most frequently selected to provide a resource of this kind are *Spondylus gaederopus, Pinna nobilis,* and *Cerastoderma glaucum.* These three species considerably extend the range of texture, form, color, and density of material available.

S. gaederopus lives at depths of up to 40 m, with one valve attached to the rocks. It can grow to more than 15 cm in length, with parts of its lower valve being a couple of centimeters or more thick. When fresh, the top valve has short, not particularly sharp spines. The valves are a dusky rose pink outside and on the inside a white-to-cream color. *Spondylus* is edible but, although some valves at Franchthi are in good condition, many look worn, smooth, and beach-rolled. It would be advantageous for the shell-worker to use beach-collected specimens since some of the arduous labor of grinding away the outer pinkish layers to reveal the inner, ivory-colored material would already have been performed by wave action.

About a quarter of the items found of worked or partially worked *S. gaederopus* are beads, flat, disc-like or barrel-shaped. All show fine polish, ivory color, and a dense-grained surface patterning. There are also a few fragments of *Spondylus* "bracelets." Such objects seem to have been used for exchange or trade over a wide area of Neolithic Europe (Vencl 1959), so the ratio of beads to non-beads of *Spondylus* may not be representative of the relative amount of energy accorded the making of different objects out of this material. Several of the artifacts of *Spondylus* found at Franchthi, though appearing to be complete, cannot as yet be given a name or function.

The "Fan Shell," *Pinna nobilis,* produces a strong visual contrast to *S. gaederopus.* It is a large bivalve, up to 80 cm long, standing upright attached by its byssus to the substrate. Though the basal part of each valve is fairly tough, the main area is quite delicate and friable. It is therefore rare that any part of this mollusc survives being washed ashore. Because of its tendency to shatter, it is likely that the species was collected alive. Since it is said not only to be edible but to be delicious, one imagines that the shell worker was able to fortify himself before beginning the difficult task of turning this brittle shell into "mother-of-pearl" objects. Though worked pieces are generally found in the form of pendants or cut into regular or irregular shapes (whether complete or incomplete is not easy to determine), there are also some small disc beads of *P. nobilis.* It is not unreasonable to suggest that many more did not survive burial (and perhaps excavation) owing to the extreme fragility of this species.

The third main mollusc used to supply "raw shell" is *Cerastoderma glaucum.* This species lives in brackish, shallow water on muddy or sandy bottoms. From the abundant shell remains it seems likely that the species formed part of the diet of the inhabitants of Franchthi before it was "quarried" for pendants and beads. The pendants were normally formed by poking rather crude holes through a valve, but the beads were manufactured with considerable care and expertise. "Manufacture" bears a double meaning here since it seems that there was a concentrated activity in time and space turning out beads from this shell and so could possibly represent a specialized activity. A description of the process is given in Appendix D.

CHAPTER EIGHT
Epilogue

This chapter is intentionally not headed "Conclusions," for such a title would be premature at this point. However, I should like to end this presentation of the marine molluscs of Franchthi Cave with a quick glance backwards, and by raising some points of interest arising from the study which, as they seem to me, may be the most fruitful in approaching the interpretation of the site as a whole and as indicators of potentially productive areas for future research.

As always, when looking back at the end of a piece of work, there are things one would do differently if the end point were the point of departure. Practical difficulties have arisen because the data presented here were gathered over a long period of time, and by two investigators with different interests. The interpretation is mine alone, but clearly other directions could have been taken. Any discrepancies which might be noted between the summary published by Nicholas Shackleton (1969) and my work are easily explained by the increased data now available and require no further comment. Problems over differences in species identification have been less easy to resolve tidily. Such as they are, they are mentioned in Chapter 1 and Appendix C. Though resources were not available to provide several months to rework material from earlier field seasons, in practice the solution adopted is unlikely to distort the picture of past gathering activities as it has been presented here.

Few comparisons have been made here to other sites in Greece. There is no single site comparable to Franchthi in time-span, let alone access to marine resources. For the earlier periods, such work as has been done is from inland sites, with the exception of Sidari (Sordinas 1969), and work on its marine molluscs has not been published. For the Neolithic period, an obvious example for comparison would be the lowest levels at nearby Lerna (Gejvall 1969). Unfortunately, not only was a rather small area of the earliest settlement uncovered, but only about 5% of the marine shell is still available for study. Nicholas Shackleton's (1968) study of the molluscan material from Saliagos is the most relevant publication, primarily for the way the material has been analyzed and presented rather than for any direct comparison by species. His report differs from this in part because fish data from the site were available to him. At the time of writing no such data are available for Franchthi. Under the circumstances, it seemed less productive than one would have wished to look for enlightenment outside the site itself. Clearly, my approach has primarily been influenced by molluscan studies in other parts of the world (e.g., Bailey 1975; Deith 1983; Koike 1979, 1980; Meehan 1977, 1982; Rowley-Conwy 1981; Voigt 1982). One author writing about Greece whom I should like to mention here is Vickery (1936). Not only is his work on food in early Greece a most informative and enjoyable study, it is also a salutary reminder to consider the data available to him fifty years ago and realize that the kinds of data collected and the way in which they are recorded are rarely adequate for succeeding generations. I hope that some of these pitfalls have been avoided by the excavation and recording techniques used at Franchthi.

One reason why the study of marine molluscan remains has proved so interesting at Franchthi has been the availability of material retrieved by water sieving. It is largely due to Sebastian Payne's enthusiasm for and commitment to the technique, as well the director's willingness to adopt it, that so much material was processed in this way. Water sieving is not the panacea for all ills. Sampling has been, I believe, an unsolved problem at the site, but I, as so many others, have found that it added new dimensions to my study.

The most dramatic recent work affecting the interpretation of the excavations at Franchthi may have been that of Gifford (1983). Data in van Andel et al. (1980) suggested that there might have been a settlement from the Neolithic period on the bank of the old Franchthi River in what is now Kiladha Bay. In the summer of 1981 Gifford set out to test this hypothesis by coring under water in the bay. The two cores taken provide sufficient evidence to suggest that there had indeed been such a settlement. Its approximate position is indicated on Figure 13. [Additional coring by Gifford in 1985 has lent further support to this hypothesis, but the precise location and limits of the submerged "settlement" remain to be established.—EDITOR] It is obvious that any full interpretation of the excavations at Franchthi will have to take into account the presence of a now virtually unexcavatable area, but one which may have been the main focus of activity for at least some of the time prior to 5,000 B.P.

An important problem which the shellfish remains may be of assistance in solving is that of the transition between hunting and gathering and the adoption of domesticated plants and animals. A long-standing discussion, for Franchthi as for other sites, is that concerned with the question of an indigenous development of domesticated plants and animals or their introduction and adoption from an external source. In 1975, Payne commented that the evidence available to him suggested "an intrusive or largely intrusive Neolithic." As far as I am aware, nothing in the faunal remains studied since that time has altered his view. If one examines the marine shell assemblage, the change between the *Cerithium* and bivalve zones, Zones III and IV, which, in cultural terms, would approximate the transition from Upper Mesolithic to Neolithic, does not coincide with the introduction into the economy of a pattern of animal exploitation dominated by ovicaprids or the use of domesticated plants. Instead, the change in marine molluscan collecting habits coincides with the introduction of pottery (Vitelli 1974). There seems little doubt that there is an aceramic phase in the Neolithic at the site. Equally, it seems clear that the pattern of shellfish collecting remained unaltered while such a radical change in the procurement of other animal and vegetable protein was effected.

It is perfectly true that gathering, whether of plants or shellfish, could co-exist with a settled farming way of life in the past, as it does now (Forbes 1976b). Given that it is very difficult to accept *Cerithium vulgatum* as the only shellfish available, and therefore its presence indicates that it was collected by choice, I am intrigued by the absence of any reflection in the molluscan record of such a major change as an intrusive Neolithic "package." If one adds the marine molluscan data to the pottery information, it would seem that perhaps a change in social behavior was delayed until some generations after the introduction of domesticated plants and animals.[10]

As a reflection of social taste I consider it possible and indeed likely that the social value, including that of "perceived edibility or desirability," of a particular species of shellfish will have fluctuated within a time-span such as the "Neolithic." This is a promising area for future study. In particular it is hoped that, when analyses of the lithics and the pottery from Paralia are completed, it will be possible to see the degree to which the two artifact types varied simultaneously and whether synchronous change is observable in the non-artifactual marine shell. Very preliminary talks with Drs. Perlès and Vitelli suggest that the factors accounting for changes in artifact manufacture may also simultaneously affect shellfish-gathering habits. Clearly, many factors are likely to be involved, but the very fact that there is a relatively small body of molluscan remains may enable one to monitor those fluctuations successfully in the future.

In terms of the results of the study as presented here, I suggest that their main interest lies in the approach used: the likely available environmental options were first reconstructed and mapped, and then the analyses of the excavated shells were compared with the inferred resource base. It is difficult to disentangle the multiplicity of factors that may have influenced behavior in the past and is now reflected through the extant material remains. Nevertheless, I consider that each species of shellfish present at the site is likely to have had a precise value or significance for its users. The approach adopted in this study leads, I hope, to a clearer presentation of some of the possible roles shellfish may have had in the communities existing, one trusts flourishing, at Franchthi during the millennia of use of the cave and its surrounding area. Proceeding from a more secure base line of available options has allowed for greater freedom in generating hypotheses and has increased the precision of understanding of this aspect of prehistoric use of marine resources.

NOTES

1. I should like to thank all those friends and colleagues who so generously and energetically gave time and assistance to reorganizing the material in Nafplion in summer 1983, in order to allow me to make checks on the newly-housed material.

2. This pattern of work was initiated by N. J. Shackleton. I reworked some of the material analyzed by him to check the degree of agreement between our counts. Such discrepancies as were found seem largely due to the better lighting conditions in Kranidhi. The main difference was that there was a tendency for my counts to be slightly higher, the difference being about 1-4%, and within what may be assumed to be the range of experimental error.

3. The top part of the trench was not water-seived; it is shown on Figure C.1 in Appendix C.

4. For a preliminary discussion of this problem, see Deith and J. C. Shackleton (1988).

5. All sizes are taken from D'Angelo and Gargiullo (1978).

6. I should like to acknowledge here the collaboration in this part of the study of Tj. H. van Andel. I first discussed the idea with him in the summer of 1980. Since then not only has this glimmer been transformed into elegant maps, but the ensuing discussions over problems involved have, during the past three years, helped both of us achieve a more truly interdisciplinary approach to the subject.

7. C. Perlès (personal communication) has collected this species alive in Corsica at a depth of less than one meter. Current information limiting the species to greater depths may partly reflect contemporary overcollecting.

8. It is hoped that experimental work may be conducted in the future to see whether amino acids can be used to detect changes caused by heating. Similar work has been attempted on bone material (Belluomini 1981) but not yet on shell.

9. The exception is the high proportion of *C. neritea* with man-made holes in Zone II inside the cave.

10. For a further discussion of this problem, see Deith and J. C. Shackleton (1988).

APPENDIX A

Water Sieving

There has been much discussion, informally if not in the literature, on the value of water sieving in archaeology. The debate, so far as I have experienced it, concerns the problem of coping with the enormous quantities of material retrieved through this method of processing finds. I do not wish to enter the debate, but I should like to make a few brief comments, on pragmatic grounds, about water sieving as it affects the marine molluscan remains from the site of Franchthi.

Stated in the most direct way, the marine shell recovered at Franchthi from sieve-mesh sizes of >10 mm and 5-10 mm make the whole study productive and worthwhile. The shell fragments retrieved from the 2.8-5 mm and <2.8 mm meshes, on the other hand, have not proved to be of significance for the main study of marine shell. The problems raised by this last body of material are of a totally different nature from those of the rest of the study (see brief discussion in Appendix B). The larger fragments contribute importantly to the main corpus of shell, while those retrieved from the smaller mesh sizes were either a few very small fragments of larger shells or very small "complete" shells, predominantly gastropods brought into the cave unintentionally.

There are two main reasons why the material from the larger fractions has proved so important. First there is the *increase in total numbers,* and secondly those numbers result in a *change in the ratios between species present.* When sediments from excavated deposits are sieved in this way, a relatively high proportion of the "total" quantity of objects contained within those deposits can reasonably be assumed to have been detected and retrieved (Payne 1972). Consequently, the number of shells recovered will be much higher than if one only has material found in the trenches or even through dry screening. Thus there are higher total counts for trenches which were water-sieved than from archaeologically comparable ones whose soil was not treated in this way. Table A.1 shows differential retrieval between trench-collected and water-sieved material. Since absolute numbers are higher, confidence limits are improved.

The ratio of species found at different mesh sizes during water sieving generally depends on shell structure and breakage patterns. As discussed in Chapter 1, the countable part of a gastropod was considered to be the apex, while that of a bivalve was the umbo. The fragmentation of the shell, which is fairly high, is caused by a number of factors, but the result of the generalized distinction just drawn is that the actual ratio between the species present changes with the methods of retrieval adopted.

Table A.2 shows the percentages of whole shells and countable fragments of shells for some of the species recorded at Franchthi. For example, the difference between the figures for species of limpets (*Patella* spp.) and *Murex trunculus* relates to differences in the strength of the respective shell structures. Mediterranean limpets are quite thin-shelled and so fragment relatively easily, though, as is generally the case with gastropods, the apex remains the least easily damaged part. On a limpet the apical area can be reduced to a very small fragment while still being recognizable and countable. *M. trunculus* has a much heavier and more substantial structure. In this way, shells of *M. trunculus* are initially less likely to break and the apexes are less readily reduced to very small fragments. Thus there is a greater chance of this species being easily recognized and retrieved from the trench during excavation than there is for the limpets. Similarly, there is a greater likelihood of the apexes being retained by the larger mesh size. Figure A.1 gives a more detailed breakdown of the data contained in Table A.2.

The main importance of water sieving to the study of marine shell lies in the fact that, unlike chipped stone or pottery, marine shell is not itself a chronological indicator. A limpet has no features to distinguish it as "Palaeolithic" or "Mesolithic." With a site like Franchthi, it is only possible to establish stratigraphic zonation of molluscan use by means of the ratios of the main species present through time. Use of water-sieved material is therefore central to such a study because of the marked differences between the ratios obtained in this way and those yielded by trench or dry-sieved samples. It is also worth noting that one cannot assume that these changes in ratio will remain constant over reasonable intervals of time, or that one need examine only a few samples to be certain that the result will hold true for the area of the site and through time. Because of this, simple and time-saving sampling procedures are less suitable and less rewarding.

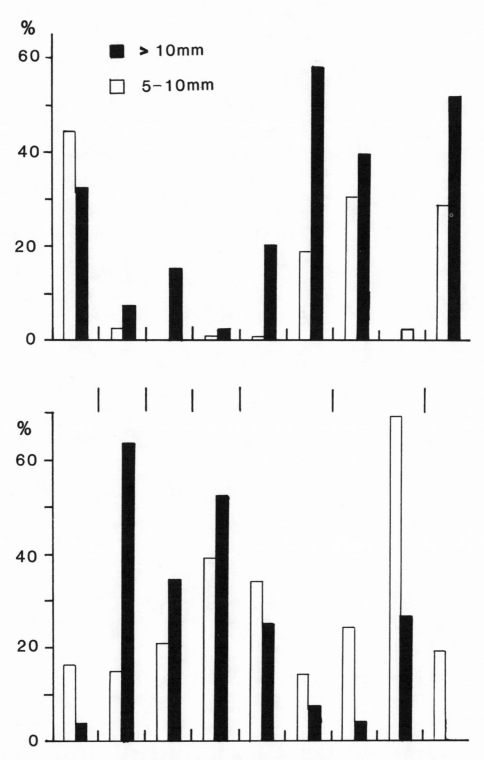

Figure A.1. Differences in species composition as a function of the mesh size of the sample (data from Trench L5, Units 55-100). *Top:* percentages of each of the nine principal species, based on counts of whole shells, separately plotted for mesh sizes 5-10 mm and >10 mm. *Bottom:* the same for fragments identifiable by species.

TABLE A.1

DIFFERENTIAL RETRIEVAL OF MARINE SHELL FROM TRENCH L5

Species: (2) *Gibbula* and *Monodonta*; (3) *Patella*; (4) *Murex*; (5) *Cerithium*; (7) *Cerastoderma*; (8) *Tapes*; (20) *Columbella*; (79) *Donax* and *Donacilla*; (91) *Cyclope*.

type	2		3		4		5		7		8		20		79		91	
unit	d	w	d	w	d	w	d	w	d	w	d	w	d	w	d	w	d	w
55	3	290			3	2	5	42	1	1	1	21		7		29		2
56	17	355	1	1		5	1	18		4	1	13		2		25		1
57	1	5						2								1		
58		82	1	2				4		1		10	1			10		
59		5										3				2		
60	3	92		1			3	14	4	6		9		4		19		
61		40		2	3	1		4	4	6		9		1		33		2
62		34	1		5	8	1	27	8	10	2	24		8		29		6
63		9						3				1				2		
64		14						1				5				5		
65		4						1				1						
66		1										4				1		
67		4					1					2				1		
68		1				4		13		10		8		7		11		1
69		3		3	2		1	14	2	4	1	5		3		8		
70		3				3		1		4		1		4		2		
71		3		1	1	1		10	1	7		7		3		6		2
72		1		1	1	4	1	6	2	4	1	6		3		6		2
73		2		1		1		9		2		6		3		6		
74				2		3		8		6		5				15		2
75			3	1	4	1		6	1	3	1	9		2		7		2
76		1		2	1	2		3	1	5		7				11		1
77		2				1		5		11		3		5		11		1
78		2		1	1	2		9	2	12		9		1		21		1
79					3	4	10	2	8		5		3		10		2	
80				4		1		11	1	11		13		3		9		5
81		1				3		8		16		15				66		3
82								7		2		2		1		7		1
83						1				2		2				2		
84		1		1				4	2	6		1						1
85	1	6					1											
86		34				4		5	2	2	1	6		1		3		
87		33		2		4		11		3		25		2		27		1
88		19		2		3	1	15	1	11		12		3		14		
89		1						9	5	9		4		2		6		1
90		7		1				1		3		3		1		3		1
91		1		2				1				1		1		2		1
92								2	1					1		1		2
93				2				5		4		1				12		
94		1		1			1	5		9		1		1		9		1
95		21						2				2				1		
96	1	59						1	1							2		
97		1																
98		1		1				1	1	6		4				2		
sum	26	1139	6	34	24	58	26	290	48	180	13	260	4	69	10	427	2	40

Note: d = dry-picked; w = water-sieved material; mesh sizes >10 mm and 5-10 mm have been combined; bottom line contains column sums.

TABLE A.2

SPECIES COMPOSITION BY SIZE FRACTIONS
FROM TRENCH L5, UNITS 55-98

Species	trench		>10mm		5-10mm		N
	who	fra	who	fra	who	fra	
Gibbula + Monodonta	2.1	0.2	32.0	4.5	44.6	16.7	1165
Patella	11.9	2.4	7.2	61.9	2.4	14.3	40
Murex	26.2	2.4	15.5	34.5	0.0	21.4	82
Cerithium	0.9	4.1	1.5	53.1	0.6	39.2	316
Cerastoderma	16.2	2.6	20.5	24.8	1.3	34.6	228
Tapes	0.7	2.1	1.8	27.4	0.0	68.0	273
Columbella	0.0	1.4	54.1	6.8	21.6	16.2	73
Donax + Donacilla	0.0	0.0	40.6	4.7	30.0	24.6	437
Cyclope	0.0	0.0	50.0	0.0	28.6	21.4	42

Note: All values are in percent of the total number (last column) of specimens of the species or species group (e.g., all *Patella*) present in the data set (Units 55-98, Trench L5; see Table A.1). The fraction labeled "trench" represents the unsieved sample. N = sum of all whole and broken specimens; *who* = whole shell; *fra* = identifiable shell fragments.

APPENDIX B

Micromolluscs

In the summer of 1980 I looked at molluscs retrieved from the finer mesh sizes of the water-sieved material (2.8-5 mm and <2.8 mm). The material that I initially examined was provided by Sebastian Payne's sub-sampling of those fractions from Trench FAS. Even though the material had undergone a preliminary sorting, it was an extremely time-consuming task to separate the marine molluscs from the remainder of the residue. Occasional tiny (but identifiable and countable) fragments of the main species present at the site were found in these fractions, but it was clear that they were basically uninformative with respect to the exploitation patterns observed in the main species of marine shell from the site. What this exercise did reveal—and it was not discovered by any other means—was the existence of many very small marine molluscs. However, it proved difficult to obtain identifications of most of the species examined. Not only is there a problem in identifying very small molluscs which have been subjected to considerable rolling and abrasion, but there is the additional difficulty of distinguishing, without adequate comparative material, the juvenile stages of various of the larger adult species of marine molluscs present in the assemblage at Franchthi. It was thus clear that a detailed study of the marine shell from these fractions would not only be immensely time-consuming, but it would require special expertise and additional funding since unit costs clearly increase exponentially with the decrease in size of the objects handled. Therefore, since there appeared to be no immediate archaeological requirement to investigate these size fractions further, I present here only my summary findings.

Figure B.1 shows the numbers of small molluscs (mainly in the size range of 3-5 mm) that were found in sub-samples of units of FAS and corrected for the fraction of the entire sample represented by the sub-sample (i.e., if the sub-sample represented 1/16, the number of molluscs counted was multiplied by 16). This imprecise approach gives at least some idea of the relative frequencies of micromolluscs in the sieved residues. The assemblages appear to be dominated by small gastropods such as those of the genus *Bittium.*

Discussion at the Franchthi Symposium in Bloomington in October, 1982, yielded various possible explanations for the presence of such small molluscs in the cave deposits. They might, for example, have been brought in with seaweed or sand together with other, larger molluscs; they might have been blown in from mud flats near the shore to the west of the site; they could have been contained in the guts of fish or octopuses or in the crops of waterfowl. No single explanation is likely to account for their presence throughout the sequence at the site.

At least in the lower part of the trench, it appears likely that their presence was due to the action of the wind and that the greater numbers of micromolluscs relative to later deposits could indicate periods of decreased human activity in the cave. For this reason I sampled selected parts of H1A and H1B in the summer of 1983, hoping to find a similar pattern. The results, shown in Figure B.2, do not seem to bear out this hypothesis. The problem is difficult but, if further work were undertaken, useful evidence regarding past human activity and its intensity in the cave might be gained from this specialized category of material.

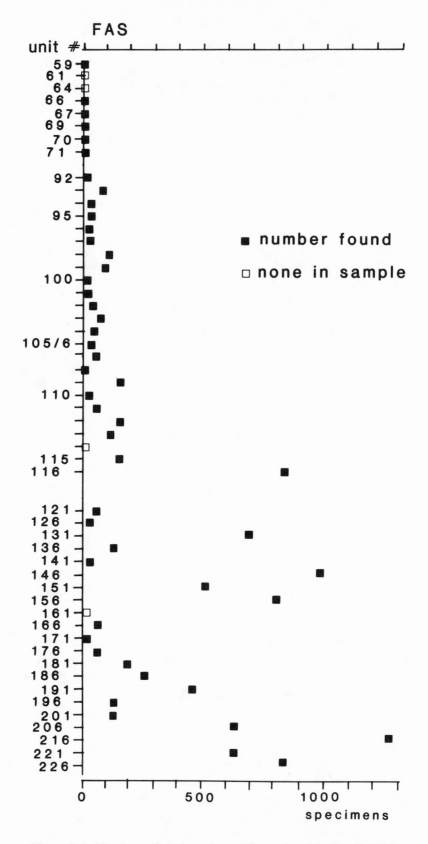

Figure B.1. Numbers of marine micromolluscs found in Trench FAS.

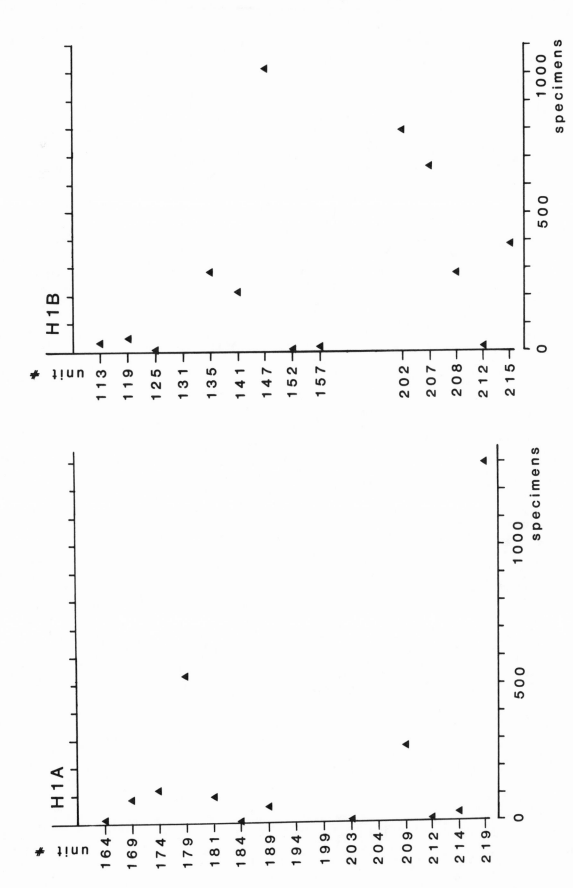

Figure B.2. Numbers of marine micromolluscs found in Trenches H1A and H1B.

APPENDIX C

Molluscan Assemblage Tables
and Trench Information

In the following tables, the composition of the marine molluscan assemblages of all excavated units analyzed in this study is shown by trench in percentages of the sum of the nine principal groups of species. The other species, occasionally not securely identified, usually comprise only a minute fraction of the total. Trenches are listed in alphabetical order beginning with those within the cave. Breaks in the numerical sequence of units mean merely that those particular units have not been analyzed. Unless otherwise indicated species counts include *both* water-sieved *and* trench material.

Note: * = only trench material counted in these units
+ = only water-sieved material counted in these units

Key

#: number of excavated unit, in numerical order
cnt1: sum of specimens of the nine principal species groups
2: *Monodonta* spp., *Gibbula* spp. combined
3: *Patella,* all species combined
4: *Murex trunculus* (L.)
5: *Cerithium vulgatum* Bruguière
7: *Cerastoderma glaucum* Bruguière
8: *Tapes decussatus* (L.), including earlier NJS counts of *Venus aurea*
20: *Columbella rustica* (L.)
79: *Donax trunculus* L. and *Donacilla cornea* (Poli)
91: *Cyclope neritea* (L.)
cnt2: sum of counted specimens of all species

As indicated in the text, the data on species identification and numbers of individuals present were collected by two different investigators over a period of 13 years. I am very grateful to Dr. Nicholas Shackleton (NJS) for generously handing over to me in 1979 all data available to him. This has been the foundation of the main data set for the trenches within the cave. I re-examined part of H1B and most of FAS, partly as a check on my own procedures and partly because of various problems that exercised me over the seasons 1979-1981. With the exception of a small part of Q5S, all work on the Paralia material was carried out by me alone between 1979 and 1981. More detailed information on the operations for the various trenches follows:

Trench FAN
NJS 105-119
JCS 105-119   (including material found in 1981)
NJS 120-193
JCS 194-230   (basal unit is 230; percentages after Unit 218 not given here because residue
               was unsorted due to limitations of time.)

Trench FAS
NJS 59-151
JCS 74-151   re-examined
JCS 152-227   (basal unit is 227; percentages for Units 212-227 not given because numbers
               are very small.)

Trench H1A
NJS 101-192   (basal unit is 219; percentages not given after Unit 181 because numbers are
               very small.)
JCS 129-164   re-examined

Trench H1B
NJS 103-164
JCS 129-164   re-examined, some new material (basal unit is 215; percentages not given
               below Unit 161 because numbers are too small.)

Paralia L5
JCS (all available material)

Paralia L5NE
JCS (all available material)

Paralia O5
JCS (all available material except Units 148-153)

Paralia Q5N
JCS (all available material)

Paralia Q5S
JCS 74-77
NJS 78-83
JCS 84-98, 136-151, 156-241 (basal unit is 241)

Paralia QR5
JCS (all available material)

Not all detailed notes for the earlier seasons were available to me, and so the total number of shells present in each unit (listed under "cnt2" in Tables C.1-10) is given simply as an undifferentiated total. The number of specimens in excess of those listed in the identified categories is usually small, especially for Zones I-III. The species most frequently represented in this undifferentiated group (in any zone) are: *Arca noae* L., *Pinna nobilis* L., *Spondylus gaederopus* L., and *Ostrea edulis* L. In addition to those species (and a very small number of unidentified specimens), the remaining specimens in the undifferentiated group belong to the following species: *Pirenella conica* (Blainville); *Bittium reticulatum* (Da Costa); *Luria lurida* (L.); *Murex brandaris* (L.); *Conus mediterraneus,* Bruguière; *Bulla striata,* Bruguière; *Dentalium,* spp.; *Arca barbata* (L.); *Mactra corallina* (L.), and *Venus verrucosa* L.

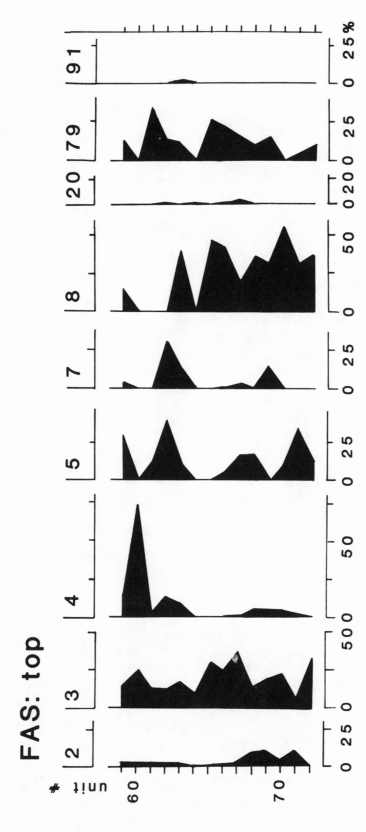

Figure C.1. Stratigraphic distribution of marine shell in upper part of Trench FAS, Units 59-72; material not water-sieved.

Judith C. Shackleton

TABLE C.1

FRANCHTHI CAVE: TRENCH FAN

#		cnt1	2	3	4	5	7	8	20	79	91	cnt2
+	105	20	5.0	0.0	0.0	25.0	10.0	35.0	10.0	10.0	5.0	23
+	108	26	3.9	0.0	23.1	11.4	15.4	23.1	0.0	23.1	0.0	27
+	109	29	6.9	0.0	0.0	27.6	27.6	27.6	0.0	10.3	0.0	29
+	110	42	2.4	0.0	0.0	19.0	16.7	45.2	4.8	11.9	0.0	44
	11	15	0.0	0.0	6.7	13.3	26.7	20.0	0.0	13.3	20.0	17
+	112	15	6.7	0.0	13.3	20.0	6.7	33.3	0.0	20.0	0.0	15
+	114	26	0.0	0.0	11.5	34.6	7.7	26.9	3.9	3.9	11.5	29
+	116	9	0.0	0.0	11.1	22.2	55.6	0.0	0.0	11.1	0.0	9
+	117	24	0.0	0.0	8.3	33.3	33.3	12.5	4.2	8.4	0.0	25
+	118	60	1.7	1.7	6.7	16.7	11.7	46.6	5.0	8.3	1.6	63
+	119	18	0.0	0.0	11.1	33.3	11.1	22.2	5.6	16.7	0.0	20
	120	245	2.0	0.0	29.0	18.7	15.5	20.0	2.9	7.8	4.1	266
	121	317	0.0	0.6	20.5	21.1	13.9	33.2	2.5	4.1	4.1	347
	122	431	0.5	1.2	13.2	9.0	11.3	53.4	4.9	4.2	2.1	480
	123	116	1.7	4.3	31.0	1.7	20.7	35.3	0.0	0.9	4.3	121
	124	83	3.6	8.4	28.9	6.0	7.2	36.3	8.4	0.0	1.2	85
+	125	18	0.0	0.0	22.2	16.7	11.1	44.4	5.6	0.0	0.0	18
	126	48	0.0	6.3	18.8	10.4	14.6	33.3	8.2	6.3	2.1	49
	127	297	1.0	6.1	21.9	7.7	10.8	37.3	9.1	3.7	2.4	308
	128	39	0.0	5.2	12.8	7.7	12.8	41.0	7.7	5.1	7.7	39
	129	102	2.9	6.7	26.6	12.8	7.8	16.7	15.7	3.9	6.9	107
	130	23	4.4	4.4	4.4	0.0	39.0	26.1	8.7	13.0	0.0	24
	131	90	2.2	5.6	7.8	8.9	12.2	46.6	6.7	3.3	6.7	97
	132	113	4.4	8.0	14.2	17.7	7.1	33.5	5.3	2.7	7.1	116
*	133	9	0.0	11.1	0.0	22.2	22.2	44.5	0.0	0.0	0.0	10
	134	173	3.5	8.1	12.1	28.3	7.5	27.2	2.9	4.6	5.8	175
	135	27	0.0	0.0	3.7	48.2	11.1	14.8	3.7	14.8	3.7	27
	136	178	0.0	1.1	5.6	48.4	7.3	9.0	2.2	26.4	0.0	180
	137	78	1.3	0.0	2.6	53.7	7.7	10.3	1.3	19.2	3.9	80
	138	20	0.0	0.0	0.0	65.0	15.0	15.0	5.0	0.0	0.0	20
	139	27	0.0	0.0	7.4	51.9	14.8	0.0	7.4	14.8	3.7	33
	140	32	0.0	0.0	3.1	37.5	31.3	6.3	0.0	18.7	3.1	33
	141	63	0.0	0.0	9.5	25.4	38.1	14.3	3.2	7.9	1.6	66
	142	60	1.7	0.0	0.0	38.3	28.3	6.7	8.3	10.0	6.7	62
	143	91	1.1	1.1	2.2	45.1	31.8	9.9	0.0	7.7	1.1	93
	144	112	0.0	3.6	1.8	29.5	39.3	9.8	1.8	8.0	6.2	120
	145	17	0.0	0.0	0.0	29.4	58.8	0.0	0.0	11.8	0.0	19
	146	101	1.0	1.0	1.0	51.4	10.9	1.0	2.0	19.8	11.9	103
+	147	12	0.0	8.3	8.3	50.0	25.0	0.0	8.4	0.0	0.0	12
	148	84	1.2	1.2	2.4	83.3	2.4	1.2	3.6	0.0	4.8	84

TABLE C.1 (continued)

	#	cnt1	2	3	4	5	7	8	20	79	91	cnt2
	149	12	8.3	0.0	0.0	58.3	0.0	0.0	16.7	0.0	16.7	12
	150	27	7.4	3.7	7.4	77.8	3.7	0.0	0.0	0.0	0.0	27
	151	77	1.3	0.0	0.0	84.4	5.2	1.3	0.0	2.6	5.2	77
+	152	80	0.0	5.0	5.0	60.0	15.0	1.3	2.5	3.8	7.4	80
	153	5	0.0	0.0	0.0	100.0	0.0	0.0	0.0	0.0	0.0	5
	154	35	0.0	0.0	2.9	97.1	0.0	0.0	0.0	0.0	0.0	35
	155	15	0.0	0.0	0.0	80.0	6.7	0.0	6.7	0.0	6.7	15
	156	7	14.3	28.6	0.0	42.9	0.0	0.0	0.0	0.0	14.3	7
*	157	3	0.0	0.0	0.0	100.0	0.0	0.0	0.0	0.0	0.0	4
	158	40	2.5	2.5	10.0	85.0	0.0	0.0	0.0	0.0	0.0	40
	159	42	4.8	0.0	9.5	85.7	0.0	0.0	0.0	0.0	0.0	42
	160	35	11.4	5.7	5.7	77.1	0.0	0.0	0.0	0.0	0.0	36
	161	74	2.7	1.3	2.7	86.5	0.0	0.0	2.7	0.0	4.1	75
	162	51	13.7	11.8	17.6	52.9	2.0	0.0	0.0	0.0	2.0	51
	163	124	5.7	6.5	4.0	76.6	0.0	0.0	2.4	0.0	4.8	125
	164	104	0.0	0.0	4.8	91.4	0.0	0.0	1.0	0.0	2.9	106
	165	149	0.0	2.0	4.0	91.3	0.0	0.0	0.7	0.0	2.0	150
	166	146	1.4	0.7	2.1	92.5	0.0	0.0	2.0	0.0	1.4	146
	167	160	0.6	0.6	2.5	87.5	0.0	0.0	3.8	0.0	5.0	160
	169	167	1.2	0.0	4.8	89.2	0.0	0.0	1.8	0.0	3.0	169
	170	208	0.5	1.0	1.0	88.9	1.0	0.0	2.4	0.0	4.8	208
	171	29	3.5	3.5	3.4	86.2	0.0	0.0	0.0	0.0	3.4	29
	172	271	0.4	5.5	6.6	69.0	0.4	0.0	2.6	0.0	15.0	273
*	173	1	0.0	0.0	100.0	0.0	0.0	0.0	0.0	0.0	0.0	2
	174	79	0.0	12.7	3.8	74.7	0.0	0.0	5.1	0.0	3.8	79
	175	110	0.9	6.4	3.6	45.5	0.9	0.0	3.6	0.0	39.1	111
	176	123	0.0	6.5	2.4	54.5	0.8	0.0	4.1	0.0	31.7	124
	177	100	1.0	9.0	3.0	43.0	0.0	0.0	3.0	0.0	41.0	101
	179	119	1.7	5.0	5.9	25.2	1.7	0.0	4.2	0.0	56.0	119
	180	38	0.0	15.8	23.7	0.0	0.0	0.0	5.3	0.0	55.3	38
+	181	6	0.0	0.0	16.7	16.7	0.0	0.0	0.0	0.0	66.6	6
	182	74	0.0	13.5	6.8	23.0	1.4	0.0	6.8	0.0	48.6	74
+	183	103	0.0	3.9	2.9	28.2	0.0	0.0	4.9	0.0	60.1	103
+	184	32	0.0	15.6	0.0	28.1	0.0	0.0	6.3	0.0	50.0	32
	185	72	1.4	5.6	8.3	8.3	5.6	0.0	5.6	0.0	65.3	73
	186	60	0.0	8.3	6.7	26.7	8.3	0.0	6.7	0.0	43.3	62
	187	219	0.5	4.1	2.3	38.4	1.4	0.0	6.9	0.0	46.6	222
	188	120	0.8	7.5	2.5	50.8	1.7	0.0	16.7	0.0	20.0	120
	189	88	0.0	20.5	9.1	47.7	0.0	0.0	3.4	0.0	19.3	88
	190	14	0.0	7.1	0.0	71.4	0.0	0.0	0.0	0.0	21.4	15
	191	31	3.2	9.7	6.5	58.0	0.0	0.0	9.7	0.0	12.9	31
+	192	43	0.0	11.6	23.3	30.2	2.3	0.0	11.6	0.0	20.9	44
+	217	54	0.0	0.0	0.0	40.7	1.9	0.0	0.0	0.0	57.4	54
+	218	152	0.7	2.6	4.6	44.7	0.7	0.0	1.3	0.0	45.4	152

Judith C. Shackleton

TABLE C.2

FRANCHTHI CAVE: TRENCH FAS

#		cnt1	2	3	4	5	7	8	20	79	91	cnt2
	73	113	21.2	8.9	5.3	18.6	1.8	41.6	0.0	1.8	0.0	119
	74	221	22.6	5.0	0.9	27.2	1.4	16.7	6.3	19.0	0.9	231
	75	91	13.2	2.2	1.1	38.4	3.3	4.4	4.4	29.7	3.3	93
	76	999	8.1	3.1	1.7	23.6	0.8	1.4	0.7	60.2	0.4	1006
	77	170	14.7	4.1	4.7	21.2	1.8	2.4	1.2	48.7	1.2	176
	78	49	10.2	2.0	2.0	32.7	2.0	6.2	10.2	32.7	2.0	51
	79	55	18.2	1.8	3.6	12.8	0.0	21.9	0.0	40.0	1.8	55
	80	11	18.2	0.0	0.0	9.1	0.0	27.3	0.0	45.4	0.0	11
	81	335	5.1	4.5	0.9	19.7	0.9	2.4	1.2	65.3	0.0	336
	82	203	3.5	2.0	4.9	18.7	6.4	36.5	2.4	25.1	0.5	206
	83	189	1.1	4.2	6.9	10.6	1.0	49.2	0.0	27.0	0.0	198
	84	113	0.0	1.8	7.1	18.6	0.9	52.1	0.0	19.5	0.0	117
	85	86	0.0	4.7	3.5	16.3	7.0	46.4	0.0	22.1	0.0	88
	86	126	0.0	5.6	0.8	3.2	0.0	62.6	1.6	26.2	0.0	127
	87	41	0.0	2.4	14.6	19.5	0.0	29.4	4.9	26.8	2.4	41
	88	58	0.0	5.2	1.7	6.9	1.7	37.9	1.8	43.1	1.7	58
	89	196	0.5	2.5	2.0	10.7	3.1	44.5	1.0	35.2	0.5	199
	90	149	0.7	0.0	12.8	13.4	1.3	55.4	2.0	14.4	0.0	152
	91	213	3.8	2.4	11.3	17.4	5.2	37.3	3.8	16.9	1.9	218
	92	16	0.0	0.0	6.3	25.0	0.0	43.8	18.7	0.0	6.2	17
	93	146	3.4	0.7	9.6	22.6	12.3	44.5	2.1	4.1	0.7	150
	94	86	1.2	3.5	7.0	38.4	4.7	39.4	1.2	3.5	1.1	87
	95	38	7.9	0.0	2.6	15.8	18.4	39.5	0.0	15.8	0.0	39
	96	20	15.0	0.0	5.0	30.0	5.0	40.0	0.0	5.0	0.0	20
	97	13	0.0	0.0	7.7	53.8	0.0	15.7	0.0	15.4	7.6	13
	98	139	5.0	2.9	4.3	30.9	7.2	32.4	2.2	12.2	2.9	142
	99	108	0.9	0.0	8.3	20.4	9.3	51.9	0.0	7.4	1.8	110
	100	36	5.6	0.0	5.6	0.0	19.4	58.3	0.0	11.1	0.0	36
	101	44	6.8	0.0	2.3	11.4	22.7	36.3	4.6	13.6	2.3	45
	102	78	5.1	0.0	5.1	18.0	18.0	46.2	0.0	7.6	0.0	78
	103	108	9.3	4.6	8.3	13.0	17.6	31.4	1.9	12.0	1.9	111
	104	77	5.2	2.6	3.9	14.3	41.6	27.2	1.3	3.9	0.0	82
*	105	16	12.5	0.0	25.0	0.0	25.0	18.7	6.3	12.5	0.0	17
*	106	6	0.0	0.0	0.0	0.0	50.0	33.3	0.0	16.7	0.0	7
	107	98	10.2	0.0	3.1	21.4	15.3	29.6	1.0	18.4	1.	100
	108	28	3.6	0.0	0.0	17.9	39.2	25.0	0.0	10.7	3.6	29
	109	137	2.2	4.4	8.0	1.5	13.9	36.4	2.2	31.4	0.0	140
	110	32	3.1	0.0	9.4	15.6	0.0	21.9	0.0	46.9	3.1	32
	111	162	0.6	2.5	4.9	21.6	3.1	60.5	2.5	3.7	0.6	163
	112	147	2.0	0.0	8.2	25.2	4.8	55.8	1.3	2.0	0.7	151
	113	83	0.0	3.6	13.3	15.7	4.8	61.4	1.2	0.0	0.0	85

TABLE C.2 (continued)

#	cnt1	2	3	4	5	7	8	20	79	91	cnt2
114	8	12.5	0.0	37.5	12.5	12.5	12.5	0.0	12.5	0.0	11
115	69	1.5	1.4	17.4	24.6	11.6	21.8	10.1	10.1	1.5	76
116	525	4.4	1.3	19.6	24.2	12.8	17.3	6.5	9.3	4.6	575
117	1002	1.1	0.8	13.9	11.5	14.2	44.4	5.7	5.6	2.9	1105
118	96	2.1	2.1	15.6	14.6	35.4	15.5	9.4	2.1	3.2	111
119	38	2.6	2.6	0.0	0.0	47.4	31.6	5.3	7.9	2.6	39
120	347	3.2	7.2	16.1	7.5	16.1	45.8	0.3	3.2	0.6	353
121	91	0.0	11.0	15.4	8.8	12.1	46.1	2.2	2.2	2.2	94
122	233	1.3	4.3	12.5	7.7	12.9	51.5	1.3	4.7	3.8	238
123	338	1.8	5.9	11.2	15.4	8.6	45.8	2.7	3.0	5.6	392
124	395	1.0	4.3	14.7	43.0	6.1	17.7	1.5	8.4	3.3	403
125	6	0.0	16.7	16.7	50	16.6	0.0	0.0	0.0	0.0	6
126	38	0.0	0.0	18.4	21.1	2.6	50.0	5.3	2.6	0.0	39
127	6	0.0	0.0	0.0	33.3	66.7	0.0	0.0	0.0	0.0	6
128	62	1.6	8.1	0.0	27.4	41.9	8.1	0.0	9.7	3.2	67
129	25	8.0	0.0	0.0	72.0	4.0	4.0	4.0	4.0	4.0	26
130	149	1.3	4.7	3.4	32.2	44.4	4.0	1.3	6.0	2.7	150
131	114	0.0	0.9	2.6	57.0	17.4	5.3	1.8	1.8	13.2	116
132	21	4.8	0.0	9.5	33.3	28.6	4.8	0.0	9.5	9.5	21
133	5	0.0	0.0	0.0	60.0	20.0	0.0	0.0	0.0	20.0	6
134	44	0.0	0.0	6.8	75.0	11.5	2.3	0.0	2.2	2.2	44
135	44	0.0	0.0	4.5	93.2	2.3	0.0	0.0	0.0	0.0	44
136	87	0.0	0.0	2.3	90.7	1.2	0.0	1.2	0.0	4.6	87
137	109	0.9	0.9	1.8	94.6	0.0	0.9	0.9	0.0	0.0	109
138	61	0.0	3.3	1.6	93.5	1.6	0.0	0.0	0.0	0.0	61
139	68	0.0	2.9	5.9	80.9	2.9	0.0	0.0	0.0	7.4	68
140	67	1.5	1.5	9.0	86.5	1.5	0.0	0.0	0.0	0.0	67
141	7	0.0	0.0	0.0	99.0	1.0	0.0	0.0	0.0	0.0	8
+ 142	30	0.0	6.7	6.7	46.7	20.0	6.7	3.3	6.7	3.3	32
143	64	1.6	6.3	4.7	82.8	0.0	0.0	1.5	0.0	3.1	65
144	133	1.5	0.8	3.8	90.9	0.7	0.0	1.5	0.0	0.8	134
145	314	4.5	4.1	4.1	82.9	0.6	0.0	1.3	0.0	2.2	314
146	191	10.0	14.1	4.2	69.0	0.0	0.0	1.1	0.0	1.6	192
+ 147	66	6.1	3.0	10.6	72.7	4.6	0.0	1.5	0.0	1.5	66
148	165	1.8	4.9	1.2	83.1	2.4	1.2	2.4	0.0	3.0	167
149	371	0.5	0.5	3.2	91.8	0.0	0.0	0.8	0.0	3.2	371
150	394	0.3	2.0	5.6	85.5	0.3	0.5	1.0	0.0	4.8	394
151	507	0.0	1.2	3.0	87.0	0.0	0.0	2.0	0.0	6.8	510
152	230	0.9	2.6	4.4	74.8	0.4	0.0	3.9	0.0	13.0	231
153	607	1.8	3.1	2.5	71.3	0.2	0.2	3.8	0.0	17.3	614
154	213	0.9	2.4	2.8	66.7	1.4	0.0	4.7	0.0	21.1	216
155	134	2.2	5.2	2.2	23.9	6.0	0.0	7.5	0.0	53.0	137
156	739	3.3	4.6	4.3	50.9	0.9	0.0	4.8	0.0	31.2	746
157	143	0.0	3.5	2.8	39.2	4.9	0.0	6.3	0.0	43.3	143
158	164	0.6	6.1	3.7	38.4	1.8	0.0	5.5	0.0	43.9	165

TABLE C.2 (continued)

	#	cnt1	2	3	4	5	7	8	20	79	91	cnt2
	159	120	0.8	4.2	15.8	36.8	0.8	0.0	8.3	0.0	33.3	122
+	160	67	0.0	10.5	3.0	35.8	0.0	0.0	3.0	0.0	47.7	70
+	161	73	0.0	2.7	4.1	52.1	0.0	0.0	9.6	0.0	31.5	75
	162	115	2.6	2.6	20.9	27.8	0.0	0.0	4.4	0.0	41.7	115
	163	39	0.0	12.7	2.6	23.1	2.6	0.0	0.0	0.0	59.0	39
	164	72	0.0	1.4	6.9	56.9	0.0	0.0	4.2	0.0	30.6	74
	165	41	0.0	2.4	4.9	17.1	0.0	0.0	0.0	0.0	75.6	42
	166	109	0.0	0.9	3.7	22.9	0.9	0.0	3.7	0.0	67.9	109
	167	16	0.0	0.0	6.3	18.7	0.0	0.0	6.3	0.0	68.7	17
	168	34	0.0	8.8	5.9	32.4	2.9	0.0	2.9	0.0	47.1	34
	169	1	0.0	0.0	0.0	100.0	0.0	0.0	0.0	0.0	0.0	1
	170	39	0.0	7.9	7.9	13.2	2.6	0.0	0.0	0.0	68.4	39
	171	17	0.0	11.8	11.8	17.7	0.0	0.0	0.0	0.0	58.7	17
+	172	35	0.0	2.9	0.0	37.1	0.0	0.0	2.9	0.0	57.1	35
+	173	26	0.0	3.9	7.7	15.4	0.0	0.0	3.9	0.0	69.1	26
	174	200	1.0	7.0	3.0	14.0	0.0	0.0	4.5	0.0	70.5	201
	175	73	0.0	10.9	2.7	6.9	0.0	0.0	0.0	0.0	79.5	74
+	176	287	0.4	3.5	5.6	3.1	0.0	0.0	2.8	0.0	84.6	288
+	177	379	0.5	0.5	0.8	6.1	0.0	0.0	1.9	0.0	90.2	382
+	178	64	0.0	3.1	1.6	4.7	0.0	0.0	0.0	0.0	90.6	64
+	179	305	0.0	1.0	0.7	18.0	0.0	0.0	3.0	0.0	77.3	307
	180	392	0.3	1.5	2.6	30.4	0.0	0.0	1.5	0.0	63.7	394
+	181	110	0.9	0.9	27.3	16.4	0.0	0.0	0.0	0.0	54.5	110
+	182	422	0.0	2.4	28.4	11.1	0.0	0.0	1.4	0.0	56.7	422
	183	338	0.6	1.5	4.7	55.9	0.6	0.0	0.3	0.0	36.4	339
	184	729	0.7	1.5	6.0	54.3	0.6	0.0	0.7	0.0	36.2	734
	185	283	1.1	0.7	13.1	36.7	3.5	0.0	0.7	0.0	44.2	284
	186	278	0.7	1.8	23.0	30.3	3.6	0.0	0.7	0.0	39.9	280
	187	210	1.4	0.0	13.3	34.9	7.6	0.0	0.9	0.0	41.9	210
	188	262	0.8	0.4	5.0	29.7	20.6	0.0	1.1	0.0	42.4	263
	189	134	1.5	2.2	7.5	28.4	18.7	0.0	0.0	0.0	41.7	136
	190	69	0.6	4.7	6.5	20.7	20.1	0.0	1.8	0.0	45.6	69
	191	276	0.4	0.7	14.5	16.7	14.9	0.0	1.8	0.0	51.0	278
	192	370	0.3	1.4	5.7	13.5	12.2	0.0	1.9	0.0	65.0	370
+	193	24	0.0	0.0	12.5	8.3	12.5	0.0	0.0	0.0	66.7	24
+	194	60	1.7	1.7	6.6	0.0	3.3	0.0	1.7	0.0	85.0	60
	195	51	0.0	13.7	13.7	13.7	13.7	0.0	13.7	0.0	31.5	54
	196	181	2.2	8.8	0.0	7.2	9.9	0.0	1.7	0.0	70.2	183
+	197	82	2.4	2.4	0.0	14.8	2.4	0.0	7.3	0.0	70.7	82
+	198	102	0.0	2.0	0.0	13.7	1.0	0.0	2.9	0.0	80.4	102
+	199	45	0.0	8.9	2.2	2.2	0.0	0.0	0.0	0.0	86.7	46
+	200	8	0.0	75.0	12.5	12.5	0.0	0.0	0.0	0.0	0.0	8
+	201	4	0.0	25.0	0.0	25.0	0.0	0.0	0.0	0.0	50.0	4
+	202	25	8.0	32.0	8.0	12.0	0.0	0.0	0.0	0.0	40.0	25
	203	57	8.8	14.0	12.3	21.0	0.0	0.0	0.0	0.0	43.9	27

TABLE C.2 (continued)

	#	cnt1	2	3	4	5	7	8	20	79	91	cnt2
+	204	138	10.1	32.6	0.0	43.5	0.0	0.0	2.9	0.0	10.9	139
	205	61	34.4	16.4	16.4	14.8	0.0	0.0	0.0	0.0	18.0	61
	206	132	21.2	37.1	1.5	34.9	0.0	0.0	0.0	0.0	5.3	134
	207	84	19.1	34.5	1.2	27.3	1.2	0.0	0.0	0.0	16.7	85
+	208	3	0.0	0.0	0.0	33.3	0.0	0.0	0.0	0.0	66.7	5
+	209	5	0.0	0.0	20.0	20.0	0.0	0.0	20.0	0.0	40.0	5

TABLE C.3

FRANCHTHI CAVE: TRENCH H1A

Note: Water sieving in this trench started at Unit 164, but no water-sieved material is included here.

#	cnt1	2	3	4	5	7	8	20	79	91	cnt2
101	58	0.0	8.6	3.5	10.3	5.2	0.0	8.6	0.0	63.8	59
102	43	0.0	4.7	0.0	9.3	4.6	0.0	0.0	0.0	81.4	43
103	14	0.0	0.0	0.0	14.3	0.0	0.0	7.1	0.0	78.6	14
104	9	0.0	0.0	0.0	0.0	0.0	0.0	0.0	0.0	100.0	11
105	15	0.0	6.6	6.6	0.0	0.0	0.0	6.7	0.0	80.0	15
106	17	0.0	0.0	0.0	17.7	5.9	0.0	0.0	0.0	76.4	17
107	23	0.0	0.0	0.0	8.7	26.1	0.0	8.7	0.0	56.5	23
108	7	0.0	0.0	14.3	0.0	28.6	0.0	0.0	0.0	57.1	7
109	4	0.0	0.0	0.0	0.0	0.0	0.0	0.0	0.0	100.0	4
110	5	0.0	20.0	0.0	20.0	0.0	0.0	40.0	0.0	20.0	5
111	20	0.0	5.0	0.0	30.0	0.0	0.0	0.0	0.0	65.0	21
112	10	0.0	0.0	0.0	20.0	0.0	0.0	20.0	0.0	60.0	10
113	6	0.0	0.0	0.0	33.3	0.0	0.0	16.7	0.0	50.0	6
114	15	0.0	6.7	0.0	6.7	0.0	0.0	6.4	0.0	80.0	15
115	3	0.0	33.3	0.0	33.3	0.0	0.0	0.0	0.0	33.4	3
116	5	0.0	0.0	0.0	0.0	0.0	0.0	20.0	0.0	80.0	5
117	36	0.0	0.0	0.0	13.9	2.8	0.0	2.8	0.0	80.5	36
118	13	0.0	7.7	0.0	30.8	0.0	0.0	0.0	0.0	61.5	13
119	13	0.0	15.4	0.0	7.7	15.4	0.0	0.0	0.0	61.5	13
123	23	0.0	8.7	4.3	13.0	0.0	0.0	4.4	0.0	69.6	23
121	8	0.0	12.5	0.0	0.0	12.5	0.0	0.0	0.0	75.0	8
122	15	0.0	0.0	0.0	0.0	0.0	0.0	0.0	0.0	100.0	15
123	7	0.0	14.3	0.0	14.3	14.3	0.0	0.0	0.0	57.1	7
124	39	0.0	2.6	2.6	7.7	2.6	0.0	5.1	0.0	79.4	39
125	27	0.0	11.1	11.1	11.1	0.0	0.0	0.0	0.0	66.7	27
126	15	0.0	0.0	0.0	6.7	0.0	0.0	6.7	0.0	86.6	15
127	42	0.0	7.1	0.0	4.7	0.0	0.0	2.4	0.0	85.8	42
128	28	0.0	3.6	0.0	14.3	7.1	0.0	7.1	0.0	67.9	28
129	64	0.0	1.6	3.1	15.6	1.6	0.0	0.0	0.0	78.1	64
130	1	0.0	0.0	0.0	0.0	0.0	0.0	0.0	0.0	100.0	1
131	78	0.0	5.1	14.1	18.0	2.6	0.0	0.0	0.0	60.2	79
132	151	0.0	2.0	5.3	31.1	2.7	0.0	0.0	0.0	58.9	152
133	14	0.0	0.0	7.1	35.7	0.0	0.0	0.0	0.0	57.2	14
134	3	0.0	0.0	33.3	33.3	33.4	0.0	0.0	0.0	0.0	3
135	100	0.0	0.0	9.0	19.0	4.0	0.0	0.0	0.0	68.0	101
136	16	0.0	6.3	6.2	6.3	0.0	0.0	0.0	0.0	81.2	16
137	14	0.0	0.0	21.4	21.4	7.2	0.0	0.0	0.0	50.0	14
138	16	0.0	0.0	12.5	25.0	12.5	0.0	0.0	0.0	50.0	16
139	15	0.0	0.0	6.7	13.3	13.3	0.0	0.0	0.0	66.7	15
140	47	0.0	0.0	4.3	14.9	12.8	0.0	0.0	0.0	68.0	47

TABLE C.3 (continued)

#	cnt1	2	3	4	5	7	8	20	79	91	cnt2
141	3	0.0	0.0	0.0	0.0	66.7	0.0	0.0	0.0	33.3	3
142	38	0.0	0.0	0.0	10.5	13.2	0.0	0.0	0.0	76.3	38
143	13	0.0	0.0	15.4	0.0	30.8	0.0	0.0	0.0	53.8	14
144	9	0.0	0.0	0.0	0.0	11.1	0.0	0.0	0.0	88.9	9
145	4	0.0	25.0	25.0	50.0	0.0	0.0	0.0	0.0	0.0	5
146	35	0.0	2.9	5.7	2.9	14.3	0.0	0.0	0.0	74.2	37
147	19	0.0	5.3	0.0	5.3	0.0	0.0	0.0	0.0	89.4	19
148	19	0.0	5.3	10.5	10.5	5.3	0.0	0.0	0.0	68.4	19
149	25	0.0	0.0	0.0	0.0	4	0.0	0.0	0.0	96	26
150	12	8.3	0.0	0.0	0.0	0.0	0.0	0.0	0.0	91.7	12
151	15	0.0	0.0	0.0	33.3	6.7	0.0	0.0	0.0	60	15
152	32	0.0	0.0	0.0	6.3	0.0	0.0	0.0	0.0	93.8	33
153	6	0.0	0.0	0.0	50.0	0.0	0.0	0.0	0.0	50.0	6
154	6	0.0	0.0	0.0	0.0	0.0	0.0	0.0	0.0	100.0	7
155	55	0.0	1.8	1.8	7.3	3.6	0.0	0.0	0.0	85.5	61
156	54	0.0	1.9	0.0	1.9	0.0	0.0	3.7	0.0	92.5	58
157	1	0.0	0.0	0.0	0.0	0.0	0.0	0.0	0.0	100.0	2
158	56	0.0	8.9	1.8	1.8	0.0	0.0	0.0	0.0	87.5	57
159	29	0.0	6.9	0.0	6.9	0.0	0.0	0.0	0.0	86.2	31
160	62	0.0	8.1	0.0	4.8	0.0	0.0	0.0	0.0	87.1	62
161	16	0.0	25.0	0.0	25.0	0.0	0.0	0.0	0.0	50.0	17
162	5	100.0	0.0	0.0	0.0	0.0	0.0	0.0	0.0	0.0	5
163	15	0.0	13.3	0.0	26.7	0.0	0.0	0.0	0.0	60.0	16
164	1	100.0	0.0	0.0	0.0	0.0	0.0	0.0	0.0	0.0	1
167	5	20.0	60.0	0.0	20.0	0.0	0.0	0.0	0.0	0.0	5
170	8	37.5	62.5	0.0	0.0	0.0	0.0	0.0	0.0	0.0	8
171	4	25.0	75.0	0.0	0.0	0.0	0.0	0.0	0.0	0.0	4
172	9	55.6	44.4	0.0	0.0	0.0	0.0	0.0	0.0	0.0	9
173	54	40.7	55.6	0.0	3.7	0.0	0.0	0.0	0.0	0.0	54
174	19	26.3	63.1	0.0	5.3	0.0	0.0	0.0	0.0	5.3	19
175	3	0.0	100.0	0.0	0.0	0.0	0.0	0.0	0.0	0.0	3
176	24	25.0	62.5	0.0	12.5	0.0	0.0	0.0	0.0	0.0	24
177	7	14.3	85.7	0.0	0.0	0.0	0.0	0.0	0.0	0.0	7
178	5	40.0	60.0	0.0	0.0	0.0	0.0	0.0	0.0	0.0	5
179	17	23.5	76.5	0.0	0.0	0.0	0.0	0.0	0.0	0.0	17
180	65	7.7	81.5	1.5	9.3	0.0	0.0	0.0	0.0	0.0	65
181	75	2.7	85.3	4.0	8.0	0.0	0.0	0.0	0.0	0.0	75

TABLE C.4

FRANCHTHI CAVE: TRENCH H1B

Note: This trench was water-sieved from Unit 101 down.

	#	cnt1	2	3	4	5	7	8	20	79	91	cnt2
*	103	2	0.0	0.0	50.0	50.0	0.0	0.0	0.0	0.0	0.0	2
	104	20	0.0	5.0	5.0	40.0	0.0	0.0	10.0	0.0	40.0	20
+	105	20	5.0	10.0	0.0	20.0	0.0	5.0	15.0	0.0	45.0	20
	106	84	0.0	10.7	1.1	25.0	0.0	0.0	11.9	0.0	51.3	84
	107	43	2.3	7.0	4.7	23.3	0.0	0.0	7.0	0.0	55.7	43
	108	93	1.1	7.5	0.0	32.3	0.0	0.0	4.3	0.0	54.8	93
	109	90	0.0	4.4	1.1	33.4	1.1	2.2	0.0	0.0	57.8	90
	110	56	8.9	1.7	3.6	35.7	1.8	0.0	1.8	0.0	46.5	63
	111	45	2.2	4.4	4.4	48.9	0.0	2.2	6.7	0.0	31.2	47
+	112	41	0.0	4.9	2.4	48.8	0.0	0.0	4.9	0.0	39.0	46
+	113	41	0.0	0.0	0.0	68.3	0.0	0.0	2.4	0.0	29.3	44
	114	35	0.0	8.6	2.9	42.8	5.7	0.0	8.6	0.0	31.4	35
	115	77	0.0	7.8	2.6	39.0	0.0	0.0	3.9	0.0	46.7	84
+	116	217	0.4	1.9	3.0	52.2	1.5	0.0	2.3	0.7	38.0	266
	117	65	0.0	0.0	1.5	23.2	1.5	0.0	4.6	0.0	69.2	66
+	118	47	0.0	0.0	4.3	8.4	0.0	0.0	6.4	0.0	80.9	49
+	119	7	0.0	0.0	0.0	0.0	0.0	0.0	14.3	0.0	85.7	7
	120	63	1.6	1.6	4.8	25.4	0.0	0.0	6.4	0.0	60.2	67
+	121	66	0.0	3.0	0.0	25.8	0.0	0.0	3.0	0.0	68.2	69
+	122	97	0.0	2.1	2.1	11.3	0.0	0.0	3.1	0.0	81.4	103
	123	148	0.0	5.4	0.7	8.1	0.0	0.0	4.1	0.0	81.7	188
+	124	220	0.0	1.4	0.9	9.6	0.0	0.0	1.8	0.0	86.3	224
	125	17	0.0	5.9	0.0	11.8	0.0	0.0	0.0	0.0	82.3	17
+	126	16	0.0	0.0	0.0	31.3	0.0	0.0	0.0	0.0	68.7	16
	127	160	0.0	0.6	1.2	23.2	0.6	0.0	0.6	0.0	73.8	160
	128	157	0.0	0.0	5.7	24.8	1.3	0.0	2.6	0.0	65.6	159
	129	122	0.0	0.0	4.8	38.7	1.6	0.0	0.0	0.0	54.9	124
	130	198	0.0	0.0	5.9	47.0	3.0	0.0	0.5	0.0	43.6	202
+	131	1	0.0	0.0	0.0	0.0	0.0	0.0	0.0	0.0	100.0	1
	132	145	0.0	2.1	11.7	38.6	5.5	0.7	0.7	0.0	40.7	146
	133	115	0.0	0.8	6.7	30.3	4.2	0.0	0.0	0.0	58.0	119
	134	155	0.0	0.5	8.0	26.4	10.0	0.0	0.0	0.0	55.1	201
	135	184	0.4	0.4	5.1	31.5	11.3	0.0	0.4	0.0	50.1	257
	136	63	0.0	1.6	1.6	14.3	14.3	1.6	0.0	0.0	66.7	67
	137	54	0.0	4.8	0.0	14.3	22.2	0.0	0.0	0.0	58.7	63
	138	123	0.0	5.7	1.6	13.8	12.2	0.0	0.0	0.8	65.9	124
	139	93	1.1	3.2	2.1	9.6	6.4	0.0	1.1	0.0	76.5	94
	140	8	0.0	0.0	0.0	11.1	0.0	0.0	11.1	0.0	77.8	9
+	141	91	0.0	2.2	1.1	7.7	6.6	0.0	0.0	0.0	82.4	97
	142	372	0.3	1.6	1.1	64.0	3.8	0.0	1.1	0.0	28.1	374
	143	59	1.7	0.0	6.8	6.8	3.6	0.0	1.7	0.0	79.4	60

TABLE C.4 (continued)

#		cnt1	2	3	4	5	7	8	20	79	91	cnt2
	144	170	0.0	2.3	0.0	7.7	0.6	0.0	0.6	0.0	88.8	178
	145	102	0.0	2.0	0.0	17.7	0.0	0.0	1.0	0.0	79.3	103
	146	16	0.0	0.0	0.0	0.0	0.0	0.0	0.0	0.0	100.0	16
+	147	204	0.5	2.0	0.5	11.3	3.9	0.0	0.0	0.0	81.8	207
	148	32	3.1	0.0	0.0	0.0	0.0	0.0	3.1	0.0	93.8	33
	149	22	9.1	4.6	0.0	0.0	4.6	0.0	0.0	0.0	81.7	22
	150	62	1.6	1.6	1.6	9.7	0.0	0.0	0.0	0.0	85.5	68
	151	20	0.0	15.0	0.0	30.0	0.0	0.0	0.0	0.0	55.0	20
+	152	2	50.0	0.0	0.0	50.0	0.0	0.0	0.0	0.0	0.0	4
	153	159	23.1	30.0	0.6	40.0	0.0	0.0	1.3	0.0	5.0	160
	154	103	32.1	33.9	0.0	16.5	0.9	0.0	0.9	0.0	15.7	109
	155	100	17.0	29.0	2.0	18.0	0.0	0.0	3.0	0.0	31.0	105
	156	153	5.3	37.9	2.6	21.6	0.0	0.0	1.3	0.0	31.3	153
	157	116	3.5	54.3	0.9	24.1	0.0	0.0	2.6	0.0	14.6	117
	158	42	0.0	35.7	7.1	7.1	2.4	0.0	2.4	0.0	45.3	44
	159	40	7.5	37.5	2.5	7.5	2.5	0.0	2.5	0.0	40.0	40
	160	39	12.8	46.2	0.0	0.0	0.0	0.0	0.0	0.0	41.0	39
	161	4	0.0	75.0	0.0	0.0	0.0	0.0	0.0	0.0	25.0	4

TABLE C.5

FRANCHTHI PARALIA: TRENCH L5

	#	cnt1	2	3	4	5	7	8	20	79	91	cnt2
*	1	12	0.0	8.3	0.0	0.0	75.0	8.3	8.4	0.0	0.0	14
*	2	3	0.0	0.0	0.0	100.0	0.0	0.0	0.0	0.0	0.0	3
*	3	4	0.0	0.0	0.0	25.0	50.0	25.0	0.0	0.0	0.0	4
	4	107	5.6	3.7	12.2	34.5	14.1	17.8	1.9	9.3	0.9	114
	5	22	9.1	0.0	0.0	9.1	40.9	13.6	0.0	22.7	4.6	22
	6	12	0.0	0.0	8.3	8.3	33.4	0.0	0.0	50.0	0.0	12
	7	10	10.0	0.0	0.0	0.0	70.0	0.0	0.0	10.0	10.0	11
	8	25	0.0	0.0	4.0	20.0	44.0	8.0	0.0	24.0	0.0	26
	9	5	0.0	0.0	20.0	0.0	60.0	20.0	0.0	0.0	0.0	5
	10	80	3.8	1.2	5.0	12.5	33.7	3.8	3.7	33.8	2.5	82
+	11	11	0.0	0.0	0.0	9.1	54.5	27.3	0.0	9.1	0.0	11
	12	31	3.2	0.0	6.5	6.5	51.5	3.2	6.5	22.6	0.0	32
	13	39	33.3	0.0	0.0	5.1	18.0	2.6	2.6	38.4	0.0	41
+	14	13	53.9	0.0	7.7	0.0	0.0	7.7	0.0	30.7	0.0	13
	15	26	7.7	0.0	0.0	0.0	53.9	19.2	0.0	19.2	0.0	29
	16	90	4.4	3.3	15.6	16.7	26.7	8.9	1.1	21.1	2.2	93
	17	181	0.6	0.6	2.7	6.1	66.9	5.5	2.2	13.8	1.6	184
	18	97	0.0	0.0	5.1	9.3	66.1	1.0	1.0	13.4	4.1	103
	19	91	4.4	2.2	6.6	17.5	33.0	7.7	3.3	16.5	8.8	94
	20	86	2.3	4.7	4.7	10.5	32.5	7.0	2.3	24.4	11.6	91
	21	53	3.8	3.8	7.6	0.0	28.2	17.0	3.8	24.5	11.3	59
	22	47	49.0	0.0	0.0	4.3	0.0	10.6	0.0	36.1	0.0	48
	23	187	2.1	4.3	5.9	17.1	30.6	12.3	3.7	17.1	6.9	197
	24	191	3.1	2.1	7.3	19.9	15.7	7.9	4.2	32.5	7.3	199
	25	125	0.8	2.4	1.6	19.2	21.6	6.4	10.4	36.0	1.6	133
	26	111	0.0	1.8	5.4	27.9	23.9	5.4	6.3	23.9	5.4	115
	27	166	1.8	1.2	8.4	25.9	21.8	3.0	2.4	29.5	6.0	171
	28	136	4.4	1.5	4.4	21.3	28.7	16.2	5.9	15.4	2.2	141
	29	154	0.7	0.0	2.6	22.7	26.6	9.7	4.6	30.5	2.6	159
	30	125	4.0	4.0	5.6	28.8	16.8	7.2	4.0	28.8	0.8	126
+	31	10	0.0	0.0	0.0	10.0	40.0	0.0	0.0	50.0	0.0	10
	32	60	1.7	3.3	0.0	41.7	18.3	10.0	3.3	20.0	1.7	64
	33	125	4.8	1.6	5.6	32.8	21.6	16.8	2.4	9.6	4.8	128
	34	113	3.5	1.8	4.4	28.3	28.4	10.6	7.1	13.3	2.6	123
	35	161	2.5	0.6	1.2	16.8	19.2	14.9	4.4	37.3	3.1	166
	36	168	1.2	0.0	0.6	20.8	27.3	19.1	4.8	23.2	3.0	170
	37	207	4.4	1.0	1.9	23.2	34.2	17.9	7.2	8.7	1.5	213
	38	180	3.9	1.1	2.8	17.8	31.0	15.0	3.9	12.8	11.7	182
	39	103	5.8	0.0	1.9	12.6	34.1	11.7	5.8	12.6	15.5	109
	40	175	1.7	1.1	2.3	21.1	40.1	12.0	10.3	10.3	1.1	180

TABLE C.5 (continued)

	#	cnt1	2	3	4	5	7	8	20	79	91	cnt2
	41	199	4.0	0.0	2.0	28.1	29.6	14.1	8.0	12.7	1.5	206
	42	128	0.8	5.5	2.3	28.9	32.0	9.4	7.0	13.3	0.8	139
	43	62	0.0	3.2	3.2	38.7	21.0	12.9	6.5	12.9	1.6	67
	44	76	1.3	3.9	1.3	34.2	35.6	6.6	1.3	14.5	1.3	77
	45	52	1.9	1.9	1.9	23.1	63.5	1.9	1.9	3.9	0.0	55
	46	65	0.0	0.0	0.0	10.8	67.6	13.9	3.1	3.1	1.5	65
	47	18	0.0	5.6	0.0	16.6	50.0	16.6	5.6	5.6	0.0	19
+	48	11	0.0	0.0	0.0	9.0	45.5	45.5	0.0	0.0	0.0	13
	49	12	0.0	0.0	8.3	0.0	83.4	0.0	8.3	0.0	0.0	12
	50	34	2.9	0.0	0.0	2.9	79.4	9.0	2.9	0.0	2.9	34
	51	2	0.0	0.0	0.0	0.0	100.0	0.0	0.0	0.0	0.0	3
	52	1	0.0	0.0	0.0	0.0	100.0	0.0	0.0	0.0	0.0	1
+	53	1	0.0	0.0	0.0	0.0	100.0	0.0	0.0	0.0	0.0	1
	55	408	71.8	0.3	1.2	14.0	0.5	2.9	1.7	7.1	0.5	416
	56	444	83.7	0.5	1.1	4.3	0.9	3.2	0.5	5.6	0.2	451
	57	9	66.7	0.0	0.0	22.2	0.0	0.0	0.0	11.1	0.0	10
	58	109	75.2	2.8	0.0	1.8	0.9	9.2	0.9	9.2	0.0	115
+	59	10	50.0	0.0	0.0	0.0	0.0	30.0	0.0	20.0	0.0	13
	60	155	61.1	0.7	0.0	11.0	6.5	5.8	2.6	12.3	0.0	185
	61	105	38.2	1.9	3.8	3.8	9.5	8.6	0.9	31.4	1.9	159
	62	161	20.5	0.6	7.5	17.3	11.2	16.2	5.0	18.0	3.7	167
+	63	15	60.0	0.0	0.0	20.0	0.0	6.7	0.0	13.3	0.0	53
	64	25	56.0	0.0	0.0	4.0	0.0	20.0	0.0	20.0	0.0	134
	65	6	66.6	0.0	0.0	16.7	0.0	16.7	0.0	0.0	0.0	63
+	66	6	16.7	0.0	0.0	0.0	0.0	66.6	0.0	16.7	0.0	76
	67	8	50.0	0.0	0.0	12.5	0.0	25.0	0.0	12.5	0.0	139
	68	50	2.0	0.0	8.0	26.0	22.0	4.0	14.0	22.0	2.0	87
	69	45	6.7	6.7	4.4	31.1	13.3	13.3	6.7	17.8	0.0	46
	70	18	16.7	0.0	16.7	5.6	22.1	5.7	22.1	11.1	0.0	19
	71	42	7.1	2.4	4.8	23.8	19.0	16.7	7.1	14.3	4.8	44
	72	37	2.7	2.7	10.8	18.9	16.2	18.9	8.2	16.2	5.4	39
	73	30	6.7	3.3	3.3	30.0	6.7	20.0	10.0	20.0	0.0	31
	74	41	0.0	4.9	7.3	19.5	14.6	12.2	0.0	36.6	4.9	46
	75	40	0.0	10.0	12.5	15.0	10.0	25.0	5.0	17.5	5.0	42
	76	34	2.9	5.9	8.8	8.8	17.7	20.6	0.0	32.4	2.9	36
+	77	39	5.1	0.0	2.6	12.8	28.1	7.7	12.8	28.2	2.7	39
	78	61	3.3	1.6	4.9	14.8	22.9	14.8	1.6	34.5	1.6	67
	79	47	0.0	0.0	14.9	21.3	21.2	10.6	6.4	21.3	4.3	52
	80	58	0.0	6.9	1.7	19.0	20.7	22.4	5.2	15.5	8.6	59
+	81	112	0.9	0.0	2.7	7.1	14.3	13.4	0.0	58.9	2.7	114
+	82	20	0.0	0.0	0.0	35.0	10.0	10.0	5.0	35.0	5.0	21
	83	6	0.0	0.0	0.0	0.0	33.3	33.3	0.0	33.4	0.0	7
	84	17	5.9	5.9	5.9	23.5	47.0	5.9	0.0	0.0	5.9	18
	85	8	87.5	0.0	0.0	12.5	0.0	0.0	0.0	0.0	0.0	8

TABLE C.5 (continued)

#	cnt1	2	3	4	5	7	8	20	79	91	cnt2
86	54	63.0	0.0	0.0	9.1	7.4	13.0	1.9	5.6	0.0	55
87	108	30.6	1.8	3.7	10.2	2.8	23.1	1.9	25.0	0.9	111
88	82	23.2	2.4	4.9	19.5	14.6	14.6	3.7	17.1	0.0	83
89	40	2.5	0.0	7.5	22.5	35.0	10.0	5.0	15.0	2.5	42
+ 90	20	35.0	5.0	0.0	5.0	15.0	15.0	5.0	15.0	5.0	20
91	9	11.1	22.2	0.0	11.2	0.0	11.1	11.1	22.2	11.1	10
92	7	0.0	0.0	0.0	28.6	14.3	0.0	14.3	14.3	28.5	7
93	24	0.0	8.3	0.0	20.8	16.7	4.2	0.0	50.0	0.0	25
94	29	3.4	3.4	0.0	20.7	31.0	3.5	3.5	31.0	3.5	30
95	26	80.7	0.0	0.0	7.7	0.0	7.7	0.0	3.9	0.0	27
96	64	93.7	0.0	0.0	1.6	1.6	0.0	0.0	3.1	0.0	64
97	1	100.0	0.0	0.0	0.0	0.0	0.0	0.0	0.0	0.0	1
98	16	6.3	6.3	0.0	6.3	43.6	25.0	0.0	12.5	0.0	16
99	17	11.8	0.0	5.9	23.5	11.8	23.5	0.0	23.5	0.0	18
100	18	5.6	5.6	5.6	38.7	5.6	22.2	5.6	11.1	0.0	20

TABLE C.6

FRANCHTHI PARALIA: TRENCH L5NE

Note: This trench was not water-sieved.

#	cnt1	2	3	4	5	7	8	20	79	91	cnt2
1	2	0.0	50.0	0.0	50.0	0.0	0.0	0.0	0.0	0.0	7
2	62	29.0	3.2	6.5	37.1	8.1	1.6	3.2	11.3	0.0	66
3	58	36.2	8.6	5.2	24.1	1.7	5.2	5.2	13.8	0.0	66
4	11	0.0	36.3	0.0	18.2	9.1	9.1	0.0	27.3	0.0	11
5	10	20.0	10.0	20.0	0.0	0.0	30.0	0.0	20.0	0.0	10
6	40	32.5	7.5	5.0	20.0	0.0	15.0	0.0	20.0	0.0	43
7	27	33.4	3.7	3.7	11.1	7.4	7.4	3.7	29.6	0.0	29
8	2	50.0	0.0	0.0	0.0	0.0	0.0	0.0	50.0	0.0	3
9	1	0.0	0.0	0.0	100.0	0.0	0.0	0.0	0.0	0.0	1
10	5	20.0	0.0	0.0	0.0	0.0	20.0	0.0	60.0	0.0	5
11	12	33.3	0.0	0.0	16.7	16.7	8.3	8.3	16.7	0.0	16
12	5	20.0	0.0	0.0	40.0	0.0	20.0	0.0	20.0	0.0	5
13	43	23.3	2.3	4.7	27.8	2.3	14.0	2.3	23.3	0.0	44
14	1	100.0	0.0	0.0	0.0	0.0	0.0	0.0	0.0	0.0	1
15	21	19.0	4.7	0.0	14.3	14.3	47.7	0.0	0.0	0.0	26
16	12	41.7	0.0	0.0	8.3	0.0	25.0	0.0	25.0	0.0	13
17	28	3.6	3.6	7.1	17.9	0.0	46.4	0.0	21.4	0.0	31
18	33	3.0	0.0	3.0	3.0	3.0	72.9	0.0	12.1	3.0	34
19	39	10.3	0.0	2.6	5.1	0.0	66.6	0.0	12.8	2.6	42
20	3	66.7	0.0	33.3	0.0	0.0	0.0	0.0	0.0	0.0	5
21	21	9.5	4.8	4.8	4.8	23.7	38.1	0.0	14.3	0.0	23
22	22	18.2	4.6	4.6	13.6	9.1	31.7	0.0	18.2	0.0	20
23	38	13.2	0.0	2.6	0.0	7.9	42.1	0.0	34.2	0.0	40
24	6	0.0	0.0	0.0	33.3	0.0	16.7	0.0	50.0	0.0	6
25	7	14.3	0.0	0.0	14.3	0.0	42.8	0.0	28.6	0.0	7
26	4	0.0	0.0	0.0	50.0	0.0	0.0	0.0	50.0	0.0	4
27	6	16.7	0.0	0.0	33.3	0.0	0.0	0.0	50.0	0.0	6
28	8	12.5	0.0	0.0	12.5	12.5	25.0	0.0	37.5	0.0	9
29	23	21.7	0.0	0.0	4.4	0.0	47.8	0.0	26.1	0.0	25
30	45	15.6	4.4	2.2	11.1	40.0	8.9	0.0	17.8	0.0	48
31	15	0.0	6.7	0.0	0.0	53.3	13.3	6.7	20.0	0.0	16
32	1	0.0	0.0	0.0	0.0	0.0	0.0	0.0	100.0	0.0	1
33	56	16.1	3.6	1.8	8.9	42.8	0.0	0.0	26.8	0.0	56
34	4	25.0	25.0	25.0	0.0	0.0	0.0	0.0	25.0	0.0	4
35	46	2.2	2.2	2.2	13.0	47.7	0.0	4.4	28.3	0.0	50
36	37	0.0	2.7	0.0	13.5	54.1	5.4	0.0	21.6	2.7	40
37	4	25.0	0.0	0.0	25.0	50.0	0.0	0.0	0.0	0.0	4
38	90	3.3	4.4	4.4	11.1	50.0	4.4	1.1	20.0	1.1	93
39	16	0.0	6.3	0.0	12.5	56.2	0.0	0.0	25.0	0.0	18
40	83	1.2	9.6	2.4	19.3	54.3	2.4	2.4	8.4	0.0	90

TABLE C.6 (continued)

#	cnt1	2	3	4	5	7	8	20	79	91	cnt2
41	2	0.0	50.0	0.0	50.0	0.0	0.0	0.0	0.0	0.0	7
41	1	0.0	0.0	100.0	0.0	0.0	0.0	0.0	0.0	0.0	2
42	31	0.0	0.0	0.0	16.1	48.4	19.4	0.0	16.1	0.	33
43	66	1.5	4.6	3.3	12.1	51.1	4.6	6.1	15.2	1.5	69
44	2	0.0	0.0	0.0	50.0	50.0	0.0	0.0	0.0	0.0	2
45	77	2.6	2.6	2.6	13.0	52.0	10.4	2.6	14.2	0.0	77
46	12	0.0	16.7	0.0	16.7	33.3	16.7	0.0	8.3	8.3	14
47	9	0.0	0.0	22.2	22.2	33.4	0.0	0.0	22.2	0.0	9
48	111	1.8	9.0	2.7	19.0	41.4	9.0	1.8	13.5	1.8	114
49	2	0.0	0.0	0.0	0.0	0.0	50.0	0.0	50.0	0.0	2
50	118	2.5	0.9	1.7	25.4	36.4	10.2	4.2	17.0	1.7	134
51	6	16.7	0.0	16.7	0.0	50.0	0.0	0.0	16.6	0.0	6
52	139	2.2	4.3	2.2	21.4	41.0	10.1	3.6	13.0	2.2	148
53	32	0.0	3.1	3.1	18.8	46.8	6.3	0.0	6.3	15.6	33
54	87	3.5	2.3	3.4	19.5	46.1	0.0	1.1	24.1	0.0	95
55	48	4.2	4.2	4.2	12.5	60.4	4.2	2.1	6.2	2.0	50
56	79	2.5	5.1	3.8	10.1	41.8	17.7	5.0	12.7	1.2	80
57	166	1.2	3.0	1.8	27.1	48.3	6.6	3.0	7.8	1.2	174
58	20	0.0	5.0	0.0	5.0	70.0	10.0	0.0	5.0	5.0	21
59	84	1.2	3.6	0.0	19.0	57.1	10.7	3.6	4.8	0.0	91
60	2	0.0	0.0	0.0	0.0	100.0	0.0	0.0	0.0	0.0	2
61	67	6.0	6.0	4.5	17.9	47.6	9.0	6.0	3.0	0.0	71
62	20	5.0	0.0	5.0	20.0	55.0	0.0	5.0	10.0	0.0	21
63	47	0.0	4.3	0.0	6.4	80.8	2.1	2.1	4.3	0.0	49
64	103	1.9	1.0	1.9	4.9	88.3	1.0	0.0	1.0	0.0	104
65	39	5.1	0.0	0.0	0.0	94.9	0.0	0.0	0.0	0.0	39
66	1	0.0	0.0	0.0	0.0	100.0	0.0	0.0	0.0	0.0	1
67	164	0.0	0.0	0.0	1.2	97.6	1.2	0.0	0.0	0.0	164
68	13	0.0	0.0	0.0	7.7	92.3	0.0	0.0	0.0	0.0	13

TABLE C.7

FRANCHTHI PARALIA: TRENCH O5

Note: This trench was not water-sieved.

#	cnt1	2	3	4	5	7	8	20	79	91	cnt2
2	72	9.7	2.8	11.1	52.7	6.9	5.6	4.2	5.6	1.4	75
3	114	2.6	5.3	10.5	62.3	4.4	3.5	1.8	9.6	0.0	119
4	153	3.9	0.7	6.5	52.3	4.6	3.9	4.6	23.5	0.0	160
5	193	2.6	0.0	5.2	48.6	1.6	0.0	3.1	38.9	0.0	199
6	89	0.0	1.1	3.4	64.0	3.4	2.3	5.5	18.0	2.3	91
7	40	0.0	5.0	7.5	65.0	7.5	0.0	5.0	10.0	0.0	44
8	28	7.1	10.7	14.3	35.8	21.4	3.6	0.0	7.1	0.0	28
9	39	5.1	0.0	10.3	61.5	7.7	5.1	0.0	10.3	0.0	42
10	32	12.5	0.0	15.6	31.3	15.6	15.6	0.0	9.4	0.0	37
11	24	4.2	4.2	4.2	25.0	41.6	12.5	0.0	8.3	0.0	25
12	10	0.0	20.0	0.0	0.0	40.0	10.0	0.0	30.0	0.0	11
13	12	0.0	8.3	6.7	25.0	33.3	8.3	0.0	18.4	0.0	13
14	41	4.9	4.9	12.2	9.8	41.4	9.8	2.4	14.6	0.0	43
15	10	0.0	20.0	20.0	0.0	50.0	0.0	0.0	10.0	0.0	13
16	41	0.0	4.9	17.1	9.8	36.6	19.5	0.0	12.1	0.0	51
17	8	12.5	0.0	0.0	12.5	50.0	0.0	0.0	25.0	0.0	10
18	23	4.4	17.4	13.0	4.4	26.1	21.7	0.0	13.0	0.0	23
19	12	8.3	25.0	0.0	0.0	41.7	8.3	0.0	16.7	0.0	12
20	44	2.3	11.4	11.4	9.1	36.2	25.0	0.0	2.3	2.3	48
21	19	5.4	0.0	26.3	0.0	26.3	26.3	5.3	10.4	0.0	20
22	7	0.0	0.0	0.0	14.3	42.8	28.6	0.0	14.3	0.0	8
23	15	0.0	6.7	0.0	6.7	46.6	33.3	0.0	6.7	0.0	20
24	30	3.3	13.3	10.0	0.0	30.0	30.0	0.0	6.7	6.7	40
25	35	0.0	5.7	14.3	17.1	31.4	20.0	0.0	8.6	2.9	38
26	38	0.0	10.5	13.2	5.3	47.3	18.4	0.0	5.3	0.0	44
27	5	0.0	0.0	20.0	0.0	40.0	20.0	0.0	20.0	0.0	5
28	22	0.0	4.6	9.1	9.1	68.1	9.1	0.0	0.0	0.0	24
29	12	0.0	16.7	16.7	16.7	33.2	16.7	0.0	0.0	0.0	13
30	8	0.0	12.5	12.5	12.5	25.0	25.0	0.0	12.5	0.0	10
31	44	0.0	13.6	15.9	6.8	31.8	20.5	2.3	6.8	2.3	47
32	21	0.0	4.8	9.5	9.5	52.4	9.5	0.0	9.5	4.8	22
33	16	0.0	12.5	6.3	12.5	37.5	12.5	0.0	18.7	0.0	20
34	20	5.0	5.0	0.0	30.0	30.0	10.0	0.0	20.0	0.0	24
35	11	0.0	27.3	9.1	9.1	18.2	27.2	0.0	9.1	0.0	12
36	12	0.0	0.0	8.3	41.7	50.0	0.0	0.0	0.0	0.0	17
37	12	0.0	0.0	0.0	16.7	83.3	0.0	0.0	0.0	0.0	15
38	32	0.0	15.6	6.3	9.4	37.4	21.9	6.3	3.1	0.0	34
39	15	0.0	0.0	0.0	0.0	66.6	6.7	0.0	26.7	0.0	17
40	27	0.0	3.7	18.5	3.7	55.6	11.1	0.0	7.4	0.0	28
41	54	0.0	5.6	11.1	5.6	66.7	7.3	0.0	3.7	0.0	64

TABLE C.7 (continued)

#	cnt1	2	3	4	5	7	8	20	79	91	cnt2
42	17	0.0	5.9	0.0	5.9	64.6	0.0	0.0	17.7	5.9	18
43	39	0.0	2.6	18.0	5.1	64.1	5.1	0.0	5.1	0.0	43
44	56	1.8	12.5	17.9	7.1	44.6	10.7	0.0	3.6	1.8	57
45	3	0.0	0.0	0.0	0.0	66.7	33.3	0.0	0.0	0.0	4
46	6	0.0	16.7	0.0	16.7	66.6	0.0	0.0	0.0	0.0	6
47	3	0.0	0.0	0.0	0.0	66.7	0.0	0.0	33.3	0.0	3
48	8	0.0	12.5	0.0	0.0	87.5	0.0	0.0	0.0	0.0	8
49	14	0.0	0.0	0.0	21.4	64.3	7.2	0.0	0.0	7.1	15
50	13	0.0	0.0	7.7	15.4	61.5	7.7	0.0	0.0	7.7	14
51	3	0.0	0.0	0.0	33.3	66.7	0.0	0.0	0.0	0.0	5
53	8	0.0	0.0	12.5	12.5	62.5	0.0	0.0	12.5	0.0	8
54	3	0.0	0.0	0.0	0.0	100.0	0.0	0.0	0.0	0.0	3
55	4	0.0	0.0	0.0	0.0	50.0	0.0	0.0	50.0	0.0	5
56	9	0.0	22.2	0.0	0.0	44.5	11.1	0.0	22.2	0.0	10
58	10	0.0	0.0	10.0	20.0	60.0	0.0	0.0	10.0	0.0	12
59	20	0.0	0.0	0.0	5.0	85.0	0.0	0.0	10.0	0.0	20
60	3	0.0	0.0	0.0	33.3	66.7	0.0	0.0	0.0	0.0	3
61	6	16.7	0.0	0.0	16.7	66.7	0.0	0.0	0.0	0.0	7
62	5	0.0	0.0	0.0	20.0	80.0	0.0	0.0	0.0	0.0	5
63	8	0.0	12.5	0.0	50.0	37.5	0.0	0.0	0.0	0.0	9
65	16	0.0	0.0	6.3	43.8	18.7	18.7	0.0	12.5	0.0	16
66	8	0.0	0.0	0.0	0.0	75.0	0.0	0.0	25.0	0.0	10
67	6	0.0	16.7	16.7	16.7	33.2	16.7	0.0	0.0	0.0	7
68	2	0.0	0.0	0.0	0.0	100.0	0.0	0.0	0.0	0.0	3
69	6	0.0	16.7	0.0	16.7	50.0	16.6	0.0	0.0	0.0	7
70	10	0.0	0.0	0.0	50.0	20.0	0.0	0.0	30.0	0.0	11
71	2	0.0	50.0	0.0	0.0	0.0	50.0	0.0	0.0	0.0	2
73	20	0.0	5.0	0.0	50.0	30.0	10.0	0.0	5.0	0.0	22
74	17	0.0	0.0	11.8	17.7	47.3	23.2	0.0	0.0	0.0	18
76	7	14.3	0.0	14.3	0.0	71.4	0.0	0.0	0.0	0.0	7
77	16	0.0	12.5	0.0	31.3	56.2	0.0	0.0	0.0	0.0	16
78	51	0.0	3.9	7.8	13.8	52.9	15.8	0.0	5.8	0.0	56
79	5	0.0	0.0	0.0	20.0	80.0	0.0	0.0	0.0	0.0	5
80	88	1.1	2.3	1.1	15.9	64.8	9.1	0.0	5.7	0.0	91
81	204	0.0	0.5	0.5	7.8	87.8	1.0	0.0	2.4	0.0	205
82	4	0.0	0.0	0.0	0.0	75.0	0.0	0.0	25.0	0.0	4
83	156	0.0	0.0	0.0	5.1	89.8	3.2	0.0	1.9	0.0	157
84	55	0.0	0.0	0.0	5.5	69.1	5.4	0.0	18.2	1.8	56
85	25	0.0	0.0	0.0	4.0	88.0	4.0	0.0	4.0	0.0	26
87	10	0.0	30.0	10.0	40.0	20.0	0.0	0.0	0.0	0.0	17
88	2	0.0	0.0	0.0	0.0	50.0	50.0	0.0	0.0	0.0	2
89	3	0.0	0.0	0.0	0.0	66.7	0.0	0.0	33.3	0.0	4
92	13	0.0	7.7	7.7	0.0	69.2	7.7	0.0	7.7	0.0	13
93	15	0.0	0.0	0.0	0.0	100.0	0.0	0.0	0.0	0.0	19
94	6	0.0	0.0	0.0	50.0	50.0	0.0	0.0	0.0	0.0	7

TABLE C.7 (continued)

#	cnt1	2	3	4	5	7	8	20	79	91	cnt2
96	1	0.0	0.0	0.0	0.0	100.0	0.0	0.0	0.0	0.0	2
97	3	0.0	0.0	0.0	0.0	100.0	0.0	0.0	0.0	0.0	5
98	10	0.0	0.0	0.0	40.0	50.0	10.0	0.0	0.0	0.0	11
99	6	0.0	16.7	0.0	16.7	33.3	0.0	0.0	33.3	0.0	8
100	2	0.0	0.0	0.0	0.0	100.0	0.0	0.0	0.0	0.0	2
101	2	0.0	0.0	0.0	0.0	100.0	0.0	0.0	0.0	0.0	2
102	29	0.0	0.0	0.0	0.0	93.1	3.5	0.0	3.4	0.0	30
103	15	0.0	0.0	0.0	0.0	100.0	0.0	0.0	0.0	0.0	16
104	4	0.0	0.0	0.0	25.0	50.0	0.0	0.0	25.0	0.0	4
106	1	0.0	0.0	0.0	0.0	100.0	0.0	0.0	0.0	0.0	1
107	5	0.0	0.0	0.0	0.0	100.0	0.0	0.0	0.0	0.0	6
108	6	0.0	16.7	0.0	0.0	83.3	0.0	0.0	0.0	0.0	6
109	2	0.0	0.0	0.0	0.0	100.0	0.0	0.0	0.0	0.0	3
110	3	0.0	0.0	0.0	33.3	66.7	0.0	0.0	0.0	0.0	3
111	86	1.2	25.6	14.0	4.7	33.6	15.1	0.0	3.5	2.3	94
112	32	0.0	6.3	50.0	0.0	0.0	34.3	0.0	6.3	3.1	38
113	31	0.0	3.2	9.7	22.6	51.6	6.4	0.0	6.5	0.0	34
114	10	0.0	20.0	30.0	0.0	40.0	10.0	0.0	0.0	0.0	10
115	12	0.0	8.3	0.0	8.3	83.4	0.0	0.0	0.0	0.0	14
116	17	5.9	0.0	0.0	35.3	58.8	0.0	0.0	0.0	0.0	17
117	23	4.3	0.0	0.0	17.4	65.2	8.7	4.4	0.0	0.0	23
118	56	1.8	5.4	25.0	5.4	51.7	7.1	0.0	3.6	0.0	61
119	9	0.0	11.1	11.1	22.2	55.6	0.0	0.0	0.0	0.0	10
120	25	0.0	12.0	16.0	4.0	64.0	4.0	0.0	0.0	0.0	28
121	3	0.0	0.0	0.0	0.0	100.0	0.0	0.0	0.0	0.0	3
122	1	0.0	0.0	0.0	100.0	0.0	0.0	0.0	0.0	0.0	1
123	11	0.0	18.2	0.0	0.0	63.6	9.1	9.1	0.0	0.0	12
124	3	0.0	0.0	33.3	0.0	0.0	66.7	0.0	0.0	0.0	5
125	19	0.0	15.8	31.6	5.3	31.5	10.5	0.0	5.3	0.0	22
126	3	0.0	0.0	33.3	33.3	0.0	33.4	0.0	0.0	0.0	3
127	22	0.0	9.1	22.7	0.0	59.1	4.6	4.5	0.0	0.0	23
128	10	0.0	0.0	10.0	0.0	40.0	40.0	0.0	10.0	0.0	13
129	3	0.0	0.0	0.0	0.0	100.0	0.0	0.0	0.0	0.0	3
130	20	0.0	5.0	30.0	5.0	40.0	10.0	0.0	10.0	0.0	22
131	10	0.0	0.0	30.0	0.0	70.0	0.0	0.0	0.0	0.0	12
132	10	0.0	0.0	30.0	20.0	50.0	0.0	0.0	0.0	0.0	11
133	5	0.0	0.0	40.0	0.0	0.0	60.0	0.0	0.0	0.0	5
134	12	0.0	0.0	25.0	8.3	41.7	16.7	0.0	0.0	8.3	15
135	9	0.0	0.0	11.1	0.0	33.3	55.6	0.0	0.0	0.0	10
136	15	0.0	0.0	26.7	0.0	40.0	26.7	0.0	6.6	0.0	16
137	5	0.0	0.0	20.0	0.0	40.0	40.0	0.0	0.0	0.0	6
138	5	0.0	40.0	0.0	0.0	60.0	0.0	0.0	0.0	0.0	5
139	29	0.0	3.5	0.0	31.0	58.5	0.0	3.5	3.5	0.0	31
140	5	0.0	0.0	20.0	0.0	40.0	0.0	0.0	40.0	0.0	5
141	12	0.0	8.3	8.3	16.7	66.7	0.0	0.0	0.0	0.0	12

Judith C. Shackleton

TABLE C.7 (continued)

#	cnt1	2	3	4	5	7	8	20	79	91	cnt2
142	4	0.0	0.0	0.0	0.0	100.0	0.0	0.0	0.0	0.0	5
143	4	0.0	0.0	0.0	25.0	50.0	0.0	25.0	0.0	0.0	4
144	7	0.0	0.0	0.0	28.6	57.1	0.0	0.0	14.3	0.0	8
145	6	16.7	16.7	0.0	66.6	0.0	0.0	0.0	0.0	0.0	6
146	9	0.0	0.0	0.0	22.2	33.3	0.0	0.0	44.5	0.0	9
147	1	0.0	0.0	0.0	0.0	0.0	0.0	0.0	100.0	0.0	1

TABLE C.8

FRANCHTHI PARALIA: TRENCH Q5N

Note: This trench was not water-sieved until Units 69 and following; Units 90, 101, and 106 contain no information from trench material.

#	cnt1	2	3	4	5	7	8	20	79	91	cnt2
1	5	0.0	0.0	0.0	100.0	0.0	0.0	0.0	0.0	0.0	5
2	35	5.7	0.0	8.6	68.5	5.7	2.9	0.0	8.6	0.0	37
3	64	10.9	4.6	20.3	0.0	0.0	10.9	9.4	35.9	7.8	67
4	211	2.8	3.3	10.9	64.6	4.7	1.9	2.8	8.5	0.5	214
5	205	7.8	1.0	8.8	65.9	4.9	1.9	0.5	6.3	2.9	210
6	62	4.8	1.6	17.7	45.2	13.0	1.6	3.2	11.3	1.6	64
7	59	1.7	3.4	11.9	22.0	40.6	3.4	3.4	11.9	1.7	66
8	45	0.0	4.4	4.4	17.7	33.3	8.9	2.2	28.9	0.0	49
9	76	1.3	1.3	1.3	29.0	36.9	9.2	0.0	19.7	1.3	82
10	166	0.0	6.0	3.0	36.2	31.3	4.8	0.6	18.1	0.0	175
11	92	0.0	5.4	3.3	30.4	43.5	4.4	1.1	11.9	0.0	95
12	66	3.0	9.1	3.0	21.2	34.9	3.0	6.1	16.7	3.0	68
13	47	0.0	2.1	0.0	31.9	36.2	12.8	0.0	17.0	0.0	50
14	24	0.0	4.2	4.2	29.2	45.7	12.5	0.0	4.2	0.0	29
15	21	0.0	0.0	0.0	33.3	57.1	4.8	0.0	4.8	0.0	28
16	20	0.0	5.0	0.0	5.0	85.0	5.0	0.0	0.0	0.0	23
18	1	0.0	0.0	0.0	0.0	100.0	0.0	0.0	0.0	0.0	2
20	27	3.7	3.7	0.0	22.2	55.6	7.4	0.0	7.4	0.0	28
21	12	0.0	0.0	0.0	25.0	33.3	33.3	0.0	8.4	0.0	18
22	18	0.0	5.6	0.0	38.9	44.3	5.6	0.0	5.6	0.0	19
23	36	2.8	13.9	5.6	30.5	11.1	11.1	2.8	22.2	0.0	43
24	33	3.0	3.0	3.0	48.6	18.2	9.1	0.0	15.1	0.0	33
25	83	2.4	1.2	2.4	59.0	13.3	4.8	0.0	16.9	0.0	85
26	233	0.0	0.9	2.6	60.3	10.3	2.6	0.9	22.3	0.0	236
27	518	0.4	0.2	3.7	78.8	7.5	0.4	0.4	8.5	0.2	525
28	341	0.6	0.3	3.8	73.9	9.1	1.2	0.6	10.6	0.0	356
29	103	1.0	1.9	0.0	38.8	21.4	2.9	0.0	34.0	0.0	103
30	7	0.0	0.0	0.0	28.7	0.0	0.0	0.0	71.3	0.0	7
31	4	0.0	0.0	25.0	50.0	0.0	0.0	0.0	25.0	0.0	4
32	55	1.8	0.0	0.0	16.4	12.7	10.9	5.5	52.7	0.0	55
33	27	7.4	7.4	0.0	11.1	11.1	18.5	7.4	29.6	7.4	29
34	45	0.0	0.0	11.1	4.4	4.4	11.1	2.3	60.0	6.7	50
34A	115	0.0	0.0	9.6	13.0	9.6	12.2	2.6	47.0	6.1	124
35	48	2.0	4.2	4.2	9.1	29.0	8.3	0.0	39.0	4.2	54
36	33	0.0	3.0	3.0	9.1	33.3	6.1	0.0	39.4	6.1	34
37	24	8.3	0.0	4.2	20.8	29.2	8.3	0.0	25.0	4.2	25
38	26	0.0	0.0	15.4	23.0	34.6	7.7	3.9	15.4	0.0	28
39	42	0.0	2.4	0.0	23.8	21.4	0.0	4.8	42.9	4.8	43
40	23	0.0	0.0	0.0	13.0	39.1	4.4	8.7	34.8	0.0	23

TABLE C.8 (continued)

#	cnt1	2	3	4	5	7	8	20	79	91	cnt2
41	48	0.0	0.0	6.3	22.9	29.2	4.2	4.2	33.3	0.0	51
42	4	0.0	0.0	0.0	0.0	25.0	0.0	0.0	75.0	0.0	4
43	97	2.1	5.2	0.0	26.8	37.0	7.2	1.0	17.6	3.1	102
44	84	3.6	1.2	2.4	22.6	30.9	7.1	3.6	23.8	4.8	88
45	76	4.0	2.6	2.6	36.8	19.7	7.9	3.9	18.4	4.0	80
46	17	0.0	0.0	17.7	23.5	5.6	29.7	5.9	17.6	0.0	18
47	75	0.0	2.7	1.3	28.0	26.7	22.7	0.0	17.3	1.3	80
48	71	1.4	2.8	1.4	31.2	16.9	29.5	4.2	9.8	2.8	79
49	56	1.8	7.1	3.6	26.8	33.9	17.9	0.0	8.9	0.0	61
50	52	5.8	3.9	3.9	26.8	34.6	11.5	3.9	9.6	0.0	60
51	36	2.8	2.8	2.8	5.6	50.0	19.3	2.8	13.9	0.0	45
52	1	0.0	0.0	0.0	0.0	100.0	0.0	0.0	0.0	0.0	1
53	64	0.0	0.0	0.0	32.5	26.6	7.8	9.4	20.3	3.3	77
54	53	5.7	13.2	0.0	18.4	30.2	9.8	3.8	17.0	1.9	59
55	51	9.8	9.8	2.0	19.6	33.3	9.8	3.9	9.8	2.0	55
56	49	4.1	12.3	0.0	16.3	36.7	6.1	8.2	14.3	2.0	52
57	32	3.1	3.1	3.1	37.5	18.9	15.6	0.0	15.6	3.1	37
58	2	0.0	0.0	0.0	50.0	50.0	0.0	0.0	0.0	0.0	4
59	10	0.0	0.0	0.0	40.0	30.0	20.0	0.0	10.0	0.0	10
60	279	1.8	0.4	2.9	76.3	6.4	2.5	2.2	6.8	0.7	287
61	335	0.9	1.2	3.0	73.3	10.8	0.6	0.9	9.0	0.3	343
62	56	1.8	1.8	3.6	26.7	10.7	7.1	5.4	42.9	0.0	59
63	75	4.0	5.3	1.3	41.4	16.0	4.0	1.3	26.7	0.0	78
64	935	1.0	0.9	1.7	51.7	13.3	1.4	0.6	29.2	0.2	951
65	607	3.1	0.8	1.5	19.1	11.1	7.6	0.3	56.3	0.2	617
66	19	10.5	0.0	0.0	15.8	10.5	0.0	5.3	57.9	0.0	20
67	1	0.0	0.0	0.0	100.0	0.0	0.0	0.0	0.0	0.0	1
69	153	1.3	1.1	7.8	25.0	18.3	12.4	6.5	24.3	3.3	159
71	178	0.0	0.0	14.6	23.9	9.6	17.4	7.9	23.9	2.5	190
73	23	0.0	0.0	8.7	13.0	21.7	30.5	8.7	13.0	4.4	23
75	45	0.0	0.0	4.4	31.1	15.7	20.0	4.4	17.7	6.7	48
77	193	0.5	0.5	14.5	9.8	14.0	34.2	3.1	19.2	4.2	199
79	28	3.6	0.0	0.0	53.5	17.9	0.0	7.1	14.3	3.6	29
80	142	0.0	2.8	14.1	13.4	21.8	27.5	1.4	17.6	1.4	150
82	18	5.6	0.0	5.6	27.7	27.7	16.7	0.0	16.7	0.0	20
83	45	4.4	0.0	2.2	24.4	35.7	4.4	11.1	15.6	2.2	48
85	8	0.0	0.0	25.0	25.0	0.0	0.0	0.0	50.0	0.0	9
86	17	0.0	5.9	0.0	17.7	11.8	0.0	5.9	52.8	5.9	19
87	5	0.0	0.0	0.0	20.0	40.0	40.0	0.0	0.0	0.0	5
89	15	6.7	0.0	6.7	20.0	0.0	20.0	26.6	20.0	0.0	17
90	1	0.0	0.0	0.0	100.0	0.0	0.0	0.0	0.0	0.0	1
97	48	2.1	0.0	6.3	2.1	31.2	31.2	0.0	25.0	2.1	51
98	33	0.0	3.0	3.0	6.1	33.3	21.2	6.1	18.2	9.1	34
99	28	0.0	3.6	0.0	14.3	21.4	17.9	21.4	14.3	7.1	31

TABLE C.8 (continued)

#	cnt1	2	3	4	5	7	8	20	79	91	cnt2
100	20	0.0	0.0	5.0	15.0	20.0	30.0	10.0	15.0	5.0	22
101	15	6.7	13.3	26.6	13.3	6.7	6.7	6.7	13.3	6.7	15
102	50	4.0	0.0	0.0	26.0	12.0	16.0	4.0	32.0	6.0	50
103	21	0.0	0.0	0.0	19.1	33.3	9.5	0.0	28.6	9.5	23
104	34	0.0	0.0	8.8	11.8	11.8	20.6	23.5	14.7	8.8	37
105	12	0.0	0.0	0.0	16.7	16.7	33.3	8.3	16.7	8.3	14
106	20	0.0	0.0	5.0	30.0	10.0	25.0	0.0	25.0	5.0	20

TABLE C.9

FRANCHTHI PARALIA: TRENCH Q5S

Note: The following units were water-sieved: 74-98, 156, and 162-168. Units 99-135 have not been studied.

	#	cnt1	2	3	4	5	7	8	20	79	91	cnt2
+	74	36	0.0	0.0	8.3	47.2	5.6	19.4	2.8	16.7	0.0	37
	75	150	0.7	0.7	8.0	28.2	11.3	18.7	2.0	26.7	4.0	155
	76	46	4.4	0.0	2.2	37.0	21.6	19.6	2.2	10.8	2.2	46
	77	187	1.6	0.5	3.7	47.6	10.2	16.6	1.1	17.6	1.1	191
	78	68	0.0	0.0	8.8	33.8	23.5	7.4	7.4	19.1	0.0	68
	79	44	2.3	0.0	9.1	40.8	11.4	18.2	0.0	15.9	2.3	44
	80	54	0.0	1.9	5.6	24.1	20.4	14.8	1.8	24.0	7.4	58
	81	7	0.0	0.0	0.0	10.0	50.0	20.0	0.0	10.0	10.0	10
	82	49	0.0	0.0	2.0	28.8	12.9	8.6	0.0	40.8	6.8	55
	83	49	0.0	0.0	10.2	30.6	8.2	20.4	4.1	22.4	4.1	51
	84	59	3.4	0.0	3.4	22.0	18.6	11.9	11.9	23.7	5.1	62
	85	48	2.1	2.1	6.3	33.3	12.5	18.7	6.3	18.7	0.0	51
	86	173	1.2	1.2	14.5	28.8	18.5	16.2	1.7	16.2	1.7	181
	87	43	2.3	0.0	4.7	11.6	18.6	16.3	13.9	27.9	4.7	45
	88	30	0.0	0.0	3.3	20.0	36.8	13.3	3.3	23.3	0.0	34
	89	32	3.1	0.0	6.3	28.1	25.0	18.7	12.5	6.3	0.0	33
+	90	11	0.0	0.0	0.0	27.5	9.1	36.4	9.1	18.2	0.0	11
	91	101	5.9	1.0	2.0	27.7	13.9	14.9	2.0	31.6	1.0	103
	92	39	0.0	0.0	7.7	23.1	20.4	7.7	10.3	20.5	10.3	43
	93	21	4.8	0.0	4.8	28.6	4.8	9.5	0.0	42.7	4.8	22
	94	34	2.9	2.9	5.9	20.7	14.7	17.6	2.9	23.6	8.8	35
	95	45	0.0	0.0	8.9	28.8	15.6	8.9	2.2	26.7	8.9	46
+	96	27	0.0	0.0	7.4	59.3	11.1	0.0	7.4	11.1	3.7	28
+	97	56	1.8	1.8	1.8	32.0	16.1	16.1	5.4	16.1	8.9	57
	98	65	0.0	1.5	0.0	24.7	36.9	12.3	4.6	15.4	4.6	67
	136	17	0.0	0.0	0.0	17.6	35.3	0.0	0.0	47.1	0.0	18
	137	1	0.0	0.0	0.0	0.0	100.0	0.0	0.0	0.0	0.0	1
	138	99	0.0	0.0	0.0	2.0	82.8	1.0	1.0	13.2	0.0	99
	139	12	8.3	0.0	16.7	16.7	0.0	16.7	16.7	25.0	0.0	13
	140	5	0.0	0.0	0.0	0.0	20.0	0.0	0.0	60.0	20.0	6
	141	84	0.0	1.2	1.2	8.3	48.8	1.2	1.2	36.9	1.2	84
	142	2	0.0	0.0	0.0	50.0	0.0	0.0	0.0	50.0	0.0	2
	143	32	0.0	0.0	18.7	34.4	21.9	3.1	0.0	15.6	6.3	33
	144	73	0.0	1.4	0.0	0.0	78.1	1.4	0.0	19.1	0.0	75
	145	19	0.0	0.0	15.8	15.8	21.1	10.5	0.0	26.3	10.5	19
	146	19	0.0	0.0	26.3	26.3	26.3	0.0	0.0	21.1	0.0	22
	147	88	0.0	0.0	1.1	3.4	81.9	0.0	0.0	13.6	0.0	91
	148	53	3.8	1.9	3.8	15.1	26.4	5.6	5.6	35.9	1.9	54
	149	21	0.0	4.8	0.0	0.0	95.2	0.0	0.0	0.0	0.0	21
	150	78	2.6	3.8	6.4	52.6	15.4	0.0	1.3	16.6	1.3	79

TABLE C.9 (continued)

#	cnt1	2	3	4	5	7	8	20	79	91	cnt2
151	12	8.3	0.0	8.3	16.7	25.0	0.0	0.0	41.7	0.0	12
156	46	6.5	0.0	2.2	15.2	26.1	0.0	2.2	47.8	0.0	46
162	15	6.7	0.0	0.0	26.6	6.7	20.0	6.7	26.6	6.7	16
163	25	4.0	4.0	4.0	32.0	20.0	4.0	0.0	32.0	0.0	26
164	58	1.7	1.7	5.2	31.0	19.0	12.1	6.9	20.7	1.7	59
165	2	0.0	0.0	0.0	50.0	0.0	0.0	0.0	50.0	0.0	2
166	34	2.9	2.9	0.0	52.9	17.7	5.9	0.0	11.8	5.9	34
167	4	0.0	0.0	0.0	25.0	25.0	0.0	0.0	50.0	0.0	4
168	15	0.0	0.0	6.7	13.3	13.3	0.0	6.7	60.0	0.0	16
169	8	0.0	0.0	0.0	25.0	0.0	0.0	0.0	75.0	0.0	8
170	81	0.0	0.0	0.0	1.2	84.0	1.2	0.0	13.6	0.0	82
171	48	0.0	0.0	0.0	2.0	81.3	0.0	2.1	14.6	0.0	50
172	65	0.0	0.0	1.5	4.1	87.2	0.0	0.0	7.2	0.0	65
174	1	0.0	0.0	0.0	0.0	100.0	0.0	0.0	0.0	0.0	1
176	56	0.0	5.4	7.1	10.7	60.7	7.1	3.6	5.4	0.0	60
177	8	0.0	12.5	0.0	0.0	0.0	0.0	25.0	62.5	0.0	8
178	5	0.0	20.0	0.0	20.0	20.0	0.0	0.0	40.0	0.0	5
179	2	0.0	0.0	0.0	50.0	50.0	0.0	0.0	0.0	0.0	2
180	38	2.6	5.3	2.6	21.1	47.3	5.3	5.3	10.5	0.0	39
181	17	0.0	5.9	5.9	17.6	41.2	5.9	0.0	23.5	0.0	20
182	7	0.0	0.0	0.0	0.0	71.4	0.0	0.0	28.6	0.0	8
183	13	0.0	7.7	0.0	0.0	46.2	7.7	7.7	30.7	0.0	14
184	27	0.0	7.4	0.0	29.6	59.3	3.7	0.0	0.0	0.0	33
185	121	0.0	5.0	4.1	14.9	65.3	4.1	0.0	6.6	0.0	129
186	47	0.0	0.0	2.1	23.5	63.8	6.4	0.0	4.3	0.0	52
187	52	0.0	7.7	0.0	13.5	59.5	11.5	3.9	3.9	0.0	60
188	27	0.0	33.3	7.4	7.4	51.9	0.0	0.0	0.0	0.0	31
189	23	0.0	60.9	4.4	0.0	30.4	0.0	0.0	4.3	0.0	25
190	59	0.0	35.6	0.0	17.0	25.4	3.4	0.0	18.6	0.0	65
191	28	3.6	7.1	7.1	10.7	21.4	21.4	3.6	25.1	0.0	32
192	10	0.0	0.0	0.0	40.0	30.0	10.0	0.0	20.0	0.0	11
193	31	0.0	3.2	6.5	29.0	35.5	0.0	0.0	25.8	0.0	32
194	10	0.0	10.0	10.0	30.0	20.0	0.0	10.0	20.0	0.0	10
195	21	0.0	57.2	0.0	14.3	9.5	9.5	0.0	9.5	0.0	22
196	10	0.0	10.0	0.0	30.0	60.0	0.0	0.0	0.0	0.0	14
197	3	0.0	0.0	0.0	0.0	33.3	33.3	0.0	33.4	0.0	4
198	6	0.0	16.7	0.0	66.6	0.0	16.7	0.0	0.0	0.0	7
199	15	0.0	0.0	0.0	26.7	46.6	6.7	0.0	20.0	0.0	17
200	33	0.0	3.0	3.0	6.1	63.7	6.1	3.0	12.1	3.0	34
201	7	0.0	0.0	0.0	42.8	28.6	14.3	0.0	14.3	0.0	9
202	55	1.8	7.2	1.8	45.5	21.8	1.8	5.5	14.6	0.0	57
203	2	0.0	0.0	0.0	0.0	0.0	0.0	0.0	100.0	0.0	2
205	20	0.0	0.0	0.0	20.0	40.0	5.0	0.0	35.0	0.0	20
208	1	0.0	0.0	0.0	0.0	0.0	0.0	0.0	100.0	0.0	1
210	28	0.0	0.0	7.1	3.6	60.7	0.0	0.0	28.6	0.0	29
211	4	0.0	0.0	0.0	25.0	25.0	0.0	0.0	50.0	0.0	4

Judith C. Shackleton

TABLE C.9 (continued)

#	cnt1	2	3	4	5	7	8	20	79	91	cnt2
212	17	0.0	0.0	0.0	0.0	76.5	0.0	0.0	23.5	0.0	18
213	140	0.7	0.0	0.7	3.6	80.0	0.7	0.7	13.6	0.0	141
214	20	0.0	0.0	0.0	15.0	50.0	5.0	0.0	30.0	0.0	22
215	23	0.0	13.0	0.0	21.7	47.9	4.4	0.0	13.0	0.0	23
217	10	0.0	0.0	0.0	10.0	50.0	10.0	0.0	30.0	0.0	10
218	19	0.0	5.3	0.0	5.3	73.6	0.0	0.0	15.8	0.0	19
219	5	0.0	0.0	0.0	60.0	40.0	0.0	0.0	0.0	0.0	6
220	10	10.0	20.0	0.0	40.0	20.0	0.0	0.0	10.0	0.0	11
221	15	6.7	33.3	13.3	0.0	40.0	6.7	0.0	0.0	0.0	15
222	21	0.0	42.9	0.0	14.3	23.7	14.3	0.0	4.8	0.0	21
223	9	0.0	11.1	0.0	22.2	55.6	0.0	0.0	11.1	0.0	9
224	5	0.0	0.0	0.0	20.0	80.0	0.0	0.0	0.0	0.0	6
225	1	0.0	0.0	0.0	0.0	100.0	0.0	0.0	0.0	0.0	1
227	1	0.0	0.0	0.0	0.0	0.0	0.0	0.0	100.0	0.0	1
228	2	0.0	0.0	0.0	0.0	50.0	0.0	0.0	50.0	0.0	2
229	63	3.2	1.6	0.0	17.4	54.0	4.8	4.8	7.8	6.4	65
230	122	3.3	41.0	2.5	15.6	18.8	4.1	1.6	12.3	0.8	126
231	62	1.6	87.1	0.0	0.0	11.3	0.0	0.0	0.0	0.0	65
232	141	2.6	44.2	3.6	22.7	9.9	7.1	2.1	7.1	0.7	146
233	41	2.4	43.9	4.9	26.9	12.3	2.4	2.4	2.4	2.4	42
234	1	0.0	0.0	0.0	0.0	0.0	0.0	0.0	100.0	0.0	1
235	1	0.0	0.0	0.0	0.0	0.0	0.0	0.0	100.0	0.0	1
236	5	0.0	0.0	0.0	0.0	0.0	0.0	40.0	60.0	0.0	5
237	77	0.0	0.0	0.0	2.6	83.1	1.3	1.3	11.7	0.0	77
238	10	0.0	0.0	0.0	0.0	80.0	0.0	0.0	20.0	0.0	10
239	14	0.0	0.0	0.0	21.4	35.7	0.0	0.0	42.9	0.0	14
240	5	0.0	0.0	20.0	0.0	20.0	0.0	0.0	40.0	20.0	5
241	3	33.3	0.0	0.0	0.0	33.4	0.0	0.0	33.3	0.0	4

TABLE C.10

FRANCHTHI PARALIA: TRENCH QR5

Note: Only Units 36-41 were water-sieved.

#	cnt1	2	3	4	5	7	8	20	79	91	cnt2
1	79	2.5	2.5	8.9	70.9	2.5	1.3	3.8	6.3	1.3	83
2	67	4.5	0.0	9.0	62.6	14.9	0.0	1.5	3.0	4.5	70
3	52	5.8	0.0	13.5	57.6	11.5	0.0	7.7	0.0	3.9	55
4	31	6.5	3.2	9.7	61.3	12.9	0.0	0.0	3.2	3.2	35
5	45	8.9	2.2	15.6	53.4	13.3	0.0	4.4	0.0	2.2	48
6	50	6.0	16.0	2.0	48.0	20.0	2.0	4.0	2.0	0.0	53
7	36	11.1	2.8	11.1	63.8	0.0	2.8	2.8	5.6	0.0	36
8	74	8.1	1.4	6.8	58.1	2.7	9.4	0.0	10.8	2.7	75
9	65	1.5	4.6	3.1	27.7	43.0	9.2	1.5	7.7	1.7	67
10	82	1.2	9.8	0.0	24.4	45.1	6.1	0.0	13.4	0.0	91
11	71	1.4	5.6	8.5	21.1	42.3	14.1	2.8	4.2	0.0	75
12	158	1.9	8.2	4.4	20.3	36.2	8.2	1.2	19.6	0.0	162
13	88	1.1	8.0	8.0	22.7	39.8	6.8	0.0	10.2	3.4	91
14	74	0.0	13.5	5.4	29.7	33.8	8.1	0.0	9.5	0.0	78
15	27	0.0	22.2	3.7	14.8	33.4	11.1	0.0	11.1	3.7	28
16	63	4.8	6.3	3.2	17.5	42.8	4.8	0.0	20.6	0.0	66
17	26	3.9	15.3	11.5	11.5	19.2	15.4	0.0	23.2	0.0	27
18	66	4.6	9.1	4.6	43.8	16.7	4.5	0.0	16.7	0.0	68
19	8	0.0	0.0	12.5	12.5	12.5	25.0	0.0	37.5	0.0	8
20	12	0.0	0.0	0.0	33.3	41.7	0.0	8.3	16.7	0.0	14
21	1	0.0	0.0	0.0	0.0	100.0	0.0	0.0	0.0	0.0	1
22	9	0.0	0.0	0.0	55.6	44.4	0.0	0.0	0.0	0.0	10
23	20	10.0	10.0	5.0	35.0	25.0	10.0	0.0	5.0	0.0	21
24	47	2.1	10.6	0.0	27.7	34.1	0.0	0.0	23.4	2.1	47
25	102	2.9	2.9	7.8	46.2	15.7	7.8	2.9	11.8	2.0	104
26	114	1.8	7.0	4.4	18.4	30.8	14.0	2.6	19.3	1.7	123
27	257	2.0	4.7	30.0	8.1	28.0	11.2	1.6	14.0	0.4	263
28	115	1.7	6.1	1.7	17.4	43.7	13.0	4.4	10.3	1.7	116
29	50	2.0	6.0	4.0	12.0	44.0	10.0	4.0	16.0	2.0	51
31	154	0.7	2.0	1.3	59.4	13.6	17.1	0.7	3.9	1.3	159
32	179	3.9	2.8	3.4	45.8	24.6	8.4	1.1	9.5	0.5	186
33	89	6.7	3.4	0.0	21.4	29.1	7.9	3.4	28.1	0.0	90
35	50	0.0	2.0	2.0	2.0	42.0	18.0	4.0	30.0	0.0	57
36	124	3.3	3.3	0.8	36.2	19.4	9.7	10.4	14.5	2.4	132
37	39	5.1	5.1	5.1	33.4	28.2	5.1	7.7	10.3	0.0	45
38	101	3.0	3.0	3.0	37.5	24.8	7.9	5.9	13.9	1.0	103
39	161	9.9	1.2	2.5	42.2	21.8	5.0	5.0	9.9	2.5	166
40	117	5.1	1.7	5.1	41.1	29.1	6.0	3.4	7.7	0.8	120
41	166	6.6	4.2	4.2	35.5	18.1	9.7	3.6	15.7	2.4	173
42	11	9.1	9.1	0.0	27.3	36.3	9.1	0.0	9.1	0.0	12
43	71	0.0	7.0	7.0	28.3	23.9	5.6	5.6	22.6	0.0	76
44	15	6.7	6.7	0.0	20.0	46.6	13.3	0.0	6.7	0.0	16

APPENDIX D

Cerastoderma Bead Making in Trench L5

An examination of shells found in the Neolithic deposits on Paralia gives the impression that there is an emphasis on the decorative aspects of marine shell as well as on its use for food value. Numbers of shells which are decorative in their natural state as well as of those which can be worked into items such as pendants and beads are found in the Paralia trenches. In L5 in particular, there is a clear concentration on the use of *Cerastoderma glaucum* Bruguière, the Mediterranean cockle, for bead making. Though the finds range over a number of units and more than one stratigraphic layer, there is a clustering of this material between L5:33 and L5:42.

Having studied several hundred fragments of *C. glaucum,* some obviously worked, others not so, I present the following suggestions regarding the bead-making process at this site. While I could offer an exception to almost any statement that follows, there appears to be enough material to deduce the general pattern.

CHOICE OF MATERIAL

Cerastoderma glaucum was the preferred shell for bead making in L5. The material from this trench represents the majority of the shell beads, incomplete or finished, for the site as a whole. (This does not take into account "beads" made of *Cyclope neritea* which have holes poked in the shell.)

STAGES OF WORKING

1. Cutting. Pieces of shell for bead blanks were cut or chipped out of the valve which had probably first been broken. This cutting was, I suspect, technically quite difficult and explains why the small objects (5-10 mm in diameter) were cut before one surface was smoothed. Otherwise, it would have been easier to grind the surface of a larger shell fragment.

Most bead blanks are relatively roughly shaped, seeming to have been chipped or cut by a crude technique. A reasonably high proportion of offcut pieces were left with straight edges.

Unless the bead blank has been partially worked, there is considerable difficulty in establishing objective criteria for identifying *C. glaucum* bead blanks. It is evident from worked examples that, in practice, a very wide range of irregular shapes was considered suitable for use. My classification has been conservative, but I was encouraged to find, during a check in the summer of 1981, that a number of pieces were classified in virtually the same manner by M. Schaeffer, who studied beads and pendants from the site manufactured from various materials (Schaeffer 1977).

99

2. Smoothing. The convex side of the blank was smoothed first, either partly or entirely. That polishing took place at this stage was no doubt meant to provide better stability during drilling. Sometimes the concave side was smoothed at the rim. Square or oblong blanks were often used, whereas nearly circular ones are in the minority (Figures D.1 and D.2).

3. Drilling. The hole was always drilled from the concave side, although sometimes additional drilling was carried out on the convex side. The hole was often drilled at an angle, perhaps unintentionally so, sometimes starting off-center (Figure D.3), and the result would not be straight-sided. The holes are usually wider towards the concave side.

I assume that drilling took place at a relatively early stage because this operation produced considerable stress on the shell and resulted in much breakage. And, indeed, many bead blanks broken at this stage are to be found. It would therefore have been economic to drill as early as possible in the process to avoid wasted effort. Stone tools from L5 peak in quantity in approximately the same units and may have been used as drills (C. Perlès, personal communication).

4. Secondary smoothing. Both sides of the blank were then completely rubbed or ground smooth to provide two flat, usually parallel, surfaces. Occasionally, a blank of uneven thickness was produced.

5. Rounding of the circumference. Rounding seems to have been carried out from several angles, sometimes producing two or three different profiles on the same blank, although the final bead is always evenly rounded (Figure D.3).

6. Finished beads. Surprisingly few completed beads have been found: less than 30 finished examples from the site as a whole can be either definitely or probably ascribed to *C. glaucum.* This small total compares with about 300 bead blanks from L5 alone. The completed beads are usually at least 5 mm in diameter and 1-2 mm thick. They tend to have a relatively large central hole and a bright, white, marble-like final appearance and polish. Faint traces of the ribs can usually be seen as a slight herringbone pattern on the surface. Material found in the excavated trenches on Paralia, especially in L5, allows one to put forward an analysis of shell bead-making techniques, though a discussion of the tools that may have been used in the process can not be presented in this outline. Given the high proportion of partly-worked beads to completed artifacts, it is not possible to indicate whether the makers worked for their own needs or intended their products to reach beyond the home settlement.

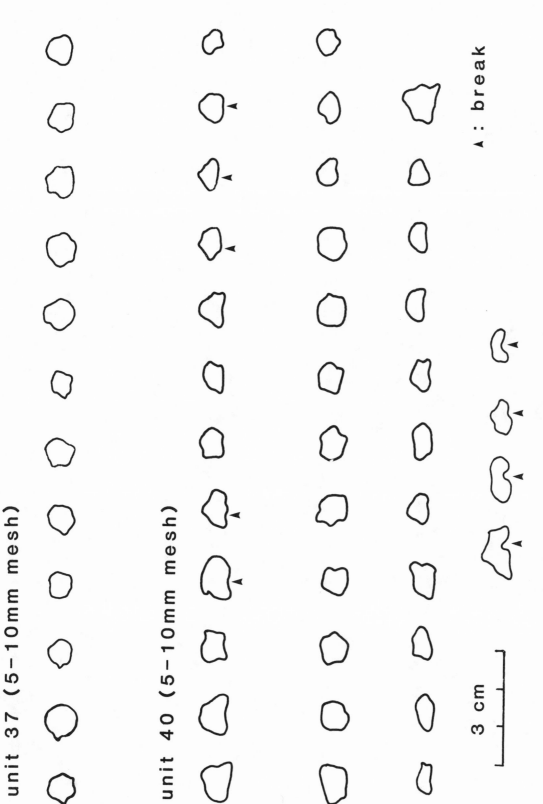

Figure D.1. Worked bead blanks of *Cerastoderma glaucum* Bruguière, from two excavated units in Trench L5. The outlines are direct tracings of the beads along their greatest perimeter. Top row is from Unit 37 (5-10 mm mesh); bottom three rows are from Unit 40 (5-10 mm mesh). All blanks in the second row are probably broken, but all unmistakable breaks have been indicated with arrows. The blanks of row four may also be broken, but there are no obvious broken edges.

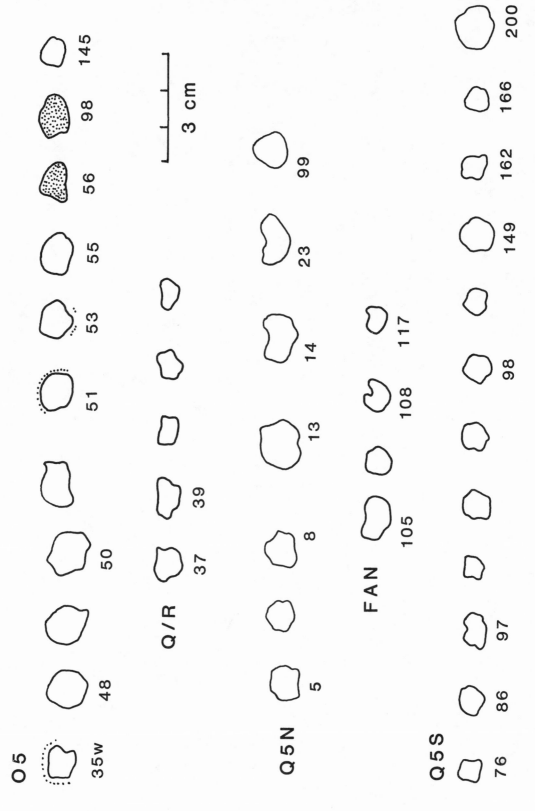

Figure D.2. Worked bead blanks of *Cerastoderma glaucum* Bruguière from trenches other than L5, for comparison with Figure D.1. The specimens shown here have been derived directly from the trenches or through water sieving.

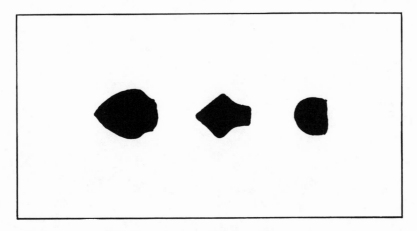

Figure D.3. Three cross sections of *C. glaucum* bead rim, outside to the left. No scale.

APPENDIX E

Worked Shell from Franchthi Cave

The following list (Table E.1) of worked shell now housed in the Nafplion Museum in Greece is not an attempt to provide a complete *catalogue raisonné* of all items of worked shell from Franchthi Cave. I have, however, examined all catalogued items at various times in order to identify what species of shell had been used.

What follows, therefore, is a list of all those items that I consider can reasonably be included under the heading of "worked shell." I give the excavation's (prefix FV) and the Nafplion Museum's identification numbers, a brief object description, the species of mollusc used (where it can be determined), and sometimes a short comment on the artifact. The purpose of presenting such an infant catalogue here is that it underpins views put forward in Chapter 7, and that it contains data which may be found useful elsewhere.

Before proceeding to the catalogue I should like to comment briefly on the manner in which this material has been handled. It is traditional on some excavations to treat small artifacts thought to have artistic qualities, aesthetic merit, and perhaps a non-utilitarian function in a manner quite different from the remainder of the finds. This means that such objects are separated from other data sets and catalogued individually, and so tend to have a higher status in the final report than seems warranted. Franchthi is no exception. Any piece of shell thought to have been worked was removed from the rest of the molluscan material, inventoried, and separated for special study.

Without entering into a discussion of the validity or rationale of this procedure, I wish to point out some problems and anomalies that have sprung from it. Every find of *Dentalium* sp., for example, a very easily recognized species, was individually catalogued until it became too cumbersome to do so. No distinction was clearly made between beach-collected specimens of *Dentalium* and those which received further modification. I have followed this pattern in the catalogue and listed beads of *Dentalium* sp., whether modified or not, without further comment unless they were burnt or I detected the possible use of pigment. I have not attempted to list here all examples of *Dentalium* sp. found at the site but not formally catalogued.

Less obvious examples of worked shell were quite frequently not detected and remained to be noted during examination of the main body of marine molluscan remains. I have not included such items found in the course of my own work in Kranidhi and which have as yet to be formally inventoried.

The catalogue does not include items which, from examination under a hand lens, appear not to have been worked at all. As a postscript I have added all FV numbers of items so excluded. I have also removed from this catalogue those items, without exception beads, which had been described as shell but which were not made from marine molluscs (Table E.2). As a result of this decision an old controversy was reopened, which led to the mineralogical analysis of a class of tiny cylindrical beads. The result of the analysis indicated that the beads were not made of an organic material.

The final section of the catalogue (Table E.3) is a reordering of the objects in sequence by trench and excavation unit rather than, as in Table E.1, in the numerical order of the inventory.

TABLE E.1

WORKED SHELL FROM FRANCHTHI CAVE

FV #	Trench:Unit	Museum #	Object Description	Mollusc Species	Commentary
2	G:25	16333	pendant frag.	Ostrea edulis ?	
3	G:6	16334	triangular frag.	Spondylus gaederopus	highly polished, broken after completion
4	A:31	16335	bracelet frag.	Spondylus gaederopus	
5	FF1:8	16336	frag. with holes	Ostrea edulis ?	two holes made from one side; "crenellated" edge
6	F1:2	16337	carved shape	Spondylus gaederopus	
7	H:9	16338	ground shell "ring"	Monodonta turbinata ?	shell heavily ground at top and base, part of central structure remaining
8	H:21	16339	frag. with drilled hole	Spondylus gaederopus	beach-worn rather than polished
9	H1:1	16340	frag. with hole	?	hole made from outside
12	H1:12	16343	pendant with 2 holes	Spondylus gaederopus	made from small valve; highly polished back
13	H1:19	16344	frag. with drilled hole	Spondylus gaederopus	
14	H1:21	16345	cowrie with groove	Luria lurida ?	carefully filed groove
15	H1:66	16346	Spondylus valve with signs of use	Spondylus gaederopus	heavy valve with signs of use; pounder ?
17	H1A:85	16348	bead	Spondylus gaederopus	polished, showing "grain"
18	FA:56A	16349	bracelet frag.	Spondylus gaederopus	well polished
19	H1A:91	16350	drilled pendant with notched edge	Ostrea edulis ?	
20	H1:69R	16351	bead	?	
23	FA:49	16354	bead	Cerastoderma glaucum	
27	H1B:79	16358	ground shell with hole	Columbella rustica	

FV #	Trench:Unit	Museum #	Object Description	Mollusc Species	Commentary
28	H:37B	16359	bead	Spondylus gaederopus ?	
29	FAS:61,63 65,68,70	16360	necklace	Cerithium vulgatum	all pieces beach-worm
30	H:37O	16361	bead	Spondylus gaederopus ?	
31	H:37E	16362	smoothed frag.	Spondylus gaederopus	
32	H:37I	16363	shell with hole	Conus mediterraneus/ Columbella rustica	
33	FAN:84	16364	bead	Spondylus gaederopus	
35	FAN:88	16366	spoon	Mytilus galloprovincialis	outer surface polished to reveal bright coloring, broken
36	FAN:101	16367	shell with hole	Conus mediterraneus	hole ground in apex
37	FAN:101	16368	ground shell "ring"	Monodonta turbinata ?	shell heavily ground at top and base, part of central structure remaining
38	FAN:111	16369	spoon	Mytilus galloprovincialis	outer surface polished to reveal brighter coloring, broken
39	FAN:119	16370	spoon frag.	Mytilus galloprovincialis	
40	FAN:119	16371	spoon	Mytilus galloprovincialis	complete small valve, finely "honed" edge
41	FAN:119	16372	spoon frag.	Mytilus galloprovincialis	
42	H:33	16373	shell frag. with cut marks	Pinna nobilis	series of cut marks, appear to be random, pieces cut out of the edges
43	FF1:25	16374	cowrie with hole	Luria lurida ?	rough hole in outer surface made by grinding/rubbing
44	G1:27	16375	polished frag.	Glycimeris sp.	

FV #	Trench:Unit	Museum #	Object Description	Mollusc Species	Commentary
45	FAS:61	16376	shell with hole	Conus mediterraneus/ Columbella rustica	hole in apex
46	H1A:104	16377	2 beads	Dentalium sp.	
47	FAN:116	16378	bead	?	
48	H1A:126	16379	shell with hole	Cyclope neritea	
49	H2A:21	16380	frag. with 2 holes	Pinna nobilis ?	holes bored from both sides
50	H2A:31	16381	pendant with 2 holes	Spondylus gaederopus	
51	H2A:35	16382	polished rod	Spondylus gaederopus	
53	H1A:151	16384	shell with hole	Conus mediterraneus	very beach-worn, hole in apex
54	H2A:38	16385	shell with hole	Cyclope neritea	
55	H2A:46	16386	smoothed rectangular piece	Cerastoderma glaucum ?	
56	H2A:54	16387	ground shell "ring"	Monodonta turbinata ?	shell heavily ground at top and base, open center, outer surface of shell partially removed
58	FAS:91	16389	bead	Spondylus gaederopus	
60	FAS:107	16391	ground shell "ring"	Monodonta turbinata ?	shell heavily ground at top and base, open center
63	FAS:91	16394	bead	Spondylus gaederopus	
64	FAS:91	16395	bead	Spondylus gaederopus	
65	FAN:121	16396	curved frag.	Spondylus gaederopus	not a broken part of bracelet, unless later modified, as tip is worked
66	FAS:82	16397	bead	?	
68	FAS:82	16399	bead	?	
70	FAS:82	16401	bead	Spondylus gaederopus	
78	FAS:82	16409	bead	?	

FV #	Trench:Unit	Museum #	Object Description	Mollusc Species	Commentary
89	Q5N:15	16420	bead	*Cerastoderma glaucum*	beach-worn fragment
90	FAN:127	16421	frag.	*Cerithium vulgatum*	
91	H2B:37	16422	oval piece	*Spondylus gaederopus*	some edges appear to have been worked
92	H2B:41	16423	disc	*Spondylus gaederopus*	polished
93	FAN:132	16424	disc	*Spondylus gaederopus* ?	polished
94	H2B:43	16425	disc	*Spondylus gaederopus*	polished
95	H2B:46	16426	disc	*Spondylus gaederopus*	polished
96	FAS:83	16427	bead	*Spondylus gaederopus*	
104	H2B:48	16435	rod	*Spondylus gaederopus*	polished
106	FAS:84	16437	bead	*Spondylus gaederopus*	
115	FAS:117	16446	scoop ?	*Pinna nobilis*	
120	H2A:88	16451	"chisel" or "celt"	*Spondylus gaederopus*	
121	FAS:88	16452	bead	*Pinna nobilis* ?	
124	H2A:89	16455	bead	*Spondylus gaederopus* ?	
127	FAS:90	16458	bead	*Cerastoderma glaucum*	
128	FAS:90	16459	bead	*Pinna nobilis* ?	
129	FAS:90	16460	bead	*Pinna nobilis* ?	since initial examination has disintegrated
136	FAS:86	16467	bead	*Pinna nobilis* ?	broken post-excavation
140	FAS:86	16471	bead	?	
144	FAS:86	16475	bead	?	
151	FAS:87	16482	bead	*Pinna nobilis* ?	broken post-excavation
152	FAS:87	16483	bead	*Pinna nobilis* ?	
168	FAN:136	16822	bead	?	
169	FAS:102	16873	bead	?	
173	FAS:120	16903	bead	?	

FV #	Trench:Unit	Museum #	Object Description	Mollusc Species	Commentary
174	FAN:120	16904	bead	?	
175	FAS:101	16905	bead	?	
176	FAS:101	16908	bead	?	
177	FAS:101	16909	bead	?	
178	FAS:101	16910	bead	?	
188	FAS:97	16929	bead	?	
190	Q5N:51	16940	bead frag.	*Cerastoderma glaucum*	
192	H1B:125	16941	bead	*Dentalium* sp.	
197	FAS:117	16987	bead	*Spondylus gaederopus*	
201	FAS:116	16991	bead	*Dentalium* sp. ?	
202	FAN:146	18019	bead	*Cerastoderma glaucum*	
203	FAN:154	18025	bead	*Dentalium* sp.	from unusually large specimen
205	H2A:138	18035	bead	*Dentalium* sp.	
206	H1B:138	18041	bead	*Dentalium* sp.	possibly burnt
207	H1B:120	18045	bead	*Dentalium* sp.	burnt
208	Q5S:46	18081	bead	*Cerastoderma glaucum*	
209	FAS:143	18082	frag. of "ring"	*Spondylus gaederopus*	surface shows natural damage from boring molluscs/sponges
210	FAS:128	18083	rod	*Spondylus gaederopus*	polished
211	L5NE:23	18113	bead	*Spondylus gaederopus*	
212	L5NE:21	18118	beach-worn, wear marks ?	*Glycimeris* sp.	probably only beach-worn specimen
214	H1B:137	18124	bead	*Dentalium* sp.	
215	FAS:136	18144	bead	?	
218	FAS:85	18155	spoon frag.	*Mytilus galloprovincialis*	small frag., but displaying type of working/shaping

FV #	Trench:Unit	Museum #	Object Description	Mollusc Species	Commentary
219	Q5NE:12	18166	bead blank	*Cerastoderma glaucum*	signs of working
221	O5NE:14	18168	frag. with notch/broken hole	*Spondylus gaederopus* ?	broken piece, shape/purpose unclear
222	Q5N:51	18169	cowrie frag.	*Luria lurida* ?	broken with groove made in dorsal surface, signs of beach wear
224	O5NE:11	18173	*Spondylus* valve	*Spondylus gaederopus*	very thick specimen, beach-worn, possible signs of working
225	FAS:116	18195	bead	*Dentalium* sp.	actually two, one inside the other
226	H1A:149	18197	bead	*Dentalium* sp.	
227	Q5S:91	18199	bead	*Dentalium* sp.	
228	Q5S:92	18200	bead	*Dentalium* sp.	
229	FAS:85	18202	bead	*Dentalium* sp.	
230	FAN:129	18203	bead	*Dentalium* sp.	
231	L5NE:52	18205	bead blank	*Cerastoderma glaucum*	signs of working
232	FAS:76	18206	bead	*Cerastoderma glaucum* ?	
234	FAS:145	18208	bead	*Cerastoderma glaucum*	complete and finely polished
235	H1A:132	18209	bead	*Dentalium* sp.	
236	H1A:135	18210	bead	*Dentalium* sp.	
237	H1A:143	18212	bead	*Dentalium* sp.	
238	H1A:152	18214	bead	*Dentalium* sp.	burnt ?
239	H1A:154	18215	bead	*Dentalium* sp.	burnt
240	H1A:155	18217	bead	*Dentalium* sp.	
241	H1A:155	18218	bead	*Dentalium* sp.	burnt
242	H1A:155	18219	bead	*Dentalium* sp.	
243	H1A:155	18220	bead	*Dentalium* sp.	

FV #	Trench:Unit	Museum #	Object Description	Mollusc Species	Commentary
244	H1A:155	18227	bead	Dentalium sp.	appears to have pigment on outer surface of shell
245	H1A:156	18228	bead	Dentalium sp.	appears to have pigment on outer surface of shell
246	H1A:156	18229	bead	Dentalium sp.	burnt
247	H1A:156	18230	bead	Dentalium sp.	appears to have pigment on outer surface of shell
248	H1A:156	18232	bead	Dentalium sp.	
249	L5NE:51	18235	bead blank	Cerastoderma glaucum bivalve, small	signs of working
251	Q5N:33	18237	bead	Cerastoderma glaucum	
252	L5NE:54	18239	bead blank	Cerastoderma glaucum	signs of working
253	FAS:119	18240	Spondylus valve	Spondylus gaederopus	beach-worn, possible signs of working
255	FAN:134	18242	scoop	Luria lurida ?	
256	FAN:121	18243	frag. scoop ?	Luria lurida ?	
257	FAS:148	18244	frag. scoop ?	Luria lurida ?	
258	FAN:147	18246	cowrie	Luria lurida ?	hole begun on dorsal surface by rubbing/grinding; groove also begun on shell surface
259	FAS:116	18247	frag. scoop ?	Luria lurida ?	
260	H1A:156	18248	bead	Dentalium sp.	
261	H1A:157	18249	bead	Dentalium sp.	
262	H1A:158	18250	bead	Dentalium sp.	
263	H1A:159	18251	bead	Dentalium sp.	
264	H1A:161	18256	bead	Dentalium sp.	
265	FAS:117	18257	shell with hole	Cerastoderma glaucum	hole near umbo

FV #	Trench:Unit	Museum #	Object Description	Mollusc Species	Commentary
266	FAS:117	18258	shell with hole	*Cerastoderma glaucum*	hole near umbo
267	FAS:117	18259	shell with hole	*Cerastoderma glaucum*	hole near umbo
268	FAS:117	18260	shell with hole	*Cerastoderma glaucum*	hole near umbo
269	FAS:130	18261	shell with hole	*Cerastoderma glaucum*	hole near umbo
270	FAS:130	18262	shell with hole	*Cerastoderma glaucum*	hole near umbo
271	FAN:122	18263	shell with hole	*Cerastoderma glaucum*	hole near umbo
272	FAN:122	18264	shell with hole	*Cerastoderma glaucum*	hole near umbo
273	FAN:122	18265	shell with hole	*Cerastoderma glaucum*	hole near umbo
274	FAS:140	18266	utilized limpet ?	*Patella* sp.	possibly shell utilized
275	L5NE:55	18267	bead blank	*Cerastoderma glaucum*	signs of working
276	FAS:138	18268	polished piece of shell	*Cerastoderma glaucum*	appears highly polished
277	FAS:136	18269	polished piece of shell	*Cerastoderma glaucum*	appears highly polished
278	FAS:77	18270	bead	*Dentalium* sp.	
279	H1B:114	18271	bead	*Dentalium* sp.	
280	H1B:115	18272	bead	*Dentalium* sp.	
281	H1B:139	18273	bead	*Dentalium* sp.	appears to have pigment on shell outer surface
282	H1B:141	18274	bead	*Dentalium* sp.	burnt
283	H1B:141	18275	bead	*Dentalium* sp.	
284	H1B:142	18276	bead	*Dentalium* sp.	burnt ?
285	H1B:142	18277	bead	*Dentalium* sp.	appears to have pigment on shell outer surface
286	H1B:142	18278	bead	*Dentalium* sp.	
287	H1B:142	18279	bead	*Dentalium* sp.	
288	H1B:142	18280	bead	*Dentalium* sp.	
289	H1B:142	18281	bead	*Dentalium* sp.	burnt ?
290	H1B:142	18282	bead	*Dentalium* sp.	

FV #	Trench:Unit	Museum #	Object Description	Mollusc Species	Commentary
291	H1B:143	18284	bead	*Dentalium* sp.	
292	FAN:123	18286	ground shell frag.	*Arca noae*	beach-collected, ground platform
293	FAS:73	18288	used valve	*Spondylus gaederopus*	edge with signs of chipping
295	FAN:124	18290	shell with hole	*Cerastoderma glaucum*	hole near umbo
296	FAN:127	18291	shell with hole	*Cerastoderma glaucum*	hole near umbo
297	FAN:127	18292	shell with hole	*Cerastoderma glaucum*	hole near umbo
298	Q5S:83	18293	shell with hole	*Cerastoderma glaucum*	hole near umbo
301	FAN:132	18298	ground shell	*Arca noae*	shell ground on dorsal surface
302	FAN:130	18300	cowrie with grinding	*Luria lurida* ?	evidence of grinding
303	FAN:130	18301	cowrie with slit	*Luria lurida* ?	beginning of slit filed in dorsal surface
304	L5NE:55	18303	bead blank	*Cerastoderma glaucum*	
305	Q5S:73	18306	shell with hole	*Cerastoderma glaucum*	hole near umbo
306	Q5S:78	18307	shell with hole	*Cerastoderma glaucum*	hole near umbo
307	FAN:144	18308	bead	*Dentalium* sp.	possibly with pigment
308	FAN:179	18309	bead	*Dentalium* sp.	
309	H1B:143	18310	bead	*Dentalium* sp.	
310	H1B:127	18311	bead	*Dentalium* sp.	
311	H1B:128	18312	bead	*Dentalium* sp.	
312	H1B:145	18313	bead	*Dentalium* sp.	
313	H1B:145	18314	bead	*Dentalium* sp.	
314	H1B:143	18315	bead	*Dentalium* sp.	with pigment
315	H1B:141	18316	bead	*Dentalium* sp.	possibly with pigment, burnt
316	H1B:133	18317	bead	*Dentalium* sp.	burnt
317	H1B:136	18318	bead	*Dentalium* sp.	

FV #	Trench:Unit	Museum #	Object Description	Mollusc Species	Commentary
318	H1B:138	18319	bead	*Dentalium* sp.	
319	H1B:135	18320	bead	*Dentalium* sp.	
320	H1B:135	18321	bead	*Dentalium* sp.	
321	H1B:135	18323	bead	*Dentalium* sp.	
322	H1B:135	18324	bead	*Dentalium* sp.	burnt
323	H1B:135	18325	bead	*Dentalium* sp.	
324	H1B:138	18326	bead	*Dentalium* sp.	
325	H1B:141	18327	bead	*Dentalium* sp.	
326	H1B:134	18328	bead	*Dentalium* sp.	burnt
327	H1B:134	18329	bead	*Dentalium* sp.	
328	H1B:134	18330	bead	*Dentalium* sp.	
329	FAN:186	18332	bead	*Dentalium* sp.	
330	FAS:137	18333	bead	*Cerastoderma glaucum*	
331	L5NE:57	18334	bead blank	*Cerastoderma glaucum*	
332	L5NE:57	18335	bead blank	*Cerastoderma glaucum*	signs of working
333	L5NE:57	18336	bead blank	*Cerastoderma glaucum*	signs of working
334	Q5N:34	18337	pendant	*Pinna nobilis*	
335	L5NE:57-58	18340	bead blank	*Cerastoderma glaucum*	
336	L5NE:57-58	18342	bead blank	*Cerastoderma glaucum*	
337	FAS:140	18344	shell with groove	?	with cut groove
338	FAS:116	18346	cowrie with hole	*Luria lurida* ?	ground hole in dorsal surface
339	H1B:142	18347	bead	*Dentalium* sp.	
340	H1B:143	18348	bead	*Dentalium* sp.	burnt
341	H1B:144	18349	bead	*Dentalium* sp.	possibly with pigment
342	H1B:146	18350	bead	*Dentalium* sp.	
343	H1B:146	18351	bead	*Dentalium* sp.	burnt
344	L5NE:59	18352	bead blank	*Cerastoderma glaucum*	

FV #	Trench:Unit	Museum #	Object Description	Mollusc Species	Commentary
345	L5NE:62	18354	bead blank	*Cerastoderma glaucum*	signs of working
346	Q5S:147	18362	bead	*Cerastoderma glaucum*	
347	Q5S:74	18363	shell with holes	*Cerastoderma glaucum*	beginnings of two holes on dorsal surface
349	FAN:22	18369	shell with hole	*Cerastoderma glaucum*	beginning of hole near umbo
350	Q5N:45	18372	bead	*Dentalium* sp.	
351	Q5N:47	18383	bead	*Cerastoderma glaucum*	
352	Q5N:36	18384	bead blank	*Cerastoderma glaucum*	
353	Q5N:36	18385	bead blank	*Cerastoderma glaucum*	
354	H1B:150	18388	bead	*Dentalium* sp.	
355	H1B:150	18389	bead	*Dentalium* sp.	
356	H1B:150	18390	bead	*Dentalium* sp.	burnt ?
357	H1B:150	18391	bead	*Dentalium* sp.	
358	H1B:150	18392	bead	*Dentalium* sp.	
359	Q5N:37	18395	cowrie frag.	*Luria lurida* ?	frag. showing signs of grinding
361	Q5N:56	18396	scoop frag.	*Luria lurida* ?	
363	FAN:121	18398	shell with ground base	?	
366	Q5S:5	18402	bead	*Dentalium* sp.	
367	Q5S:75	18425	bead	*Dentalium* sp.	
368	H1B:133	18403	shell with hole	*Glycimeris* sp.	burnt, with ground hole, broken
370	Q5N:50	18405	shell with groove	*Columbella rustica*	grooved hole of kind normally observed on *Luria lurida* ?
371	FAS:118	18406	shell with hole	*Columbella rustica*	ground hole in dorsal surface
372	FAN:132	18407	shell with groove	*Columbella rustica*	grooved hole, see FV 370

FV #	Trench:Unit	Museum #	Object Description	Mollusc Species	Commentary
373	FAN:132	18408	shell with hole	Columbella rustica	ground hole in dorsal surface, additional grinding on ventral surface ?
374	FAS:76	18409	shell with holes	Columbella rustica	natural holes in apex and dorsal surface
375	FAS:115	18410	shell with hole	Columbella rustica	beach-worn, coarse ground hole on dorsal surface
376	FAS:120	18411	shell with hole	Columbella rustica	ground hole in dorsal surface, further grinding on ventral surface
377	FAN:122	18412	shell with hole	Columbella rustica	ground hole in dorsal surface
378	FAN:126	18413	shell with hole	Columbella rustica	ground hole in dorsal surface, broad area of grinding with start of another hole
379	FAN:127	18414	shell with hole	Columbella rustica	double facet, grinding on dorsal surface
380	FAN:129	18415	shell with hole	Columbella rustica	ground hole in dorsal surface
381	Q5S:79	18416	shell with hole	Columbella rustica	ground hole in dorsal surface
382	H1B:145	18418	bead	Dentalium sp.	
383	FAS:91	18419	spoon ?	?	worn, three cut (?) marks
384	H1B:160	18420	shell with hole	Glycimeris sp.	with ground hole at umbo
385	H1B:160	18421	shell with hole	Glycimeris sp.	with hole in umbo, burnt ?
386	H1B:151	18426	bead	Dentalium sp.	
387	FAN:185	18427	bead	Dentalium sp.	
388	Q4:2	17449	bead	Cerastoderma glaucum	
390	Q4:3	17433	shell with hole	Cerastoderma glaucum	hole partially cut, near umbo
392	Q4:6	17438	bead	Cerastoderma glaucum ?	unfinished (?), burnt ?
393	O5:4SW	17444	shell with hole	Cerastoderma glaucum	hole near umbo

FV #	Trench:Unit	Museum #	Object Description	Mollusc Species	Commentary
394	Q4:15	17446	bead	*Cerastoderma glaucum*	unfinished
395	H1B:147	17456	bead	*Dentalium* sp.	
396	H1B:147	17457	bead	*Dentalium* sp.	
397	H1B:147	17458	bead	*Dentalium* sp.	
398	O5:20	17460	pendant	*Pinna nobilis* ?	burnt
400	P5:35	17480	pendant	*Spondylus gaederopus*	
401	Q5S:180	17516	pendant ?	*Spondylus gaederopus*	3 holes drilled from both sides
402	Q4:88	17520	cowrie with groove	*Luria lurida* ?	notch cut in dorsal surface, small hole
403	L5:21	17532	pendant	*Pinna nobilis*	
404	H1B:185	17543	bead	*Dentalium* sp.	
405	H1B:185	17544	bead	*Dentalium* sp.	
406	H1B:188	17545	bead	*Dentalium* sp.	
407	H1B:188	17546	bead	*Dentalium* sp.	
408	H1B:188	17547	bead	*Dentalium* sp.	
409	H1B:188	17548	bead	*Dentalium* sp.	
410	L5:27	17554	bead blank	*Cerastoderma glaucum*	signs of working
411	Q4:109	17555	bead	*Spondylus gaederopus*	
412	Q4:90	17557	cowrie with groove	*Luria lurida* ?	groove cut in dorsal surface
413	Q4:79	17558	cowrie with hole	*Luria lurida* ?	large ground hole in dorsal surface
414	L5:30	17565	rod	*Spondylus gaederopus*	
415	H1B:157	17573	bead	*Dentalium* sp.	
416	H1B:182	17574	bead	*Dentalium* sp.	
417	H1B:182	17575	bead	*Dentalium* sp.	
418	H1B:191	17587	bead	*Dentalium* sp.	

FV #	Trench:Unit	Museum #	Object Description	Mollusc Species	Commentary
419	P5:88	17588	cowrie with hole	*Luria lurida* ?	circular hole, carefully ground on dorsal surface, additional grinding on ventral surface
420	L5:38	17595	shell with hole	*Arca noae*	ground hole
421	L5:42	17596	shell with holes	*Pinna nobilis*	frag. with 3 holes, probably man-made
422	P5-Q5:4	17611	spatula ?	*Spondylus gaederopus*	
423	O5:111	17638	pendant	*Spondylus gaederopus*	
424	Q5S:217	17650	pendant frag. ?	*Pinna nobilis*	
425	P5:136	17657	frag. with holes	*Spondylus gaederopus*	beach-worn frag. with drilled hole, ground near umbo
426	P5:134	17658	cut frag.	*Spondylus gaederopus*	signs of workings
427	Q6N:72	17686	bead blank	*Cerastoderma glaucum*	broken piece with drilled hole
428	FA QSE:13	17700	"bracelet" frag.	*Spondylus gaederopus*	
429	FF1 scarp	17702	carved piece	*Spondylus gaederopus*	carved, decorated piece, buckle ? fish-hook ?
430	Q6N:008	17707	disc ?	*Spondylus gaederopus* ?	
431	L5:001	17708	bead	*Cerastoderma glaucum*	
432	Q5S:164	16331	bead	*Cerastoderma glaucum*	
433	FAS:195	16314	bead	*Dentalium* sp.	with pigment
434	L5:28	16316	bead blank	*Cerastoderma glaucum*	signs of working
435	L5:28	16318	bead blank	*Cerastoderma glaucum*	signs of working
436	L5:28	16320	bead blank	*Cerastoderma glaucum*	
437	L5:28	16321	bead blank	*Cerastoderma glaucum*	signs of working
438	L5:28	16323	bead blank	*Cerastoderma glaucum*	signs of working
439	L5:19	16325	bead blank	*Cerastoderma glaucum*	signs of working
440	L5:17	16327	bead blank	*Cerastoderma glaucum*	signs of working

FV #	Trench:Unit	Museum #	Object Description	Mollusc Species	Commentary
441	Q5N:98	16328	worked frag.	Spondylus gaederopus	polished rod with groove, broken
442	L5:24	17713	bead blank	Cerastoderma glaucum	signs of working
443	L5:18	17716	bead blank	Cerastoderma glaucum	signs of working
444	L5:37	17718	bead blank	Cerastoderma glaucum	signs of working
445	L5:34	17719	bead blank	Cerastoderma glaucum	signs of working
446	L5:27	17721	bead blank	Cerastoderma glaucum	signs of working
447	L5:25	17722	bead blank	Cerastoderma glaucum	signs of working
448	L5:39	17723	bead blank	Cerastoderma glaucum	signs of working
449	L5:39	17725	bead blank	Cerastoderma glaucum	signs of working
450	L5:39	17726	bead blank	Cerastoderma glaucum	signs of working
451	L5:42	17727	bead	Cerastoderma glaucum	
452	L5:42	17729	bead blank	Cerastoderma glaucum	signs of working
453	L5:42	17730	worked frag.	Spondylus gaederopus	frag. of bead or pendant
454	L5:42	17731	bead blank	Cerastoderma glaucum	signs of working
455	L5:33	17733	bead blank	Cerastoderma glaucum	signs of working
456	L5:33	17734	bead blank	Cerastoderma glaucum	
457	L5:33	17735	bead blank	Cerastoderma glaucum	signs of working
459	L5:30	17737	bead blank	Cerastoderma glaucum	
460	L5:30	17738	bead blank	Cerastoderma glaucum	signs of working
462	L5:30	17742	bead blank	Cerastoderma glaucum	signs of working
463	L5:41	17743	bead	Cerastoderma glaucum ?	burnt
464	L5:41	17744	bead	Cerastoderma glaucum ?	burnt
465	L5:41	17745	bead blank	Cerastoderma glaucum	signs of working
466	L5:41	17746	bead blank	Cerastoderma glaucum	signs of working
467	L5:41	17747	bead blank	Cerastoderma glaucum	signs of working
468	L5:41	17748	bead blank	Cerastoderma glaucum	signs of working

FV #	Trench:Unit	Museum #	Object Description	Mollusc Species	Commentary
469	L5:41	17749	bead blank	*Cerastoderma glaucum*	signs of working
470	L5:35	17750	bead blank	*Cerastoderma glaucum*	signs of working
471	L5:35	17751	bead blank	*Cerastoderma glaucum*	signs of working
472	L5:35	17752	bead blank	*Cerastoderma glaucum*	signs of working
473	L5:35	17753	bead blank	*Cerastoderma glaucum*	signs of working
474	L5:35	17754	bead blank	*Cerastoderma glaucum*	signs of working
475	L5:35	17755	bead blank	*Cerastoderma glaucum*	signs of working
476	L5:32	17756	bead blank	*Cerastoderma glaucum*	
477	L5:32	17757	bead blank	*Cerastoderma glaucum*	signs of working
478	L5:32	17758	bead blank	*Cerastoderma glaucum*	signs of working
479	L5:32	17759	bead blank	*Cerastoderma glaucum*	
482	L5:32	17762	bead blank	*Cerastoderma glaucum*	signs of working
483	L5:32	17763	bead blank	*Cerastoderma glaucum*	signs of working
484	L5:32	17764	bead blank	*Cerastoderma glaucum*	signs of working
485	L5:38	*17765	bead blank	*Cerastoderma glaucum*	signs of working
486	L5:38	*17765	bead blank	*Cerastoderma glaucum*	signs of working
487	L5:38	17766	bead blank	*Cerastoderma glaucum*	signs of working
488	L5:38	17767	bead blank	*Cerastoderma glaucum*	signs of working
489	L5:38	17768	bead blank	*Cerastoderma glaucum*	signs of working
490	L5:38	17769	bead blank	*Cerastoderma glaucum*	signs of working
491	L5:38	17770	bead blank	*Cerastoderma glaucum*	signs of working
492	L5:29	17771	bead blank	*Cerastoderma glaucum*	signs of working
493	L5:29	17772	bead blank	*Cerastoderma glaucum*	signs of working
494	L5:29	17773	bead blank	*Cerastoderma glaucum*	signs of working
495	L5:29	17774	bead blank	*Cerastoderma glaucum*	signs of working

*FV 485 and FV 486 appear to have been given the same museum number

FV #	Trench:Unit	Museum #	Object Description	Mollusc Species	Commentary
496	L5:29	17775	bead blank	Cerastoderma glaucum	signs of working
497	L5:29	17776	bead blank	Cerastoderma glaucum	signs of working
498	L5:29	17777	bead blank	Cerastoderma glaucum	signs of working
499	L5:36	17778	bead blank	Cerastoderma glaucum	signs of working, burnt
500	L5:36	17779	bead blank	Cerastoderma glaucum	signs of working
501	L5:36	17780	bead blank	Cerastoderma glaucum	signs of working
502	L5:36	17781	bead blank	Cerastoderma glaucum	signs of working
503	L5:36	17782	bead blank	Cerastoderma glaucum	signs of working
504	L5:36	17783	bead blank	Cerastoderma glaucum	signs of working
505	L5:36	17784	bead blank	Cerastoderma glaucum	signs of working
506	L5:36	17785	bead blank	Cerastoderma glaucum	signs of working
507	L5:40	17786	bead	Cerastoderma glaucum	
508	L5:40	17787	bead frag.	Cerastoderma glaucum	
509	L5:40	17788	bead blank	Cerastoderma glaucum	signs of working
510	L5:40	17789	bead blank	Cerastoderma glaucum	signs of working
511	L5:40	17790	bead blank	Cerastoderma glaucum	signs of working
512	L5:40	17791	bead blank	Cerastoderma glaucum	signs of working
515	P5-Q5:35	17814	bead blank	Cerastoderma glaucum	signs of working
521	P5:180	17871	bead blank	Cerastoderma glaucum	signs of working
522	P5-Q5:40	17879	bead blank	Cerastoderma glaucum	
526	FAS:109	17903	bead	?	
527	L5NE:50	17909	bead blank	Cerastoderma glaucum	
528	L5NE:52	17910	bead blank	Cerastoderma glaucum	
529	L5NE:54	17911	bead blank	Cerastoderma glaucum	
530	FAS:109	17913	bead	?	
534	L5NE:62	17918	bead blank	Cerastoderma glaucum	signs of working
535	L5NE:62	17921	bead blank	Cerastoderma glaucum	
536	L5NE:56	17922	bead blank	Cerastoderma glaucum	

FV #	Trench:Unit	Museum #	Object Description	Mollusc Species	Commentary
537	QR:32	17926	bead	*Cerastoderma glaucum*	
538	QR:32	17927	bead	*Cerastoderma glaucum* ?	
539	FAS:91	17933	bead	*Pinna nobilis* ?	
540	L5:55	17934	bead blank	*Cerastoderma glaucum*	
541	L5:60	17935	bead	*Cerastoderma glaucum*	
542	L5:72	17939	bead	*Conus mediterraneus* ?	burnt, cut, ground hole
543	L5:71	17940	bead	*Columbella rustica* ? *Columbella rustica* ?	apex and ventral surface ground, beach-worn
544	QR:35	17941	bead blank	*Cerastoderma glaucum*	signs of working
545	QR:35	17942	bead blank	*Cerastoderma glaucum*	signs of working
546	QR:32	17945	bead blank	*Cerastoderma glaucum*	
547	QR:32	17946	bead blank	*Cerastoderma glaucum*	
548	FAS:115	17947	bead	*?*	
551	P5:191	17958	bead	*Cerastoderma glaucum*	broken
552	FAS:131	17976	bead blank	*Cerastoderma glaucum*	signs of working
553	QR:43	17977	bead	*Cerastoderma glaucum*	broken
555	QR:43	17979	bead blank	*Cerastoderma glaucum*	signs of working
557	FAS:92	17973	bead	*?*	
559	FAS:112	17975	bead	*?*	
560	FAS:117	17980	bead frag.	*Cerastoderma glaucum* ?	
561	FAS:104	17988	bead	*?*	
562	FAS:104	17989	bead	*Cerastoderma glaucum*	
563	FAS:102	17990	bead	*Cerastoderma glaucum* ?	
570	FAS:98	18435	bead	*Cerastoderma glaucum* ?	
571	FAS:98	18436	bead	*Cerastoderma glaucum* ?	
572	QR:41	18437	bead blank	*Cerastoderma glaucum*	signs of working
573	L5:77	18438	bead blank	*Cerastoderma glaucum*	signs of working
575	FAS:103	18440	bead	*?*	post-excavation break

TABLE E.2

ITEMS NOT INCLUDED IN THE CATALOGUE OF WORKED SHELL FROM FRANCHTHI CAVE[a]

Not Made of Shell				*Not Worked*	*Inadequate Information*
57	102	147	195	11	81
61	103	148	198	130	82
62	110	149	200	250	83
67	111	150	220	254	122
69	112	153	233	299	123
71	113	154	517	300	294
72	114	156	518	360	364
73	116	157	519	369	365
74	117	158	520	458	
75	118	159	525	478	
76	119	160	531	480	
77	125	161	532	481	
79	126	162	533	513	
84	131	163	549	514	
85	132	164	550		
86	133	165	556		
87	137	166	564		
88	138	172	565		
97	141	173	566		
98	142	179	567		
99	143	180	568		
100	145	193	569		
101	146	194	574		

[a]Items are listed by FV number alone.

TABLE E.3

LIST OF WORKED SHELL

FV #	Trench:Unit	Museum #	FV #	Trench:Unit	Museum #
4	A:31	16335	387	FAN:185	18427
428	FA:13	17700	329	FAN:186	18332
23	FA:49	16354	349	FAN:228	18369
18	FA:56A	16349			
33	FAN:84	16364	45	FAS:61	16376
35	FAN:88	16366	29	FAS:61, 63,	16360
36	FAN:101	16367		65, 68, 70	
37	FAN:101	16368	293	FAS:73	18288
38	FAN:111	16369	374	FAS:76	18409
47	FAN:116	16378	232	FAS:76	18206
39	FAN:119	16370	374	FAS:76	18409
40	FAN:119	16371	278	FAS:77	18270
41	FAN:119	16372	66	FAS:82	16397
174	FAN:120	16904	68	FAS:82	16399
65	FAN:121	16396	70	FAS:82	16401
256	FAN:121	18243	78	FAS:79	16409
363	FAN:121	18398	96	FAS:83	16427
377	FAN:122	18412	106	FAS:84	16437
271	FAN:122	18263	229	FAS:85	18202
272	FAN:122	18264	218	FAS:85	18155
273	FAN:122	18265	136	FAS:86	16467
292	FAN:123	18286	140	FAS:86	16471
295	FAN:124	18290	144	FAS:86	16475
378	FAN:126	18413	151	FAS:87	16482
379	FAN:127	18414	152	FAS:87	16483
90	FAN:127	16421	121	FAS:88	16452
296	FAN:127	18291·	127	FAS:90	16458
297	FAN:127	18292	128	FAS:90	16459
380	FAN:129	18415	129	FAS:90	16460
230	FAN:129	18203	539	FAS:91	17933
302	FAN:130	18300	63	FAS:91	16394
303	FAN:130	18301	58	FAS:91	16389
93	FAN:132	16424	383	FAS:91	18419
301	FAN:132	18298	64	FAS:91	16395
372	FAN:132	18407	557	FAS:92	17973
373	FAN:132	18408	188	FAS:97	16929
255	FAN:134	18242	570	FAS:98	18435
168	FAN:136	16822	571	FAS:98	18436
307	FAN:144	18308	175	FAS:101	16905
202	FAN:146	18019	176	FAS:101	16908
258	FAN:147	18246	177	FAS:101	16909
203	FAN:154	18025	178	FAS:101	16910
308	FAN:179	18309	563	FAS:102	17990

TABLE E.3 (continued)

LIST OF WORKED SHELL

FV #	Trench:Unit	Museum #	FV #	Trench:Unit	Museum #
169	FAS:102	16873	3	G:6	16334
575	FAS:103	18440	2	G:25	16333
561	FAS:104	17988	44	G1:27	16375
562	FAS:104	17989			
60	FAS:107	16391	7	H:9	16338
526	FAS:109	17903	8	H:21	16339
530	FAS:109	17913	42	H:33	16373
559	FAS:112	17975	28	H:37*B*	16359
375	FAS:115	18410	30	H:37*O*	16361
548	FAS:115	17947	31	H:37*E*	16362
259	FAS:116	18247	9	H1:1	16340
338	FAS:116	18346	12	H1:12	16343
225	FAS:116	18195	13	H1:19	16344
201	FAS:116	16991	14	H1:21	16345
197	FAS:117	16987	32	H1:37*I*	16363
560	FAS:117	17980	15	H1:66	16346
265	FAS:117	18257	20	H1:69R	16351
266	FAS:117	18258			
267	FAS:117	18259	17	H1A:85	16348
268	FAS:117	18260	19	H1A:91	16350
115	FAS:117	16446	46	H1A:104	16377
371	FAS:118	18406	48	H1A:126	16379
253	FAS:119	18240	235	H1A:132	18209
376	FAS:120	18411	236	H1A:135	18210
173	FAS:120	16903	237	H1A:143	18212
210	FAS:128	18083	226	H1A:149	18197
269	FAS:130	18261	53	H1A:151	16384
270	FAS:130	18262	238	H1A:152	18214
552	FAS:131	17976	239	H1A:154	18215
277	FAS:136	18269	240	H1A:155	18217
215	FAS:136	18144	241	H1A:155	18218
330	FAS:137	18333	242	H1A:155	18219
276	FAS:138	18268	243	H1A:155	18220
337	FAS:140	18344	244	H1A:155	18227
274	FAS:140	18266	245	H1A:156	18228
209	FAS:143	18082	246	H1A:156	18229
234	FAS:145	18208	247	H1A:156	18230
257	FAS:148	18244	248	H1A:156	18232
433	FAS:195	16314	260	H1A:156	18248
429	FF1:scarp	17702	261	H1A:157	18249
5	FF1:8	16336	262	H1A:158	18250
43	FF1:25	16374	263	H1A:159	18251
6	F1:2	16337	264	H1A:161	18256

TABLE E.3 (continued)

LIST OF WORKED SHELL

FV #	Trench:Unit	Museum #	FV #	Trench:Unit	Museum #
27	H1B:79	16358	342	H1B:146	18350
279	H1B:114	18271	343	H1B:146	18351
280	H1B:115	18272	395	H1B:147	17456
207	H1B:120	18045	396	H1B:147	17457
192	H1B:125	16960	397	H1B:147	17458
310	H1B:127	18311	354	H1B:150	18388
311	H1B:128	18312	355	H1B:150	18389
316	H1B:133	18317	356	H1B:150	18390
368	H1B:133	18403	357	H1B:150	18391
326	H1B:134	18328	358	H1B:150	18392
327	H1B:134	18329	386	H1B:151	18426
328	H1B:134	18330	415	H1B:157	17573
320	H1B:135	18321	384	H1B:160	18420
321	H1B:135	18323	385	H1B:160	18421
322	H1B:135	18324	416	H1B:182	17574
323	H1B:135	18325	417	H1B:182	17575
319	H1B:135	18320	404	H1B:185	17543
317	H1B:136	18318	405	H1B:185	17544
214	H1B:137	18124	406	H1B:188	17545
206	H1B:138	18041	407	H1B:188	17546
324	H1B:138	18326	408	H1B:188	17547
318	H1B:138	18319	409	H1B:188	17548
281	H1B:139	18273	418	H1B:191	17587
282	H1B:141	18274			
315	H1B:141	18316	49	H2A:21	16380
325	H1B:141	18327	50	H2A:31	16381
283	H1B:141	18275	51	H2A:35	16382
284	H1B:142	18276	54	H2A:38	16385
285	H1B:142	18277	55	H2A:46	16386
339	H1B:142	18347	56	H2A:54	16387
286	H1B:142	18278	120	H2A:88	16451
287	H1B:142	18279	124	H2A:89	16455
288	H1B:142	18280	205	H2A:138	18035
289	H1B:142	18281			
290	H1B:142	18282	91	H2B:37	16422
291	H1B:143	18284	92	H2B:41	16423
309	H1B:143	18310	94	H2B:43	16425
314	H1B:143	18315	95	H2B:46	16426
340	H1B:143	18348	104	H2B:48	16435
341	H1B:144	18349	105	H2B:50	16436
382	H1B:145	18418			
312	H1B:145	18313	431	L5:001	17708
313	H1B:145	18314	440	L5:17	16327

TABLE E.3 (continued)

LIST OF WORKED SHELL

FV #	Trench:Unit	Museum #	FV #	Trench:Unit	Museum #
443	L5:18	17716	503	L5:36	17782
439	L5:19	16325	504	L5:36	17783
403	L5:21	17532	505	L5:36	17784
442	L5:24	17713	506	L5:36	17785
447	L5:25	17722	444	L5:37	17718
410	L5:27	17554	420	L5:38	17595
446	L5:27	17721	485*	L5:38	17765
434	L5:28	16316	486*	L5:38	17765
435	L5:28	16318	487	L5:38	17766
436	L5:28	16320	488	L5:38	17767
437	L5:28	16321	489	L5:38	17768
438	L5:28	16323	490	L5:38	17769
492	L5:29	17771	491	L5:38	17770
493	L5:29	17772	448	L5:39	17723
494	L5:29	17773	449	L5:39	17725
495	L5:29	17774	450	L5:39	17726
496	L5:29	17775	507	L5:40	17786
497	L5:29	17776	508	L5:40	17787
498	L5:29	17777	509	L5:40	17788
459	L5:30	17737	510	L5:40	17789
460	L5:30	17738	511	L5:40	17790
462	L5:30	17742	512	L5:40	17791
414	L5:30	17565	463	L5:41	17743
476	L5:32	17756	464	L5:41	17744
477	L5:32	17757	465	L5:41	17745
479	L5:32	17759	466	L5:41	17746
482	L5:32	17762	467	L5:41	17747
483	L5:32	17763	468	L5:41	17748
484	L5:32	17764	469	L5:41	17749
455	L5:33	17733	451	L5:42	17727
456	L5:33	17734	452	L5:42	17729
457	L5:33	17735	453	L5:42	17730
445	L5:34	17719	454	L5:42	17731
470	L5:35	17750	421	L5:42	17596
471	L5:35	17751	540	L5:55	17934
472	L5:35	17752	541	L5:60	17935
473	L5:35	17753	543	L5:71	17940
474	L5:35	17754	542	L5:72	17939
475	L5:35	17755	573	L5:77	18438
499	L5:36	17778			
500	L5:36	17779	212	L5NE:21	18118
501	L5:36	17780	211	L5NE:23	18113
502	L5:36	17781	527	L5NE:50	17909
			249	L5NE:51	18235

*FV 485 and 486 have same Museum #.

TABLE E.3 (continued)

LIST OF WORKED SHELL

FV #	Trench:Unit	Museum #	FV #	Trench:Unit	Museum #
231	L5NE:52	18205	89	Q5N:15	16420
528	L5NE:52	17910	251	Q5N:33	18237
252	L5NE:54	18239	334	Q5N:34	18337
529	L5NE:54	17911	352	Q5N:36	18384
275	L5NE:55	18267	353	Q5N:36	18385
304	L5NE:55	18303	359	Q5N:37	18395
536	L5NE:56	17922	350	Q5N:45	18372
331	L5NE:57	18334	351	Q5N:47	18383
332	L5NE:57	18335	370	Q5N:50	18405
333	L5NE:57	18336	222	Q5N:51	18169
335	L5NE:57-58	18340	190	Q5N:51	16940
336	L5NE:57-58	18342	361	Q5N:56	18396
344	L5NE:59	18352	441	Q5N:98	16328
345	L5NE:62	18354			
534	L5NE:62	17918	219	Q5NE:12	18166
535	L5NE:62	17921			
			366	Q5S:5	18402
398	O5:20	17460	208	Q5S:46	18081
423	O5:111	17638	305	Q5S:73	18306
393	O5:4SW	17444	347	Q5S:74	18363
			367	Q5S:75	18425
224	O5NE:11	18173	306	Q5S:78	18307
221	O5NE:14	18168	381	Q5S:79	18416
			298	Q5S:83	18293
400	P5:35	17480	227	Q5S:91	18199
419	P5:88	17588	228	Q5S:92	18200
425	P5:136	17657	346	Q5S:147	18362
426	P5:134	17658	432	Q5S:164	16331
521	P5:180	17871	401	Q5S:180	17516
551	P5:191	17958	424	Q5S:217	17650
422	P5-Q5:4	17611	430	Q6N:008	17707
515	P5-Q5:35	17814	427	Q6N:72	17686
516	P5-Q5:36	17815			
522	P5-Q5:40	17879	537	QR:32	17926
			538	QR:32	17927
388	Q4:2	17449	546	QR:32	17945
390	Q4:3	17433	547	QR:32	17946
392	Q4:6	17438	544	QR:35	17941
394	Q4:15	17446	545	QR:35	17942
413	Q4:79	17558	572	QR:41	18437
402	Q4:88	17520	553	QR:43	17977
412	Q4:90	17557	555	QR:43	17979
411	Q4:109	17555			

PART II

M. R. Deith
and
N. J. Shackleton

CHAPTER NINE

Oxygen Isotope Analyses of Marine Molluscs from Franchthi Cave

The questions of seasonality of occupation at Franchthi Cave and of changes in the seasonal usage of the cave during its long depositional history have not yet been satisfactorily resolved. The kinds of data which bear on these questions have produced no clear picture so far, except that there is no evidence of winter occupation (Jacobsen 1976, 1981). This study of shellfish remains is a contribution to the interpretation of seasonality at the site. The distinctive value of those shells which are the remains of meals lies in the fact that they represent a food resource available throughout the year and are therefore potentially a source of more comprehensive seasonal information than other indicators. The relationship between seasonality of shellfish collection and seasonality of occupation is not necessarily simple and direct, however (Deith, forthcoming a). It depends upon the role of shellfish in the diet of the groups using the cave. Yet, despite the problems of negative evidence, whereby a lack of data cannot be equated with the absence of people from the site, the positive evidence does provide a baseline, indicative of a minimal presence, which can be added to the evidence from other classes of data.

OXYGEN ISOTOPE ANALYSIS

The oxygen isotopic composition of carbonate mollusc shell contains seasonally related information (Emiliani et al. 1964). The ratio of ^{18}O to ^{16}O in calcium carbonate is determined by two factors: the ratio of ^{18}O to ^{16}O in the water in which the carbonate was laid down and a small, temperature-dependent factor. In water whose $^{18}O/^{16}O$ ratio is stable, as it is for example in seawater over geologically short time spans, variations in the ratio in the carbonate are attributable to temperature fluctuations. Seasonal changes in water temperature should therefore be reflected in the isotopic composition of the shell material. If samples of carbonate, representing growth increments, are taken at intervals along a shell, from the oldest to the youngest part, the isotope ratios should chart the seasonal fluctuations in seawater temperature that have taken place during the lifetime of that mollusc. The position of the final value on the curve indicates the point in the seasonal cycle when the animal died (N. J. Shackleton 1973).

A standard procedure was followed for preparing and analyzing the shell material. After the shell had been cleaned, by being dipped briefly into a weak (about 1%) solution of HCl to remove post-depositional accretions, samples in the order of 0.3 mg of carbonate were removed, either by drilling, using a burr of 0.5 mm, or, in the case of the growing edge, by filing. The samples were baked under vacuum for 30 minutes at 400 °C to remove organic contaminants. CO_2 gas was released from the carbonate by reacting it with 100% ortho-phosphoric acid at 50 °C, and the ratio of the mass 46 ($^{12}C/^{18}O/^{16}O$) to mass 44 ($^{12}C/^{16}O/^{16}O$) was counted in a V. G. Micromass 903 triple collector mass spectrometer and compared with the ratio in a reference gas. Calibration was achieved by analyzing international circulating standards under identical conditions. The isotopic composition of the carbonate is expressed in terms of its relationship to the PDB standard, in parts per thousand ($^o/_{oo}$).

$$\delta = \left(\frac{R \quad sample}{R \quad standard} - 1 \right) \times 1000$$

Analytical precision is about $\pm 0.06^o/_{oo}$.

If the shell has been sampled at intervals, the sequence of $\delta^{18}O$ values should form a temperature-related curve. The fractionation coefficient is approximately $0.2^o/_{oo}$ for each degree Celsius, so that an annual seawater temperature range of 10 °C would give rise to a $2^o/_{oo}$ range of δ values. A more positive δ value is indicative of cold temperatures and a more negative one of warm temperatures. In the isotopic profiles that follow (Figures 17-20), the more negative (summer) values are at the top of the graphs and the more positive values at the bottom. Edge values are on the right.

SAMPLING STRATEGY

Shellfish were not collected in any quantity and taken back to the cave until towards the end of the Palaeolithic, around 11,000 B.P., and were from that time a consistent feature of the deposits until the end of the Neolithic (see Chapter 2). The shell remains therefore cover the end of the Upper Palaeolithic, the whole of the Mesolithic, and the whole of the Neolithic in a 6,000-year sequence spanning major changes in economic activities, most significantly the change to farming from hunting and gathering.

A good suite of species was represented in the deposits, in good condition. The shells did not appear to have been chemically changed. The species occurring most frequently in the deposits were: *Patella* spp., *Monodonta/Gibbula* spp., *Cerithium vulgatum* Bruguière, *Cerastoderma glaucum* Bruguière, *Tapes decussatus* (Linné), *Cyclope neritea* (Linné), and *Donacilla cornea* (Poli) (Plates 1-3 and Figure 14). Modern specimens of these species, mainly beach-collected, were analyzed to determine how well the isotopic profiles of each species reflected the modern sea-temperature curve and what species were shown to be reliable seasonal indicators. Where possible, complete shells were used and were sampled at intervals from the umbo or apex to the growing edge. This allows the edge value to be examined in relation to the whole shell profile. Virtually all the *Cerithium* shells were broken by the prehistoric inhabitants of the site (J. C. Shackleton, this volume), so that we were not able to analyze complete profiles of the majority of specimens of this species. Although it is impossible to distinguish between spring and autumn collection from edge values alone, it was hoped that analysis of these fragments would lend weight to the data obtained from the shell profiles.

The sampling strategy was constrained by the fact that each shell investigated requires at least a day of laboratory work. A second constraint on sampling strategy lay in the fact that whole, or very nearly whole, shells are preferable for analysis. The Mesolithic is dominated by two species, of which one (*Cyclope*) is considered to have been collected for decorative purposes (N. J. Shackleton 1969), while the other (*Cerithium*) was systematically broken to obtain the meat, leaving only a very small edge fragment of about 5 mm. The development of a sampling strategy, such as concentrating on specific periods of time when economic change took place, or a less intensive sampling of the whole sequence, was therefore not a practical possibility. Our sampling is thus somewhat ad hoc and does not represent a set of deliberate choices designed to answer the questions we should like to have asked. Whatever was available and suitable for analysis has been used, as long as it was considered to represent probable food remains and not material gathered for decoration.

Shells used for decorative purposes appear in two stratigraphic zones. In the Lower Mesolithic (Molluscan Zone II), there are large numbers of *Cyclope* shells with holes in them. From the Upper Mesolithic onwards, this species ceased to be used and *Cerastoderma* was one of the main species chosen for decoration in the Neolithic (Molluscan Zone IV). The latter shells were more extensively modified than *Cyclope* had been; in addition to having holes made in them, they were cut into rectangular pieces and polished (see Appendix D). *Cerastoderma*, however, comes from the same habitat as the other bivalves that occur in the Neolithic levels. No other species shows signs of having been worked, and it is probable that they were all collected for food. *Cerastoderma* is good for eating, and its meat is not difficult to extract. Despite our view that the cockles were collected for food, we have excluded from our analyses any that show signs of working. The *Cyclope* shells, on the other hand, are very small (8-10 mm in diameter), the small amount of meat difficult to extract, and we think it likely that they were collected dead from the shore, ready-cleaned and not smelling unpleasant. No shells of this species have been used.

PRELIMINARY WORK WITH MODERN SPECIMENS

Mean monthly sea temperatures for the Argolid are given in Figure 15, demonstrating an annual range of 11 °C. The overall range is, of course, larger, with greater variation about the means in summer than in winter. These variations are likely to be reflected in the isotopic profiles that are both less smooth than that of the mean monthly sea-temperature curve, especially in the summer, and in a range of isotopic values that is somewhat greater than would be predicted from the sea temperature curve (i.e. 2.2 $^{\circ}/_{\circ\circ}$).

Patella spp. occur mainly in the late Palaeolithic levels. In other contexts, such as northern Spain and the Inner Hebrides, limpets have produced erratic readings and isotopic profiles which have been impossible to interpret as seasonal records (Bailey et al. 1983; Deith 1988b). In the Mediterranean, *P. caerulea* appears to produce anomalous readings for summer growth in shells from Sicily (Schifano and Censi 1983). In view of this work and the availability of other species, no *Patella* shells were analyzed.

Monodonta turbinata (Figure 14:3), the predominant species of trochid, is a rocky-shore species from a fully marine habitat. It is a fast-growing species. On the Mediterranean coast of France, where growth in this species has been monitored, the rate of growth of the shell is between 21 mm and 56.4 mm a year, measured around the whorls (Régis 1972). Monthly growth in shells from this area is shown in Figure 16. There is ample material for sampling at intervals around the whorls to produce a detailed seasonal record, even at times of minimal growth such as in May. In the Mediterranean, where growth rates are fast and growth continues throughout the year, maximum height is attained at the end of about 18 months, and the life span is proportionately short (Régis 1972). The isotopic profile of a modern

1a

1b

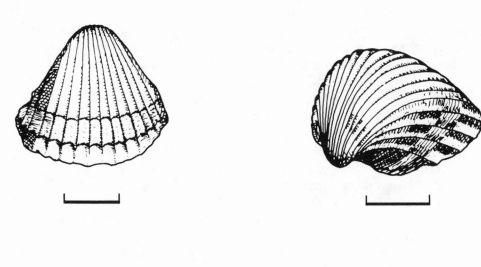

2

3

Figure 14. Species used for analysis from the Franchthi deposits: **1a-b.** *Cerastoderma glaucum*; **2.** *Cerithium vulgatum*; **3.** *Monodonta turbinata*. Scale bars = 1 cm.

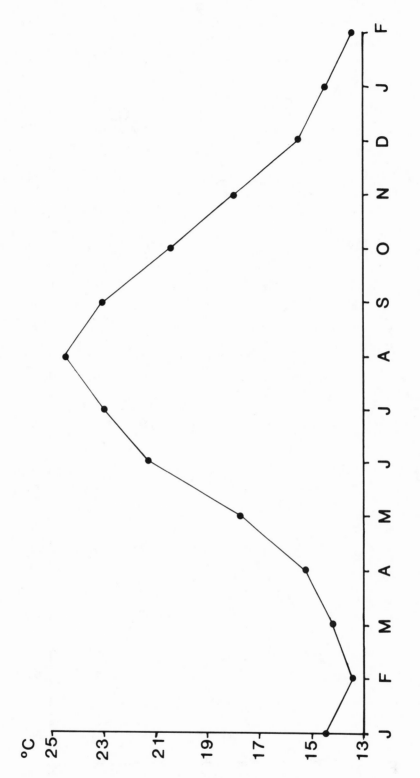

Figure 15. Mean monthly sea temperatures for the Argolid.

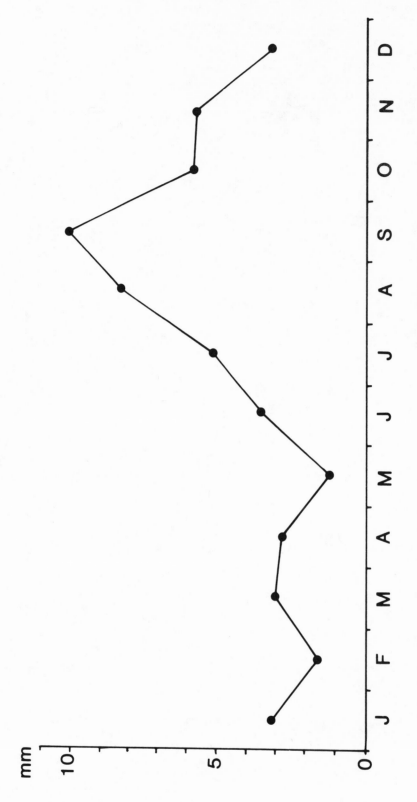

Figure 16. Growth rate of shells of *Monodonta turbinata* from Bandol, southern France (after Régis 1972).

specimen, collected live from the shore near Franchthi in June, 1980, is shown in Figure 17. It covers the period from about August, 1979 (the month when sea temperatures are highest) to June, 1980, the samples having been taken as far back towards the apex as possible. The samples were taken at regular 2 mm intervals around the whorls. The range of $\delta^{18}O$ values in this specimen is $3°/_{oo}$, reflecting growth throughout the year in this species and the probable range of actual sea temperatures through the period of growth. The slowest growth takes place in May, during spawning, when sea temperatures are rising rapidly. Because of this slow phase of growth, the isotopic profile of a shell sampled at equal intervals has a steeply sloping spring section, when $\delta^{18}O$ values become rapidly more negative as the water temperature rises by its fastest rate, while shell growth is correspondingly minimal. This is a characteristic feature of the *Monodonta* profile, in both modern and archaeological specimens. It is essential to sample the absolute edge of a shell collected at this time of year to obtain a precise seasonal dating. Growth rates slow down progressively with age. This effect can be seen particularly clearly, for example, in a sample from Unit 204 in FAS (Appendix F, FAS:204:1). Better resolution is therefore obtained from younger shells.

Cerithium vulgatum is a species that inhabits both rocky and sandy shores. Although literature on its growth rate is not available, a certain amount of information can be derived from the isotopic profile of a modern specimen (Figure 18). *C. vulgatum* is a gastropod whose shell is ornamented with knobs, large ones along the center of the whorls and smaller ones on either side of the large ones (Figure 14:2 and Plate 2b). Samples were taken from every third large knob. This proved to be an adequate sampling technique when growth was fast, but it has sometimes been necessary to take additional samples near the edge of the shell if the trend has not been clear because of slower growth. It is obvious from Figure 18 that growth is faster in the summer months than it is in winter. A comparison with the *Monodonta* profile in Figure 17 suggests that the shell may, in fact, stop growing in the coldest part of the winter because the positive values are not as extreme and are generally represented by a single sampling point, in contrast with the clusters of points with winter values in *Monodonta*. To check whether the apparent stoppage in winter was simply a function of coarse sampling techniques (sampling was a great deal coarser than for *Monodonta*), additional samples were taken around the points with most positive $\delta^{18}O$ values. However, there was no significant variation or increase in δ value in the areas around the original sampling points, either in this case or, indeed, in any of the archaeological specimens from which additional samples were taken. In both the second and third autumns in the modern shell, there was a sudden sharp increase in $\delta^{18}O$ values, indicating that growth slowed down in autumn. Similar slow growth in *Monodonta* was related to spawning. Slight variations in peak summer values from one year to the next may well be the effects of annual variations in sea temperature. Again, additional samples taken around the most negative values have yielded no changes in peak values for each summer. As with *Monodonta*, the rate of growth slows down with increasing age.

Cerastoderma glaucum (Figure 14:1a-b and Plate 2c) is a sandy- or muddy-shore bivalve, more commonly found in lagoonal or estuarine habitats than on the open shore (d'Angelo and Gargiullo 1978; Boyden and Russell 1972; Russell 1971). Our only modern example is a beach-collected one whose exact habitat is therefore uncertain. Contiguous samples were taken from this shell, along the middle rib and along the 27 mm of the outer shell layer nearest to the growing edge. Specimens from the Lago Lungo in southern Italy reach a height of 27 mm in nine months from spawning at the less saline end of the lagoon and somewhat less at the seaward end (Ivell 1979). The samples from this Greek shell can therefore be expected to cover the best part of a year's growth. Figure 19 indicates that this is so. The isotopic range is somewhat more negative than for *Monodonta* and *Cerithium*,

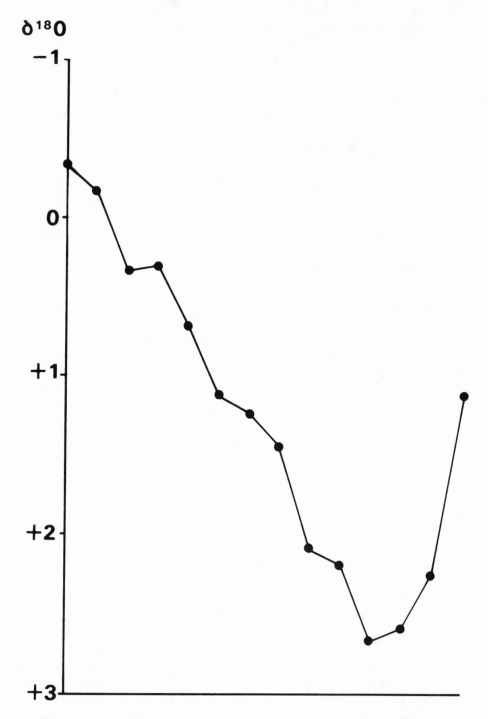

Figure 17. Isotopic profile of a modern specimen of *Monodonta turbinata* collected live from the shore near Franchthi Cave in June, 1980. Edge value on the right. Points represent samples taken at approximately 2 mm intervals.

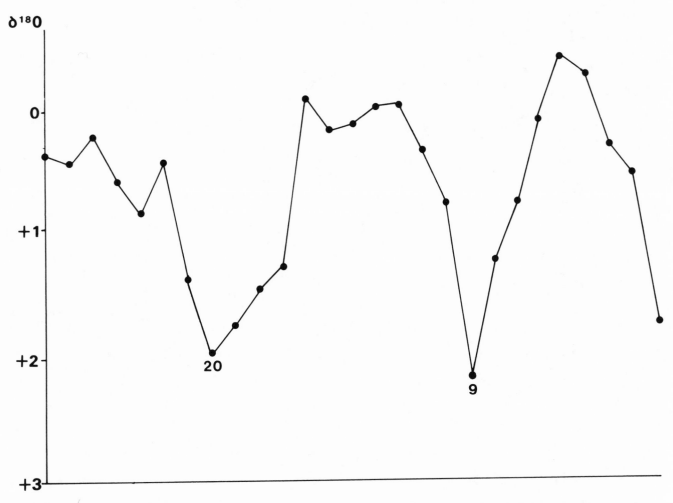

Figure 18. Isotopic profile of a modern specimen of *Cerithium vulgatum*, beach collected. Points represent samples taken at approximately 2 mm intervals.

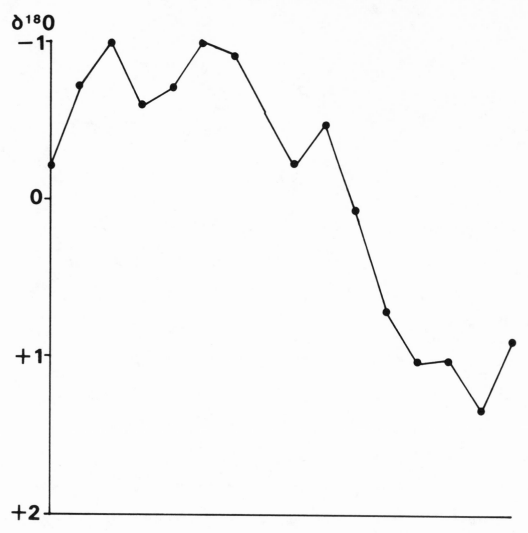

Figure 19. Isotopic profile of a modern specimen of *Cerastoderma glaucum*, beach collected. Points represent samples taken at approximately 2 mm intervals.

indicating that it probably came from a more brackish environment. It is therefore important that, in this species, the edge value should be related to the remainder of the isotopic profile and not to the average profile for fully marine species. The more brackish habitat of *Cerastoderma* may, however, constitute a problem, in that there may be fluctuations in salinity, perhaps on a seasonal basis. These would affect the isotopic composition of the water and hence that of the shell carbonate. For this reason, it is preferable to use fully marine species wherever they occur.

The profile of a modern specimen of *Tapes decussatus,* a sandy-shore bivalve, demonstrates the problems of interpretation with this species (Figure 20). The profile is not smooth enough for general trends to be distinguishable. On the basis of this profile and of some archaeological shells which were similarly difficult to interpret, this species has not been used in the study.

Donacilla cornea is a very small shell, on which it would be difficult to achieve fine enough resolution in the sampling. It is found only in Neolithic contexts. In view of the variety of species which are also found in the Neolithic and are known to be good seasonal indicators, it was decided not to use this fragile shell.

Analysis of modern material therefore indicates that the three best species to use are *Monodonta/Gibbula, Cerithium* and *Cerastoderma* (Figure 14), all of which appear through much of the sequence and are not restricted to any one period. The archaeological analyses have been concentrated on these three species.

INTERPRETATION OF ARCHAEOLOGICAL SHELLS

The analysis of modern shells highlights certain problem areas which need to be considered in the approach to the interpretation of the isotopic profiles of archaeological shells:

1. The variation in isotopic range from one year to another makes the distinction between a late autumn or winter edge difficult to make. For example, in Figure 18, sampling point 20 (counting from right to left) is $0.2°/_{oo}$ more negative than sampling point 9, representing the peak winter value one year later. Because of this variation, there is some uncertainty about whether, in certain cases, a shell was collected in autumn or winter. The absolute value, in other words, is not an infallible guide.

2. In the summer, when shell growth is fast and sea temperatures fluctuate considerably, the isotopic curve is not smooth. An edge value which registers a downward turn on the graph may thus be part of the summer fluctuations or may be the beginning of the autumn change to more positive values.

3. The ageing process slows down growth. A sample taken from the edge of an old shell probably represents a longer span of time than one taken from a younger shell (Bailey et al. 1983).

Because of year-to-year variability, differences in micro-habitat between individual shells and within-season variations, the establishment of specific $\delta^{18}O$ values as cut-off points between seasons is too arbitrary, offering a spurious appearance of precision and objectivity. In interpreting the edge measurement, it is important to take into account the shape of the curve and to relate it both to other shells from the same levels of the deposit and to the annual range within the individual shell. The growth characteristics of the species, the age and the absolute $\delta^{18}O$ value of the edge must also be taken into account.

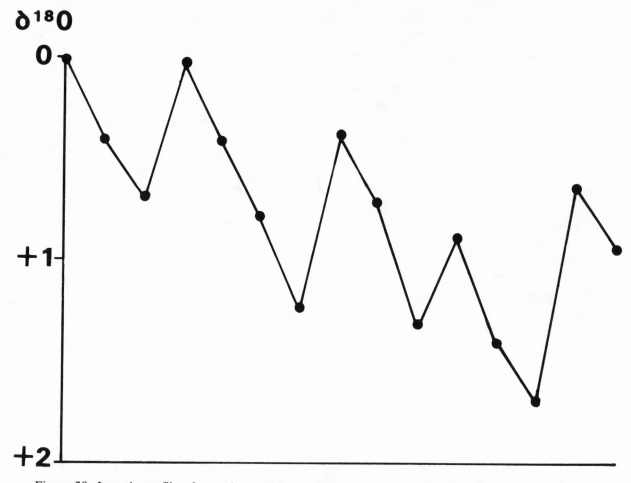

Figure 20. Isotopic profile of a modern specimen of *Tapes decussatus*, beach collected. Points represent samples taken at approximately 2 mm intervals.

The starting point for dividing the year into seasons is the sea-temperature curve. Because sea temperatures lag a little behind air temperatures, the division of the curve into the section representing the warmest sea temperatures, the section representing the coldest ones, and the two intermediate sections is slightly out of phase with the conventional way of dividing up the calendar months into the four seasons. For example, autumn is usually considered to be September, October, and November, rather than October, November, and December, as here. However, this is the most convenient way of dividing up the data (Figure 21). The problems of the erratic summer fluctuations can only be accommodated by including the whole of that zone in one category. The "autumn" category is then well clear of the zone of summer fluctuations, as is the "spring" category.

There is also a slight error caused by the fact that the carbonate removed from the edge for sampling does not represent the temperature of the water at the instant of collection, but integrates a period of time prior to collection. The length of time sampled will depend on the rate of growth during this time and on the size of the sample removed. The edge sample is removed with a small file which takes about 0.25 mm of growth from along the edge of the shell. In a fast-growing shell such as *Monodonta,* this could represent between ten days in May when growth is slowest and a single day in September when growth is at its most rapid (Régis 1972). Thus, it is not sufficient to re-form the seasonal categories according to air temperatures.

Since growth slows down with age, the edge sample of an older shell represents a slightly longer time span than an edge sample from a young shell. Likewise, a year's growth is covered by fewer samples in an older shell, so that each sample is the mean value of a longer time period than an equivalently sized sample from a younger shell. The net effect is to reduce slightly the total annual range of $\delta^{18}O$ values, especially in the region of winter deposition, when growth is slow. This can be seen in the profiles of several shells in the study, especially *Monodonta* and *Cerithium,* where it has been possible to sample two or three years' growth in a single shell.

Because of their year-round growth and the reliability of the results gained from *Monodonta* species, both modern and archaeological, from Franchthi and from other sites in the Mediterranean (N. J. Shackleton 1974) and elsewhere (Deith 1983a), the shells of *Monodonta/Gibbula* were analyzed wherever they occurred. In fact, they occur in small numbers through almost the entire sequence. Analyses from the late Palaeolithic are solely of these species. There are few *Monodonta* specimens in the Lower Mesolithic, and the majority of the analyses from this phase have been performed on *Cerithium* and *Cerastoderma.* In the late Mesolithic, the latter disappears, but there are more *Monodonta* available. *Cerastoderma* reappears in the Neolithic; all three species have been used for analysis of Neolithic material.

RESULTS

A list of the numbers of shells analyzed from each of the excavation units sampled is given in Table 5. Isotopic profiles for each of these shells appear in Appendix F, while the seasonal interpretation of each shell is given in Table 6. Each shell has been given an identification which includes the excavation unit number, the species, and a number for that species within that particular excavation unit. Histograms of the seasonal distribution within each excavation unit are presented in Figure 22.

The samples cluster in certain parts of the sequence. Correspondingly, there are also very considerable gaps where no suitable material is available for analysis. To present the

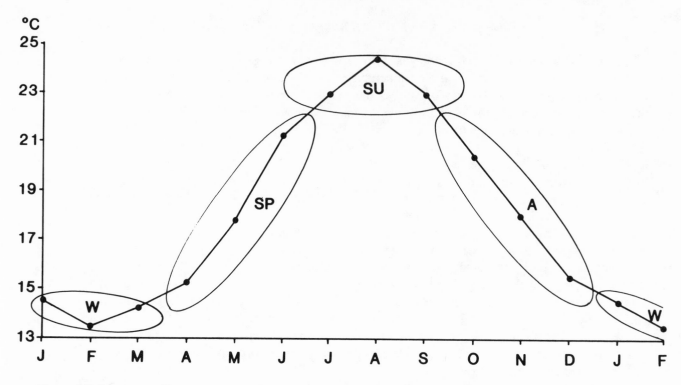

Figure 21. Mean monthly sea-temperature curve for the Argolid, showing the division of the curve into seasons. This forms the basis for dividing the similarly shaped isotopic profiles into seasonal segments.

TABLE 5

NUMBERS OF SHELLS ANALYZED BY EXCAVATION UNIT

FAS

74	1	*Monodonta*
81	7	*Monodonta*
91	1	*Monodonta*
93	3	*Cerastoderma*
111	1	*Cerastoderma*
112	2	*Monodonta*
120	2	*Monodonta*
122	1	*Cerastoderma*
130	1	*Cerastoderma*, 1 *Cerithium*
145	4	*Monodonta*
146	2	*Monodonta*
148	1	*Monodonta*
151	1	*Monodonta*, 1 *Cerithium*
159	1	*Cerithium*
183	1	*Cerithium*
184	4	*Cerithium*
185	1	*Cerithium*
191	5	*Cerastoderma*
192	1	*Cerithium*
195	5	*Cerastoderma*
196	2	*Monodonta*, 4 *Cerastoderma*
204	2	*Monodonta*
207	4	*Monodonta*

FAN

102	5	*Cerastoderma*
114	1	*Cerastoderma*
163	7	*Monodonta*
167	1	*Cerithium*
170	1	*Monodonta*
187	2	*Cerastoderma*

H1A

173	3	*Monodonta*

L5

22	4	*Monodonta*
28	2	*Monodonta*
36	5	*Cerastoderma*, 1 *Cerithium*
40	1	*Monodonta*
41	1	*Cerithium*

H1B

130	2	*Cerithium*
134	1	*Cerithium*
135	2	*Cerastoderma*
142	1	*Cerithium*
153	3	*Monodonta*
154	8	*Monodonta*
155	8	*Monodonta*

L5NE

57	1	*Monodonta*, 1 *Cerithium*

TABLE 6

SEASONAL DISTRIBUTION OF EDGES OF SHELLS ANALYZED

	Spring	Summer	Autumn	Winter
Final Palaeolithic		FAS:204:3	FAS:204:1	H1B:154:6
		FAS:207:2	FAS:207:1	H1A:173:2
		FAS:207:4	FAS:207:3	
		H1B:153:1	H1B:155:1	
		H1B:153:2	H1B:155:2	
		H1B:153:3	H1B:155:3	
			H1B:155:4	
			H1B:155:6	
			H1B:155:7	
			H1B:155:8	
			H1B:155:9	
			H1B:154:1	
			H1B:154:2	
			H1B:154:3	
			H1B:154:4	
			H1B:154:5	
			H1B:154:7	
			H1B:154:8	
			H1A:173:1	
			H1A:173:3	
Lower Mesolithic	FAS:195:7[b]	FAS:196:1	FAS:196:1[b]	FAS:196:2[b]
	FAS:191:1[b]	FAS:196:2	FAS:195:1[b]	FAS:196:3[b]
	FAS:191:2[b]	FAS:185[a]	FAS:195:6[b]	FAS:196:4[b]
	FAS:184:3[a]	FAS:184:1[a]	FAS:191:5[b]	FAS:195:3[b]
	FAS:183:1[a]	H1B:135:2[b]	FAS:192[a]	FAS:191:3[b]
	H1B:135:1[b]	H1B:134:1[a]	H1B:130:1[a,c]	FAS:191:4[b]
	FAS:195:2[b]		H1B:130:2[a]	FAS:184:2[a]
			H1B:142:1[a]	FAS:184:4[a]
			FAN:187:4[b]	
			FAN:187:5[b]	
Upper Mesolithic		FAS:159[a]		
Final Mesolithic	FAS:151[a]	FAS:148	FAS:151[b]	
		FAN:167[a]	FAN:170	
		FAN:163:2	FAN:163:1	
		FAN:163:3	FAN:163:5	
		FAN:163:4	FAN:163:6	
		FAS:145:2	FAN:163:7	
		FAS:146:1	FAS:145:1	
		FAS:146:2	FAS:145:3	
			FAS:145:4	

TABLE 6 (continued)

	Spring	*Summer*	*Autumn*	*Winter*
Early and Middle Neolithic	FAS:130[a] L5:22:1 L5:22:2 L5:36[a] L5:36:3[b] L5:36:4[b] L5NE:57 L5:41[a]	FAS:130[b] FAS:122:1[b] FAS:120:1 FAS:120:2 L5:22:8 L5:36:1[b] L5:36:2[b] L5:36:5[b] L5:40	L5:28:3 L5NE:57[a]	L5:22:4 L5:28:1
Late Neolithic	FAS:91 FAS:93:2[b] FAS:93:3[b]	FAN:102:4[b] FAN:114[b] FAS:112:1 FAS:112:2 FAS:93:1[b]	FAS:111:1[b]	FAN:102:1[b] FAN:102:2[b] FAN:102:3[b] FAN:102:5[b]
Final Neolithic	FAS:81:2	FAS:81:4 FAS:81:5 FAS:81:6 FAS:81:7 FAS:74	FAS:81:3	FAS:81:1

[a] Denotes *Cerithium.*
[b] Denotes *Cerastoderma*; the remainder are *Monodonta.*
[c] No profile available.

results in terms of the molluscan zones observed by J. C. Shackleton (Chapter 2) might imply, quite misleadingly, that the distribution of samples is more even than it is. For example, Zones II and III are represented by a cluster from the very earliest phase of the Lower Mesolithic and another from the Final Mesolithic, with only a single shell representing the vast period of time between. It therefore seems to us more appropriate to define those phases in the sequence for which we have samples in terms of their cultural or chronological affinities, rather than in terms of the molluscan zonation, which includes material from excavation units throughout the deposits.

The earliest phase for which there are data is the latest part of the Palaeolithic, around 10,500 B.P. It includes FAS:204 and 207, H1A:173 and H1B:153, 154, and 155. All shells analyzed from this period were *Monodonta/Gibbula*. The majority were collected in autumn, with a second major grouping of summer-collected shells. Of the two shells classified as "winter-collected," one (H1B:154:6 *Monodonta*) may in fact have been collected in late autumn. The absolute value of the shell edge is very close to that of H1B:154:7 *Monodonta*, which has been classified as "autumn-collected." Because of the more negative summer reading in H1B:154:6 *Monodonta*, the profile covers a reasonable range of isotopic values for a year's growth, but the assignation remains slightly dubious. Almost the entire sample from H1B:154-155 is autumn-collected.

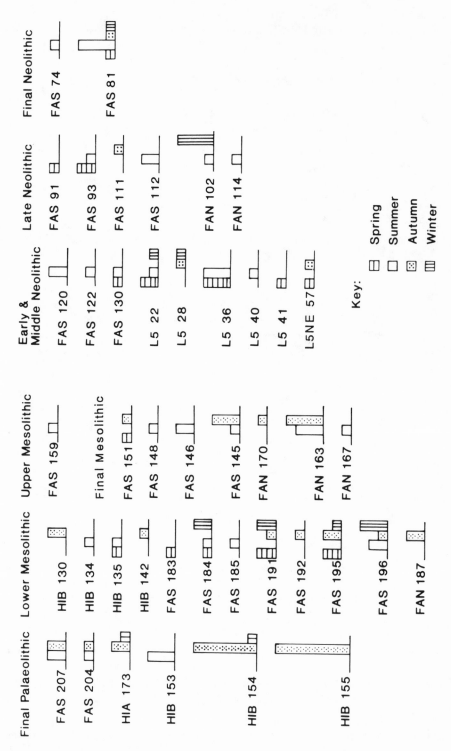

Figure 22. Histograms of seasonal classifications of shell profiles for excavation units arranged in chronological order.

It is dangerous to attach too much significance to single shells as evidence for winter occupation of the site. It is always possible to pick up the occasional dead shell during shellfish collection, perhaps more especially with bivalves than with gastropods. The hard evidence here indicates that the site was visited in autumn and summer during the latest Palaeolithic.

The second major cluster comes from the earliest phases of the Lower Mesolithic and includes material from H1B:130, 134, 135, and 142, FAS:183, 184, 185, 191, 192, 195, and 196 and FAN:187. A wider seasonal distribution is indicated here, within individual units where the sample consists of several shells. There are no samples like H1B:154 and 155, where an entire group of shells was collected in a single season.

Evidence of collection in all seasons comes from *Cerithium* shells. Analyses have also been made on the edges of fragments of *Cerithium* shells. The results are shown in Figure 23 (hatched histogram), set against the values of samples taken through complete shells and thus representing the entire seasonal range. (The larger numbers of summer readings from the whole shells are indicative of the more rapid summer growth in this species.) When the edge values of the fragments are compared with the edge values of the seasonally classified profiles of this species (see Appendix F), they can be roughly grouped as follows: summer *9*, spring or autumn *10*, winter *7*. These analyses thus lend support to the seasonally diverse classifications obtained from the complete shells.

Much of the evidence suggesting that the cave was visited in winter comes from a group of *Cerastoderma* shells from FAS:184-196. Because winter readings had not been expected, the edges were re-sampled and additional samples were taken from the carbonate nearest the shell edges to ensure that there had been no contamination in the original samples and to provide a more detailed picture of the edge areas. The results confirmed the original readings and demonstrated that there was no error in the analysis.

Cerastoderma glaucum is a euryhaline species (i.e., tolerant of a wide range of salinities) and is restricted only by its need for sheltered conditions, not by any narrow salinity requirements. It is therefore found primarily in lagoons, estuaries and sheltered bays. In the earliest phase of the Mesolithic, around 9,500 B.P., a shallow bay with thick, muddy, silty sediments originally laid down during the stillstand of 40,000 to 30,000 B.P. dominated the shoreline near the cave (see Chapter 4). This sheltered bay would have been a suitable habitat for *C. glaucum*, as would the estuary of the "Kiladha River," which appears to have been more substantial at that time, with greater runoff than today (van Andel et al. 1980).

How would these habitats affect the shell chemistry? Is it possible that variations in salinity could override the effects of temperature variations on the annual sequence of isotopic ratios in the carbonates? The Mediterranean pattern of winter precipitation and summer drought might then reverse the seasonal relationship between enrichment and depletion in ^{18}O in the shell material, causing it to be enriched in the summer and depleted in the winter. If the shells were gathered from the bay, this could certainly not happen. If they were collected from the estuary, the combination of summer temperatures and summer drought would lead to ratios no more enriched than those in species from a marine habitat. In order to produce a reversed curve, winter values would then have to be depleted in $\delta^{18}O$ by $4^\circ/_{\circ\circ}$ or $5^\circ/_{\circ\circ}$ relative to winter values in shells from the open shore. If we compare the *Cerithium* profiles with those of *Cerastoderma*, the most negative values in each set are around $-1^\circ/_{\circ\circ}$, while the most positive ones vary more but are somewhat more enriched in *Cerastoderma* than in *Cerithium*. Allowing for a winter recession in growth in the latter species, the curves are quite closely similar. The values are consistent with collection from the shallow waters of the bay and with an interpretation of those edges with the most positive $\delta^{18}O$ values as winter-collected. They are *not* consistent with collection from a habitat

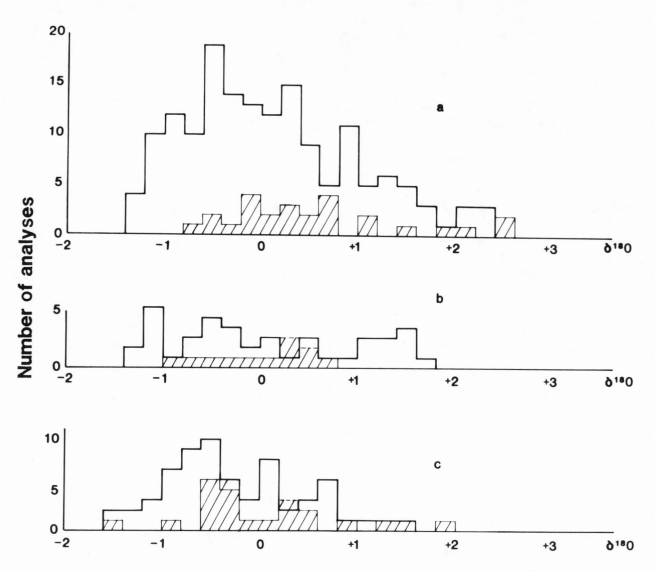

Figure 23. Histograms of isotopic values of the edges of fragments of *Cerithium vulgatum* (*hatched*), set against histograms of isotopic values through complete shells of *C. vulgatum* (*solid lines*): **a.** Lower Mesolithic; **b.** Final Mesolithic; **c.** Early and Middle Neolithic.

with a markedly divergent salinity regime. If the *Cerastoderma* and *Cerithium* data are taken together, there is good evidence for winter collection in the early part of the Mesolithic.

Only one of the Upper Mesolithic shells (FAS:159) comes from the Upper Mesolithic proper, the remainder coming from the Final Mesolithic. Of these, six shells are from FAS:145 and 146, which are mixed units in which both Mesolithic and Neolithic material occurs (C. Perlès, personal communication). The other analyses in this cluster come from FAS:148 and 151 and FAN:163, 167, and 170. There is no evidence of winter collection in this cluster and only one spring edge which is, in fact, in the borderline zone between spring and summer. The sample from the Final Mesolithic is evenly distributed between summer and autumn. As in the Lower Mesolithic, the additional *Cerithium* edges from fragments generally confirm the results of analyses of complete shells. There are three values which can be classified as summer edges, nine which fall into the spring or autumn groupings, but no winter edges (Figure 23).

During the Neolithic occupation of the site, there were certain distinctive occupational phases. In the Early and Middle Neolithic, both the cave and the terraced area outside it (Paralia) were used, but in the Late Neolithic, usage was restricted to the cave. A second major change occurred with the Final Neolithic, when the Paralia was again brought into use. The possibility of additional Neolithic habitation in what is now Kiladha Bay (Gifford 1983) adds to the complexity of the Neolithic occupation of the area and suggests a variety of possible uses for the cave. In view of these problems, we conclude that the largest units that can be considered as relatively homogeneous entities are (a) the Early and Middle Neolithic, (b) the Late Neolithic and (c) the Final Neolithic. Since the samples are small, it is desirable to make the units as large as possible if any patterning in the data is to be discerned.

(a) Early and Middle Neolithic. Samples FAS:120, 122, and 130 come from the cave and L5:22, 28, 36, 40, and 41 and L5NE:57 from Paralia. The majority from both the cave and Paralia are clustered in the spring and summer quadrants, but there are two shells in each of the autumn and winter categories, all from Paralia. A good measure of support for a spread of seasonal collection comes from the edge fragments of *Cerithium*. Seasonal attributions are summer *7,* spring or autumn *10,* winter *5.*

(b) The samples from the Late Neolithic come from FAS:91, 93, 111, and 112 and FAN:102 and 114. The numbers are small and cluster in the spring and summer categories, as in the Early and Middle Neolithic. Here, however, there is a group of *Cerastoderma* shells which appears to have been collected in winter. The same comments apply here as to the group in the Lower Mesolithic (see above), and they may as confidently be ascribed to ''winter'' as those in FAS:93 and FAN:114 are to ''spring'' and ''summer.'' Evidence for collection in both winter and summer is incontrovertible in the Late Neolithic.

(c) The Final Neolithic is represented by two excavation units, FAS:74 and 81. Here, there is a strong bias towards summer, with minimal evidence for collection in other seasons.

The results have been presented according to preliminary excavation stratigraphy (Figure 22), but the question arises as to whether shells demonstrating the same season of collection can be the remains of a single meal. One of the problems here is that the excavation units are wholly arbitrary and do not represent depositional episodes. A unit may cover a number of years, even decades, and perhaps five to ten years in the early Mesolithic when sedimentation rates were high. Shells from a single meal could equally well be found in different excavation units, given the kind of blurring of resolution that results from trampling. There is clearly no systematic way in which the possibility of statistical bias can be allowed for, and it was felt that a direct presentation of the data was preferable to statistical treatment, which is more likely to distort than to clarify the evidence.

DISCUSSION

The small size of the samples obviates any attempt to apply statistical analysis to the data. What the analyses do, therefore, is to point to times of year when people were visiting the cave and collecting shellfish. Lack of evidence for shellfish collecting at other times of year is not evidence that people were not there (Deith forthcoming a).

There is a strongly seasonal bias in the data from the latest Palaeolithic. The use of the cave in summer and autumn fits well with the botanical evidence of the harvesting of fruit and nuts such as pistachio, almond, and wild pear (Hansen 1980). The advantages of the cave during the warmer months emerge from surveys of the area. A lowered sea level during the late Palaeolithic exposed a wide coastal plain (see Chapter 4), which could have supported herds of grazing herbivores. In winter and spring, when there was an adequate water supply and the grass was renewed by the rains, this plain would have been a very attractive place for Palaeolithic man. In the summer, when the water supply dried up and the grass shrivelled, it would have been an inhospitable place for both man and beast, whereas one of the great advantages of Franchthi Cave as a summer base was its year-round water supply in the form of natural springs (van Andel and Sutton 1987). It may therefore have been used as a summer/autumn base camp.

The lack of other evidence for winter occupation of the site (Jacobsen 1976) gives the results from the Lower Mesolithic an especial interest. They indicate at least a human presence at times of the year hitherto unsuspected. There are several different ways of organizing the movements of the community which might give rise to the seasonal pattern observed in the data:

1. The cave might have continued to be used as a summer/autumn base camp, with occasional visits in winter and spring. The Nunamiut Eskimo, for example, sometimes use one seasonal base as an overnight stopover between two other base camps (Binford 1982).

2. All visits to the cave might have been brief and occasional, whatever the season (cf. Deith 1983b).

3. The seasonal data may represent a more radical extension of the usage of the site, to a permanent, sedentary home base.

The fact that, in the Final Mesolithic, the shellfish-gathering pattern appears to revert to that of the Final Palaeolithic, together with all other evidence for seasonal abundances and shortages in the resources exploited by the hunter-gatherer groups that visited Franchthi, is perhaps suggestive that the first alternative is the most likely of the three. Nevertheless, the hunter-gatherer phase at Franchthi covers a long period of time and it cannot be assumed that there were no major changes during that period. One change which might be very relevant here is that the sedimentation rate became much more rapid in the earliest Mesolithic, by comparison with the latest Palaeolithic. This may be indicative of a more intensive use of the cave.

In the Neolithic levels, there is a perceptible change in emphasis, from the summer and autumn bias of the hunter-gatherers to a summer and spring bias. Autumnal collection is relatively insignificant in all phases, replaced by a stronger spring component in the Early to Late Neolithic. Although the numbers are small, there is some indication of collection in each season, especially in the Late Neolithic. Together with the bone and plant data, these data support the evidence for the existence of a settled farming community in the Neolithic. Sample sizes are too small for comparisons to be made between Neolithic phases. A summer bias in each, however, appears to be a common feature and could be a reflection of the role of shellfish among subsistence farmers in this region (cf. Deith 1988a). A bias towards summer shellfish gathering has been observed in present-day subsistence farming communities in the Argolid (Forbes 1976a). Gathered foods are used today to add flavor and vitamins to a predominantly cereal diet. From October to May, wild greens such as leaves, stems, shoots and some bulbous roots are gathered two or three times a week but, by the summer, they have disappeared (Forbes 1976b). While shellfish are gathered throughout the year, they are collected much more frequently in the summer, partly to compensate for the loss of the wild greens and partly because shellfish gathering is more pleasant in summer (Forbes 1976a). Since the "spring" category of the archaeological shell data includes May and June, the bias in the Franchthi data is much the same as the present-day seasonal bias among the farming communities of the area.

CONCLUSION

The use of oxygen isotope analysis to establish seasonal patterns of shellfish collection has revealed certain variations in human behavior through time at Franchthi Cave, especially at the transition between the hunter-gatherer way of life and that of farming. It constitutes an important beginning in attacking the problem of seasonality at Franchthi, especially the question of evidence for winter use of the cave, which is otherwise difficult to attain. In addition to providing new information, it has raised questions about the occupation of the cave, the answers to which must be looked for by reviewing the entire body of evidence, both from the site itself and from survey work in the area.

ACKNOWLEDGMENTS

We thank the Science and Engineering Research Council for funding this project. The analyses have been run over an extended period of time and we should like to thank Su Wanek, Mike Hall, and Chandrakant Solanki for their sample analyses. We are particularly grateful to Judith Shackleton, who provided the modern shells and has been most generous in allowing us unrestricted access to her data. In the later stages of the work, we have had many valuable and stimulating discussions with her and also with Tjeerd van Andel on the more general aspects of the Franchthi environment and economy. The final presentation of the material has been speeded by John Line's computer program for drawing graphs of each shell profile.

APPENDIX F

Isotopic Profiles of Shells Analyzed

The profiles that follow are arranged alphabetically by trench and numerically by excavation unit within trenches. In those cases where more than one shell has been analyzed in an excavation unit, the unit number (followed by a colon) includes a second number and the name of the species analyzed (e.g., FAS:204:3 *Monodonta,* H1B:134:1 *Cerithium,* H1B:135:1 *Cerastoderma*).

In these profiles, a more positive δ value is indicative of cold temperatures and a more negative one of warm temperatures. The more negative (summer) values are at the top of the graphs and the more positive (winter) values are at the bottom. Edge values are on the right.

[*N.B.* Appendix F should be used in conjunction with Tables 5 and 6. This will explain those excavation units where it may appear to the reader that the analyses of some samples are missing. See, for example, Unit FAS:195 where five *Cerastoderma* shells were analyzed: 1, 2, 3, 6, and 7. — EDITOR]

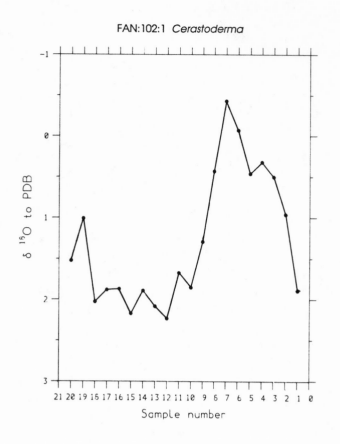

FAN:102:1 *Cerastoderma*

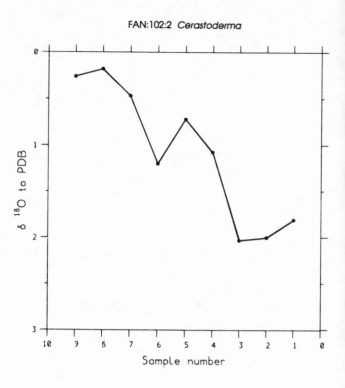

FAN:102:2 *Cerastoderma*

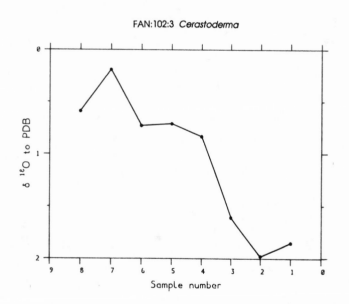

FAN:102:3 *Cerastoderma*

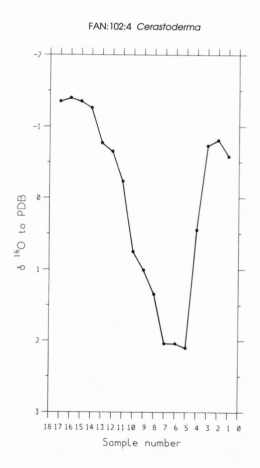

FAN:102:4 *Cerastoderma*

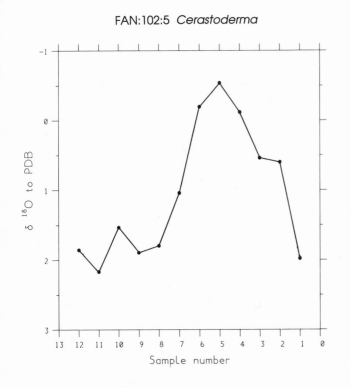

FAN:102:5 *Cerastoderma*

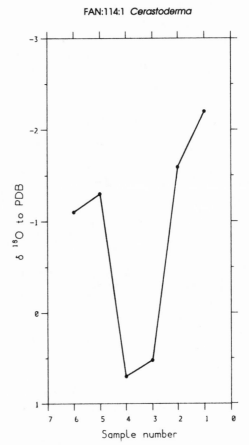

FAN:114:1 *Cerastoderma*

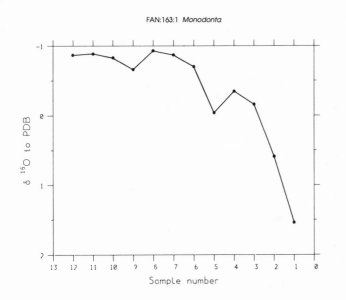

FAN:163:1 *Monodonta*

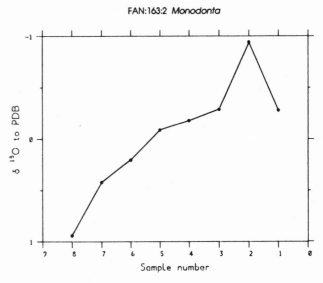

FAN:163:2 *Monodonta*

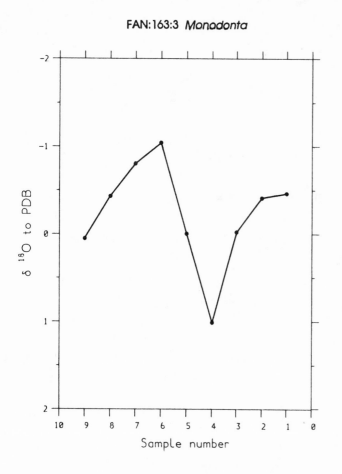

FAN:163:3 *Monodonta*

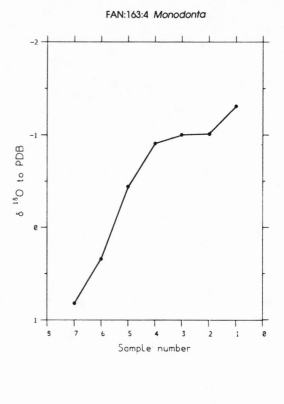

FAN:163:4 *Monodonta*

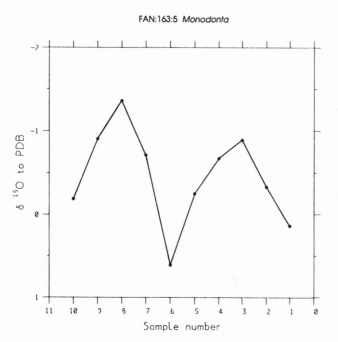

FAN:163:5 *Monodonta*

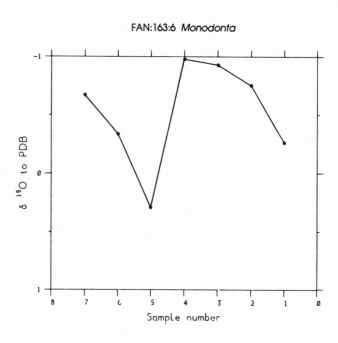

FAN:163:6 *Monodonta*

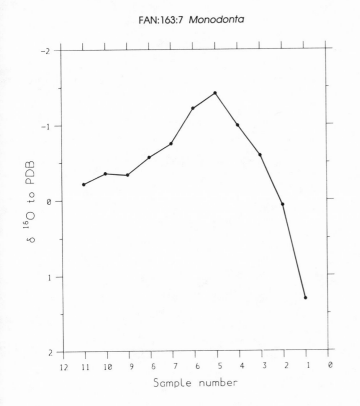

FAN:163:7 *Monodonta*

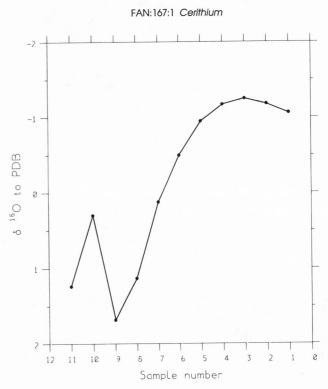

FAN:167:1 *Cerithium*

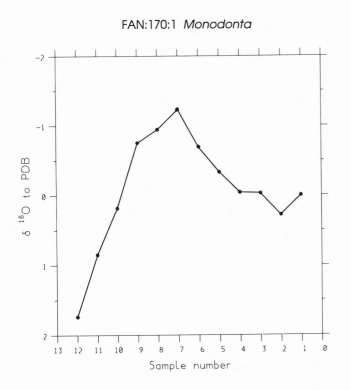

FAN:170:1 *Monodonta*

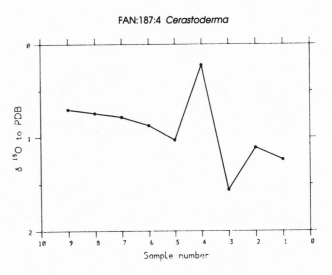

FAN:187:4 *Cerastoderma*

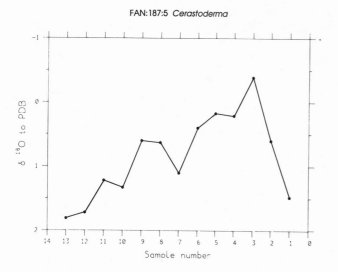

FAN:187:5 *Cerastoderma*

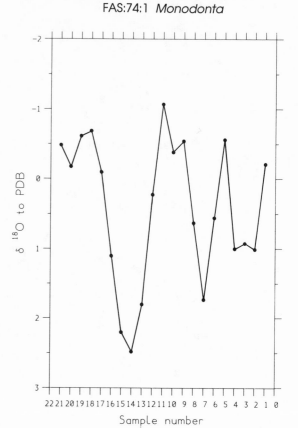

FAS:74:1 *Monodonta*

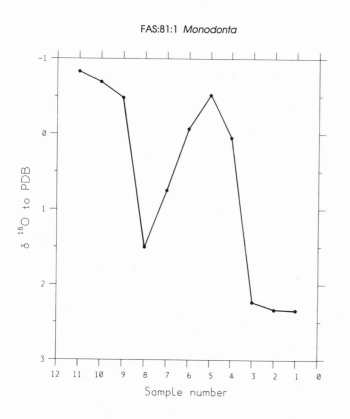

FAS:81:1 *Monodonta*

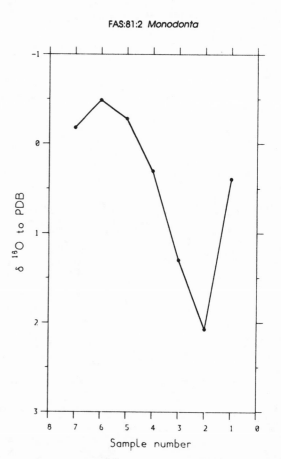

FAS:81:2 *Monodonta*

FAS:81:3 *Monodonta*

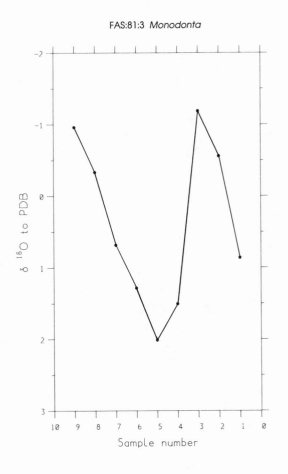

FAS:81:4 *Monodonta*

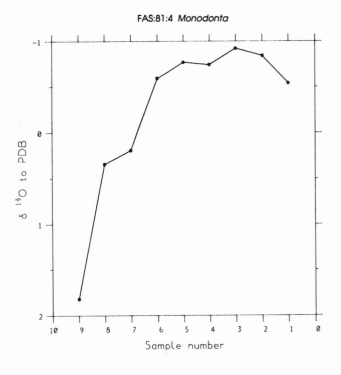

FAS:81:5 *Monodonta*

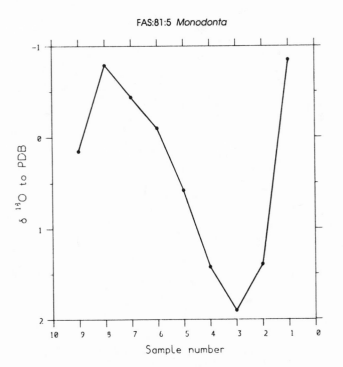

FAS:81:6 *Monodonta*

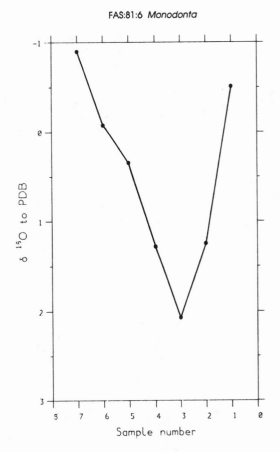

FAS:81:7 *Monodonta*

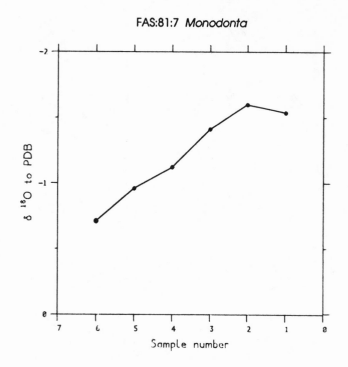

FAS:91:1 *Monodonta*

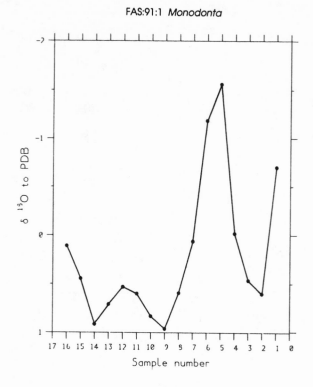

FAS:93:1 *Cerastoderma*

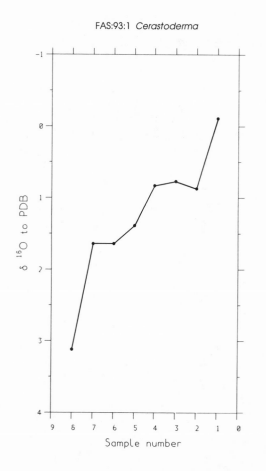

FAS:93:2 *Cerastoderma*

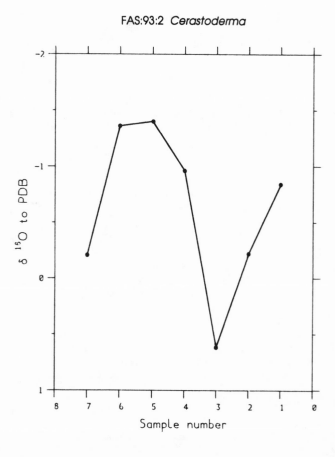

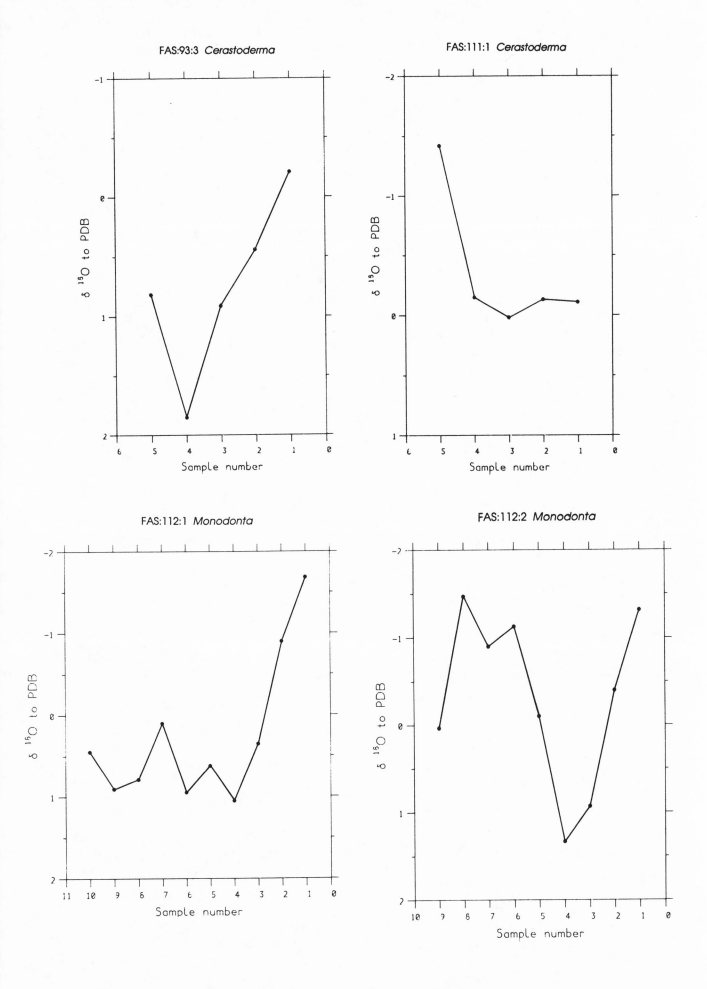

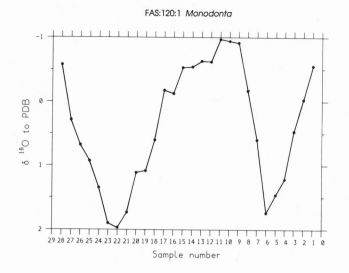

FAS:120:1 *Monodonta*

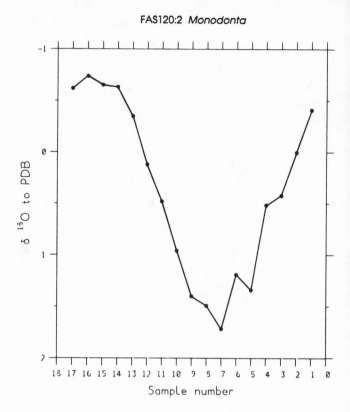

FAS120:2 *Monodonta*

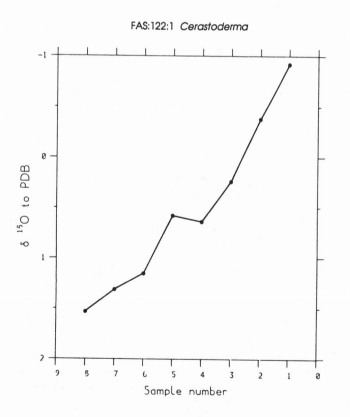

FAS:122:1 *Cerastoderma*

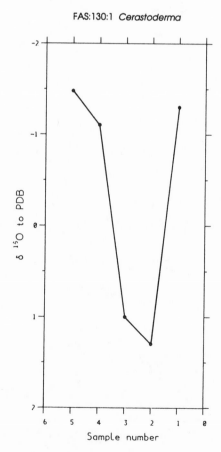

FAS:130:1 *Cerastoderma*

FAS:130:1 *Cerithium*

FAS:145:1 *Monodonta*

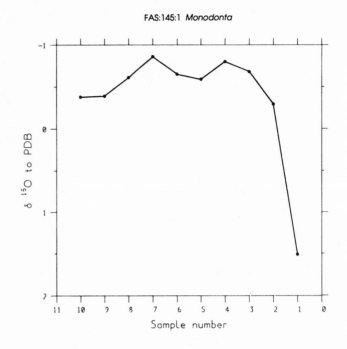

FAS:145:2 *Monodonta*

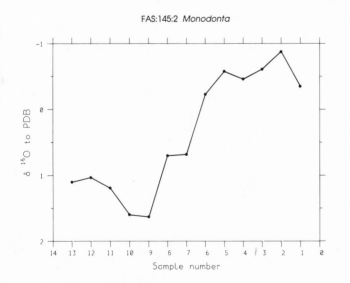

FAS:145:3 *Monodonta*

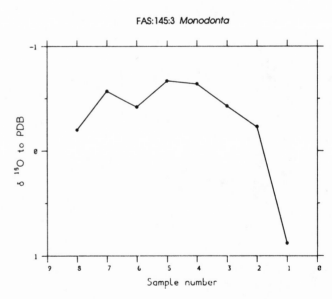

FAS:145:4 *Monodonta*

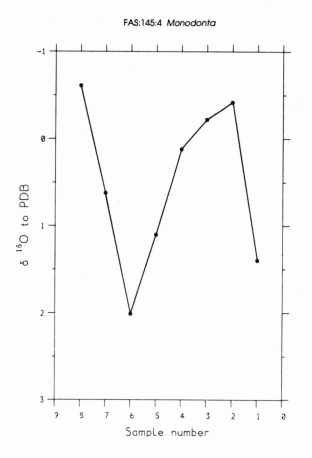

FAS:146:1 *Monodonta*

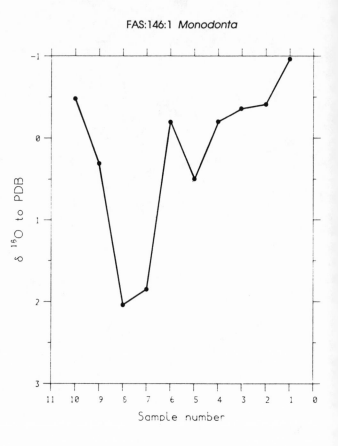

FAS:146:2 *Monodonta*

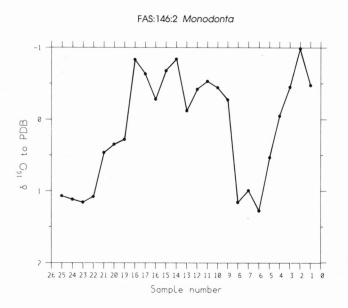

FAS:148:1 *Monodonta*

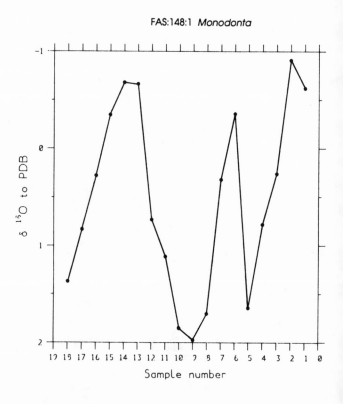

FAS:151:1 *Cerithium*

FAS:151:1 *Monodonta*

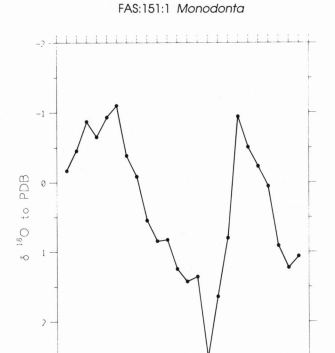

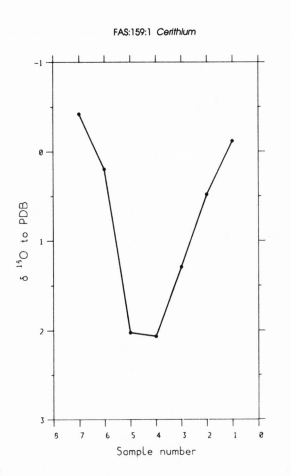

FAS:159:1 *Cerithium*

FAS:183:1 *Cerithium*

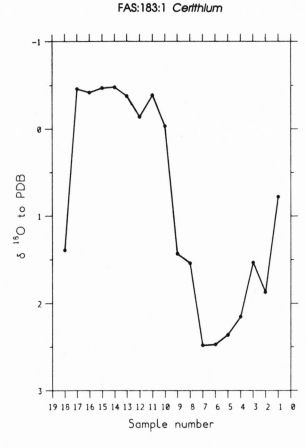

FAS:184:1 *Cerithium*

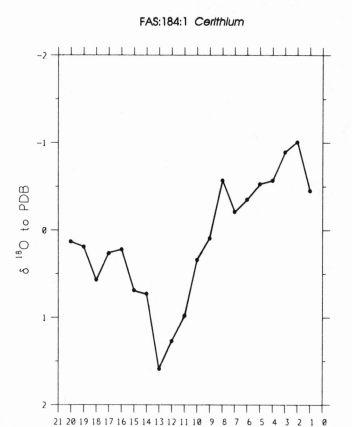

FAS:184:2 *Cerithium*

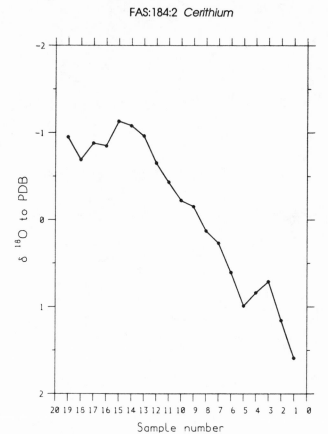

FAS:184:3 *Cerithium*

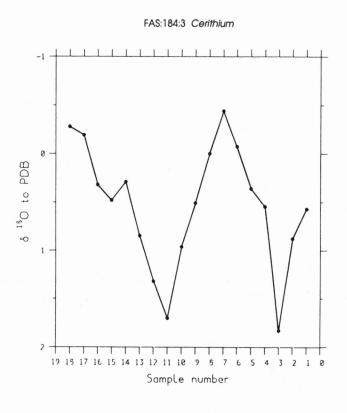

FAS:184:4 *Cerithium*

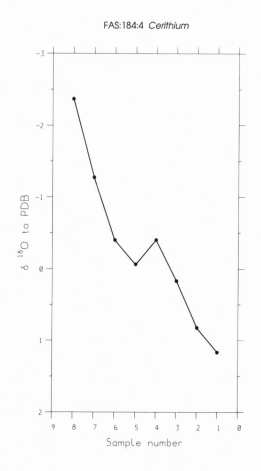

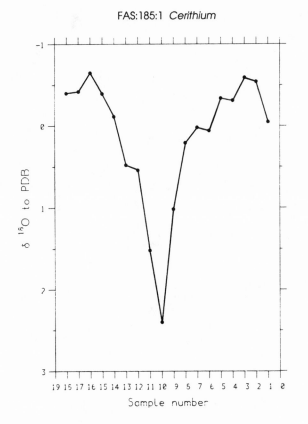

FAS:185:1 *Cerithium*

δ¹⁸O to PDB

Sample number

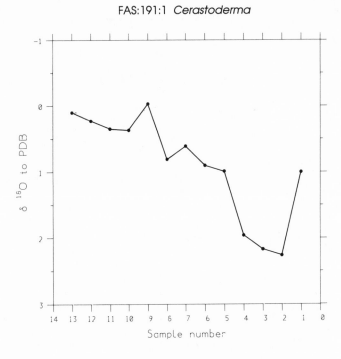

FAS:191:1 *Cerastoderma*

δ¹⁸O to PDB

Sample number

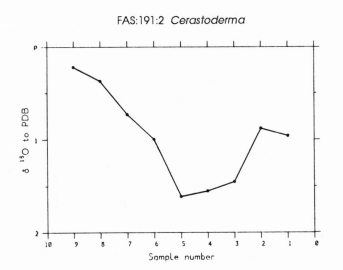

FAS:191:2 *Cerastoderma*

δ¹⁸O to PDB

Sample number

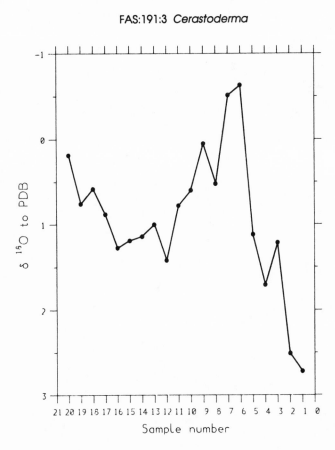

FAS:191:3 *Cerastoderma*

δ¹⁸O to PDB

Sample number

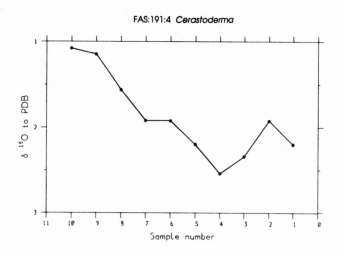

FAS:191:4 *Cerastoderma*

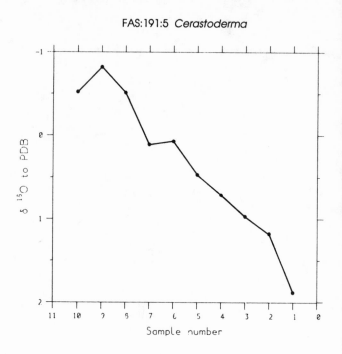

FAS:191:5 *Cerastoderma*

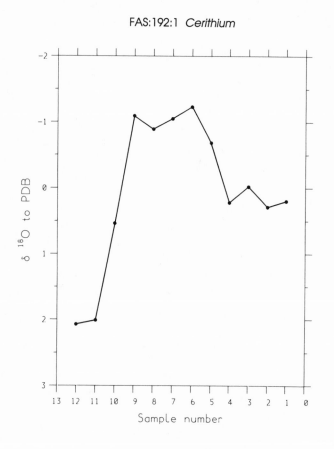

FAS:192:1 *Cerithium*

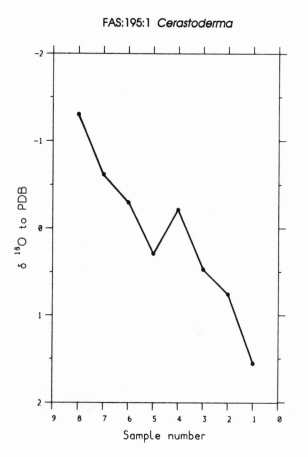

FAS:195:1 *Cerastoderma*

FAS:195:2 *Cerastoderma*

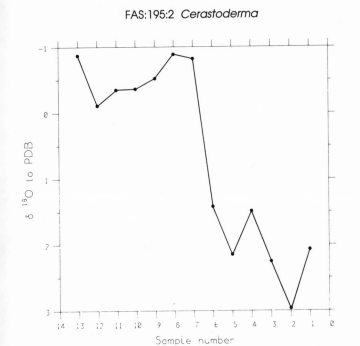

FAS:195:3 *Cerastoderma*

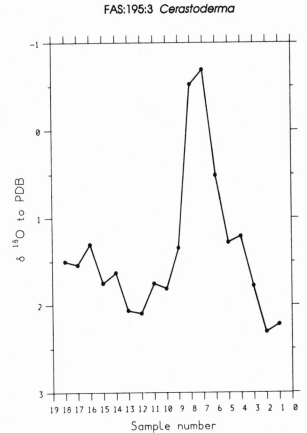

FAS:195:6 *Cerastoderma*

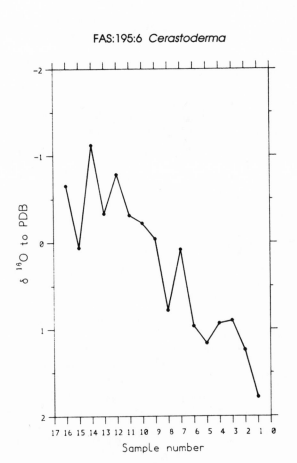

FAS:195:7 *Cerastoderma*

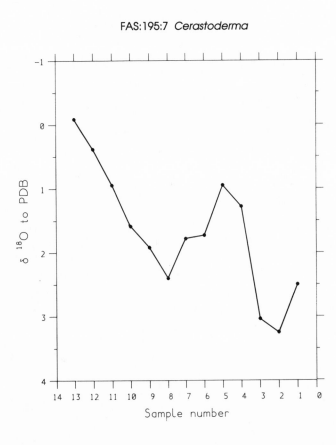

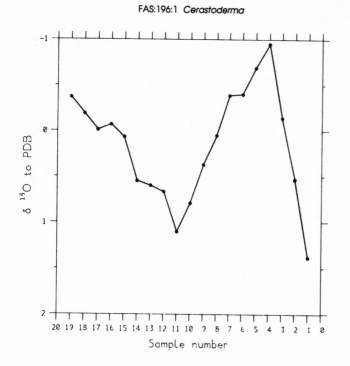

FAS:196:1 *Cerastoderma*

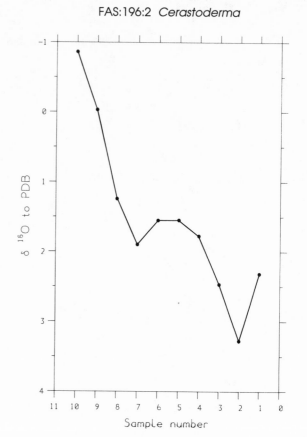

FAS:196:2 *Cerastoderma*

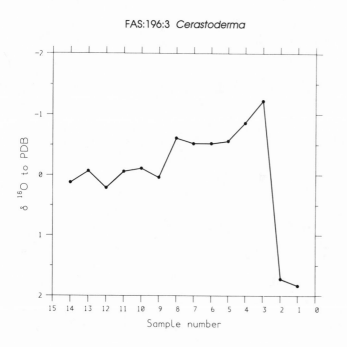

FAS:196:3 *Cerastoderma*

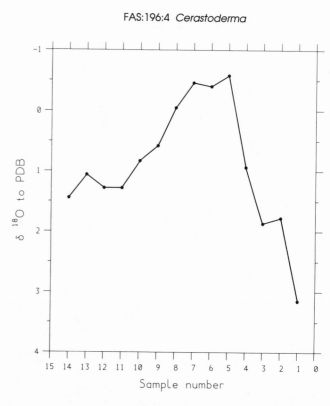

FAS:196:4 *Cerastoderma*

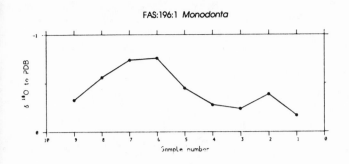

FAS:196:1 *Monodonta*

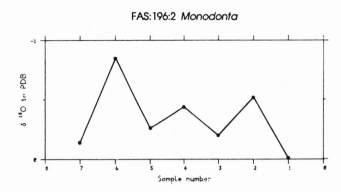

FAS:196:2 *Monodonta*

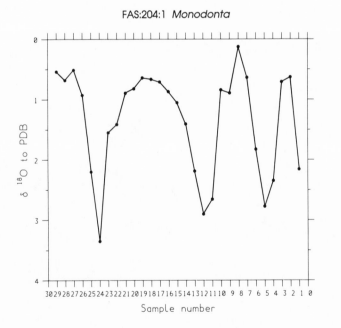

FAS:204:1 *Monodonta*

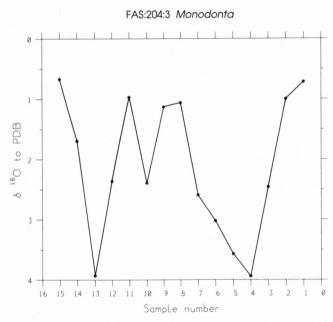

FAS:204:3 *Monodonta*

FAS:207:1 *Monodonta*

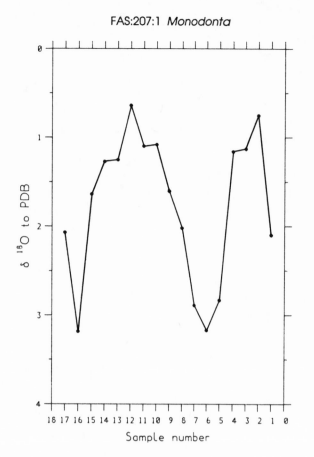

FAS:207:2 *Monodonta*

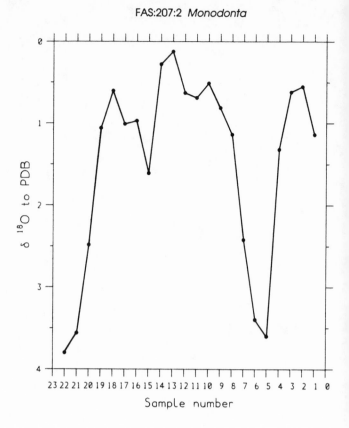

FAS:207:3 *Monodonta*

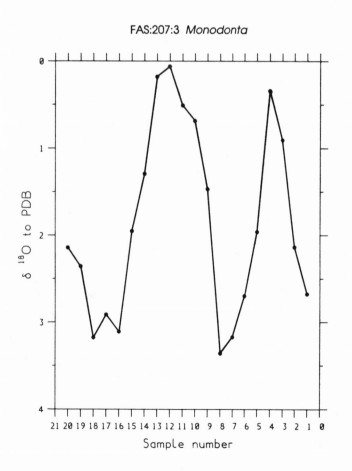

FAS:207:4 *Monodonta*

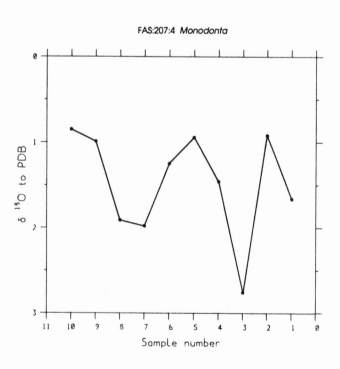

H1A:173:1 *Monodonta*

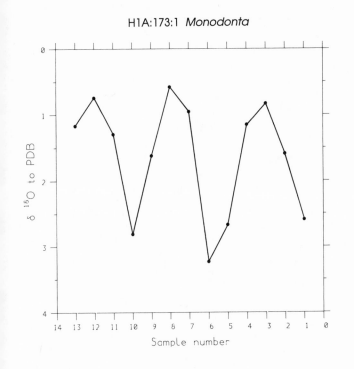

H1A:173:2 *Monodonta*

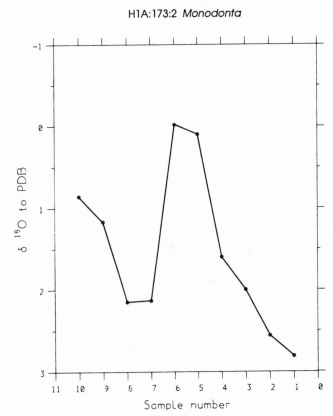

H1A:173:3 *Monodonta*

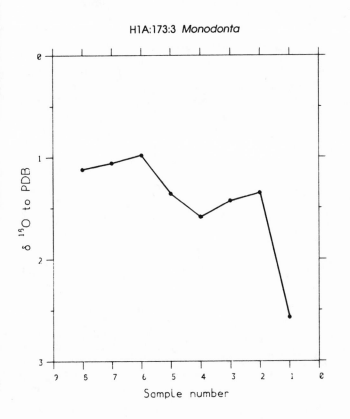

H1B:130:2 *Cerithium*

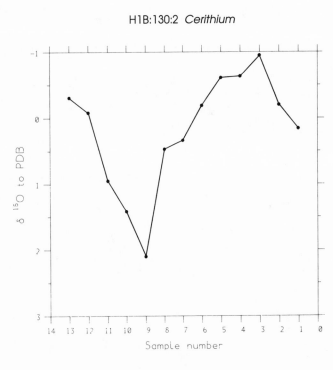

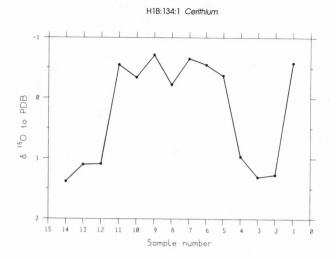

H1B:134:1 *Cerithium*

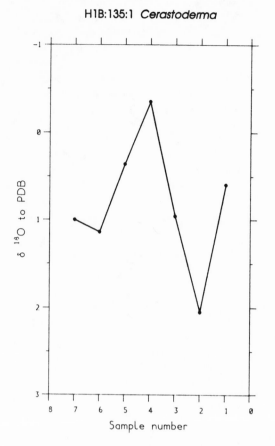

H1B:135:1 *Cerastoderma*

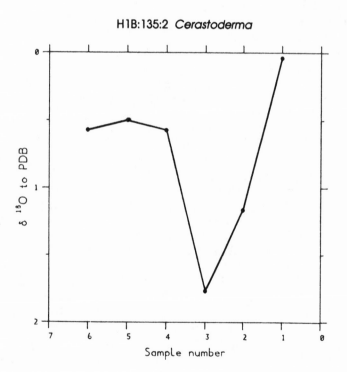

H1B:135:2 *Cerastoderma*

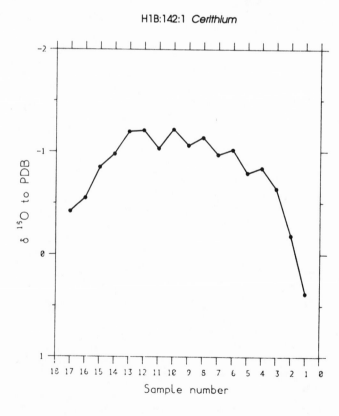

H1B:142:1 *Cerithium*

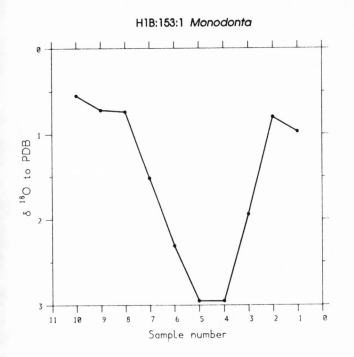

H1B:153:1 *Monodonta*

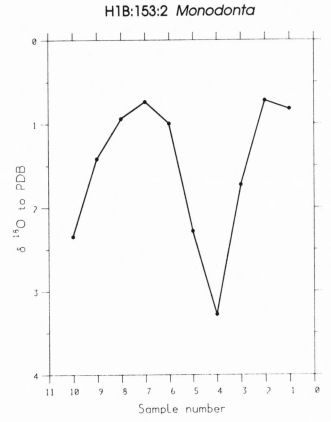

H1B:153:2 *Monodonta*

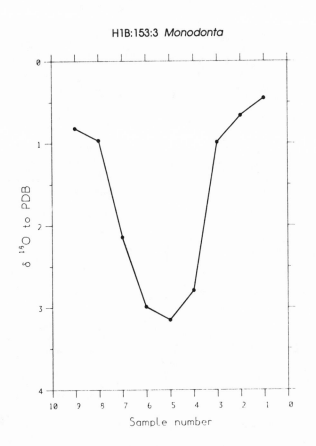

H1B:153:3 *Monodonta*

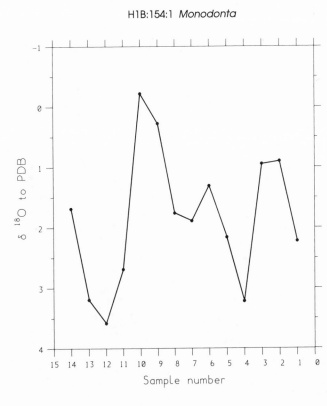

H1B:154:1 *Monodonta*

H1B:154:2 *Monodonta*

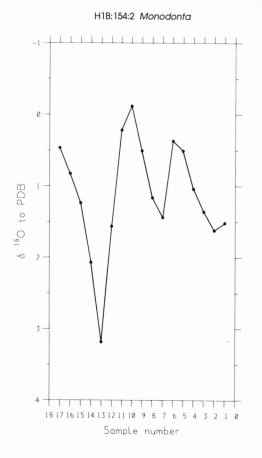

H1B:154:3 *Monodonta*

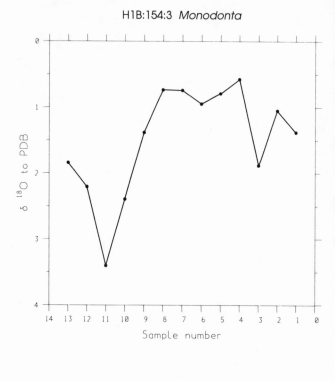

H1B:154:4 *Monodonta*

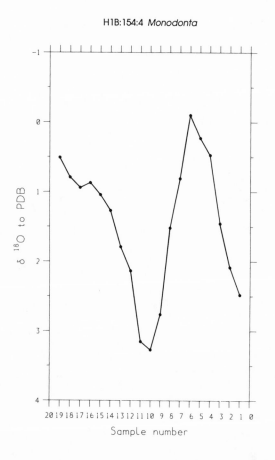

H1B:154:5 *Monodonta*

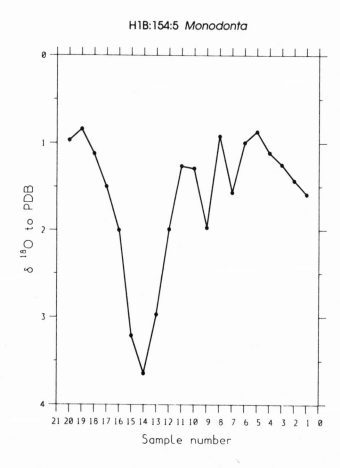

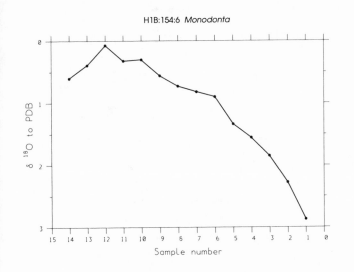

H1B:154:6 *Monodonta*

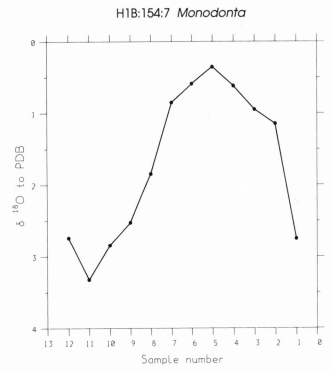

H1B:154:7 *Monodonta*

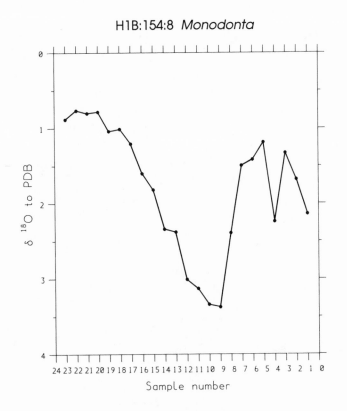

H1B:154:8 *Monodonta*

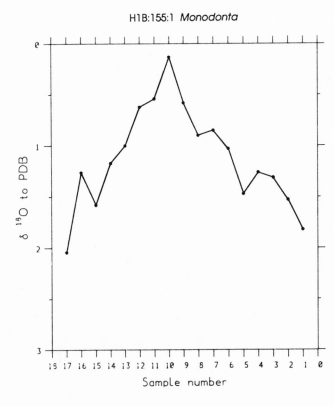

H1B:155:1 *Monodonta*

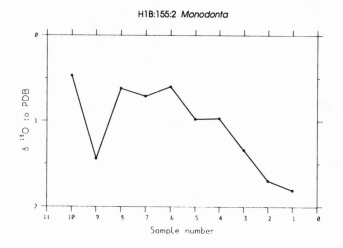

H1B:155:2 *Monodonta*

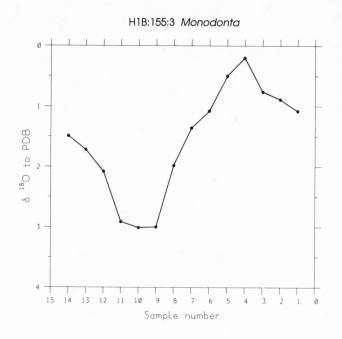

H1B:155:3 *Monodonta*

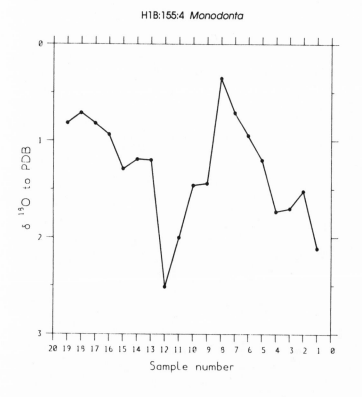

H1B:155:4 *Monodonta*

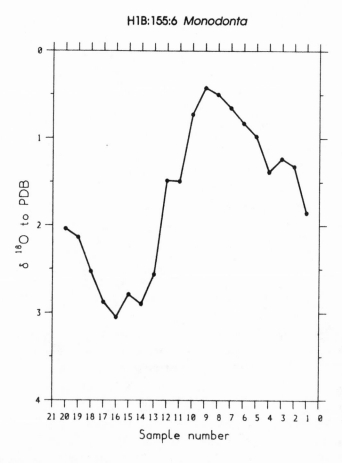

H1B:155:6 *Monodonta*

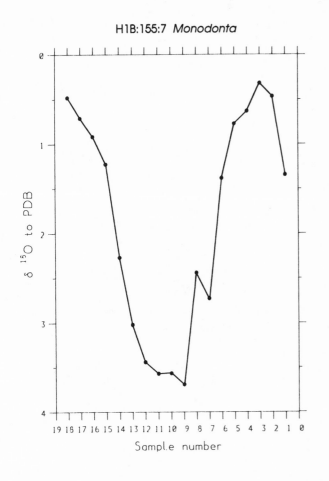

H1B:155:7 *Monodonta*

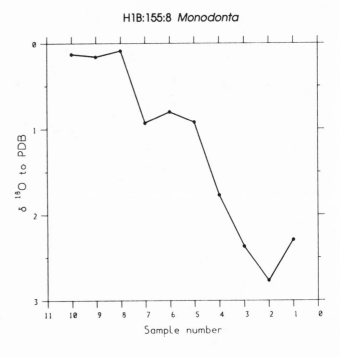

H1B:155:8 *Monodonta*

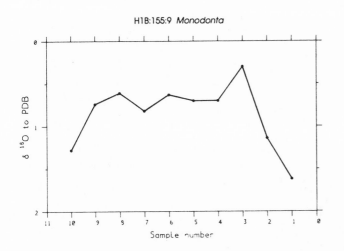

H1B:155:9 *Monodonta*

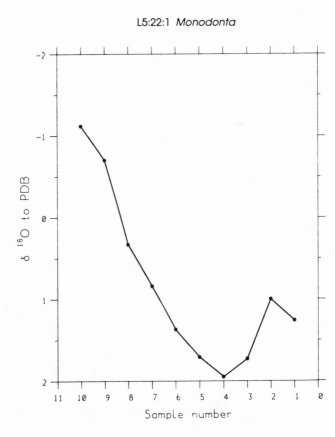

L5:22:1 *Monodonta*

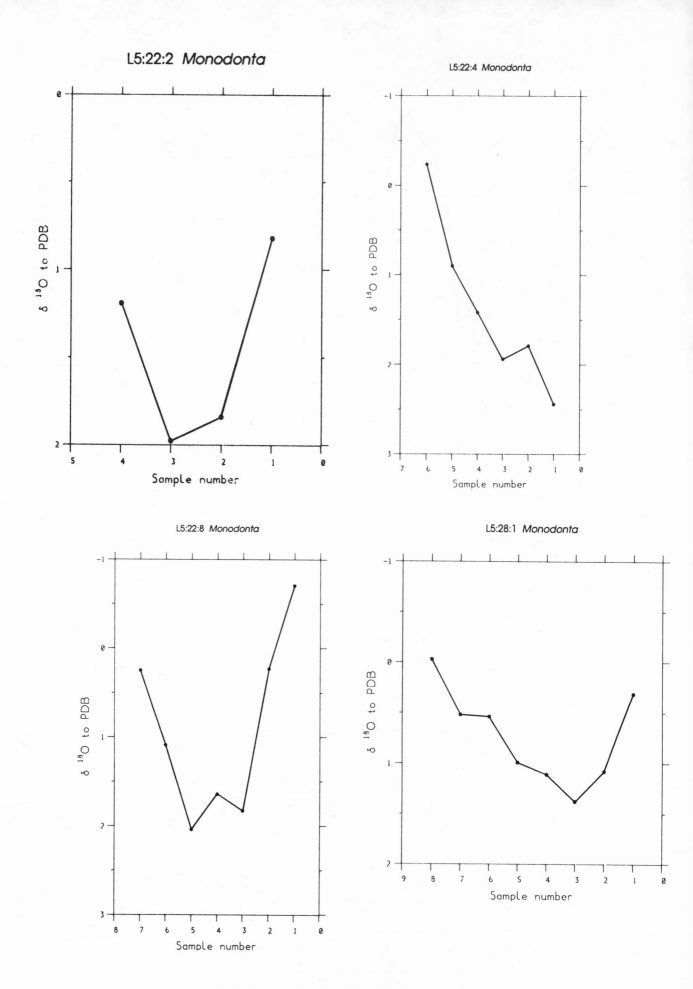

L5:28:3 *Monodonta*

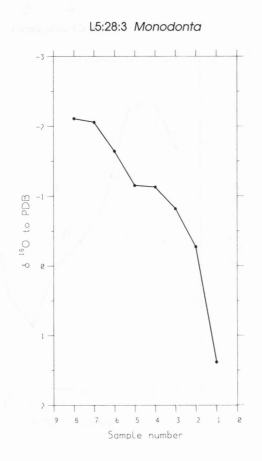

L5:36:1 *Cerastoderma*

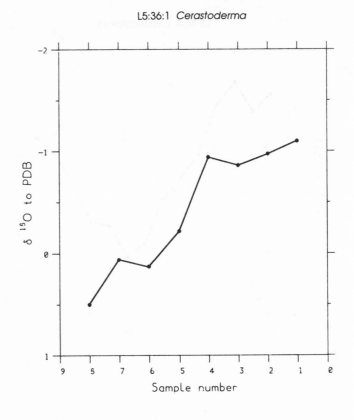

L5:36:2 *Cerastoderma*

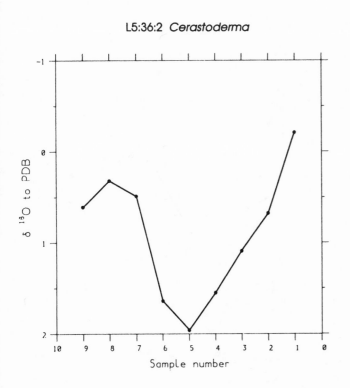

L5:36:3 *Cerastoderma*

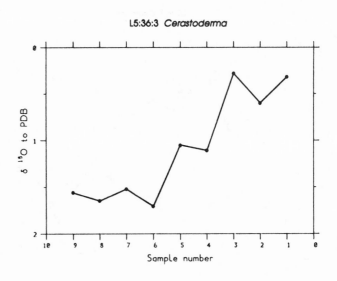

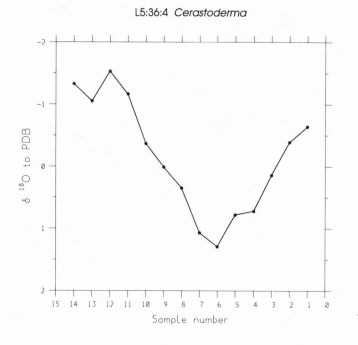

L5:36:4 *Cerastoderma*

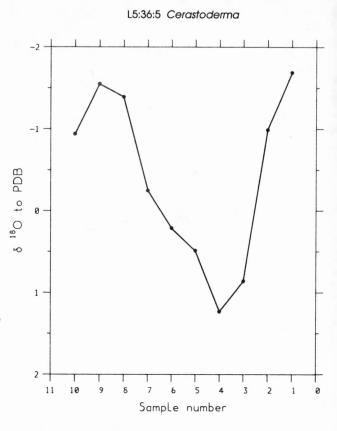

L5:36:5 *Cerastoderma*

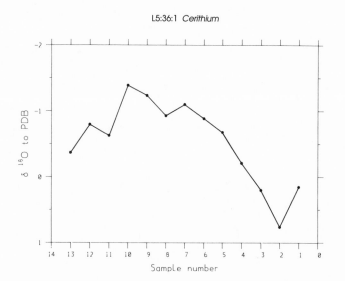

L5:36:1 *Cerithium*

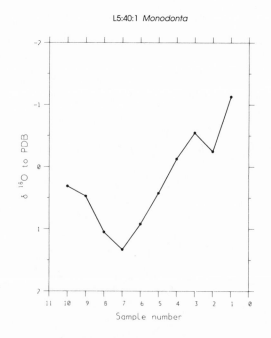

L5:40:1 *Monodonta*

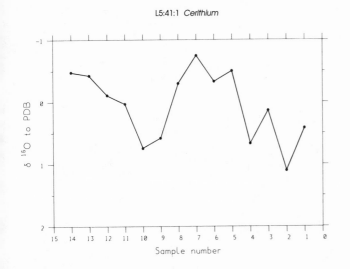

L5:41:1 *Cerithium*

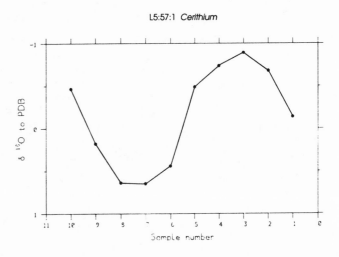

L5:57:1 *Cerithium*

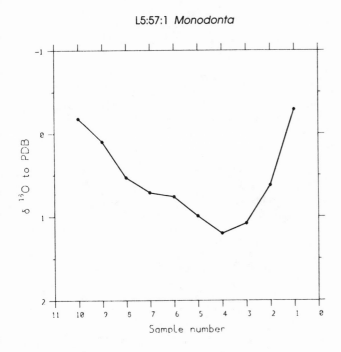

L5:57:1 *Monodonta*

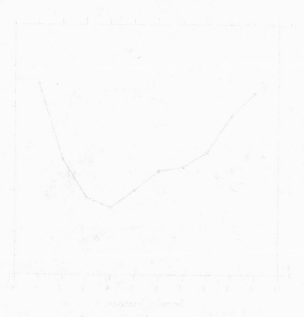

REFERENCES FOR PARTS I AND II

General (including seasonality and isotopic studies)

Bailey, G. N.
1975 The Role of Molluscs in Coastal Economies: The Results of Midden Analysis in Australia. *Journal of Archaeological Science* 2:45–62.

Bailey, G. N., M. R. Deith, and N. J. Shackleton
1983 Oxygen Isotope Analysis and Seasonality Determinations: Limits and Potential of a New Technique. *American Antiquity* 48:390–398.

Belluomini, G.
1981 Direct Aspartic Acid Racemization Dating of Human Bones from Archaeological Sites of Central Southern Italy. *Archaeometry* 23:125–137.

Binford, L. R.
1982 The Archaeology of Place. *Journal of Anthropological Archaeology* 1:5–31.

Boyden, C. R., and P. J. C. Russell
1972 The Distribution and Habitat Range of the Brackish Water Cockle (*Cardium* (*Cerastoderma*) *glaucum*) in the British Isles. *Journal of Animal Ecology* 41:719–734.

Chambers, M. R., and H. Milne
1979 Seasonal Variation in the Condition of Some Intertidal Invertebrates of the Ythan Estuary, Scotland. *Estuarine and Coastal Marine Science* 8:411–419.

Clark, J. G. D.
1954 *Excavations at Star Carr.* Cambridge University Press, Cambridge.

Clarke, D.
1976 Mesolithic Europe: The Economic Basis. In *Problems in Economic and Social Archaeology,* edited by G. de G. Sieveking, I. H. Longworth, and K. E. Wilson, pp. 449–481. Duckworth, London.

Davidson, A.
1972 *Mediterranean Seafood.* Penguin Books, London.

Davis, J. C.
1973 *Statistics and Data Analysis in Geology.* John Wiley, New York.

Deith, M. R.
1983a Seasonality of Shell Collecting, Determined by Oxygen Isotope Analysis of Marine Shells from Asturian Sites in Cantabria. In *Animals and Archaeology.* Vol. 2, *Shell Middens, Fishes and Birds,* edited by C. Grigson and J. Clutton-Brock, pp. 67–76. British Archaeological Reports, Oxford.

1983b Molluscan Calendars: The Use of Growth-line Analysis to Establish Seasonality of Shellfish Collection at the Mesolithic Site of Morton, Fife. *Journal of Archaeological Science* 10:423–440.

Forthcoming a Clams and Salmonberries. Interpreting Seasonality Data from Shells. In *The Mesolithic in Europe,* edited by C. Bonsall.

Deith, M. R.

1988a A Molluscan Perspective on the Role of Foraging in Neolithic Farming Economies. In *The Archaeology of Prehistoric Coastlines,* edited by G. N. Bailey and J. Parkington, pp. 116–124. Cambridge University Press, Cambridge.

1988b Shell Seasonality: An Appraisal of the Oxygen Isotope Technique. In *Recent Developments in Environmental Analysis in Old and New World Archaeology,* edited by R. Esmée Webb, pp. 37–49. British Archaeological Reports, Oxford.

Deith, M. R., and J. C. Shackleton

1988 The Contribution of Shells to Site Interpretation: Approaches to Shell Material from Franchthi Cave. In *Conceptual Issues in Environmental Archaeology,* edited by J. Bintliff, D. Davidson, and E. Grant, pp. 49–58. Edinburgh University Press, Edinburgh.

Dennell, R.

1983 *European Economic Prehistory: A New Approach.* Academic Press, London.

Diamant, S.

1979 A Short History of Archaeological Sieving at Franchthi Cave, Greece. *Journal of Field Archaeology* 6:203–217.

Emiliani, C., L. Cardini, T. Mayeda, C. B. M. McBurney, and E. Tongiorgi

1964 Palaeotemperature Analysis of Fossil Shells of Marine Mollusks (Food Refuse) from the Arene Candide Cave, Italy, and the Haua Fteah Cave, Cyrenaica. In *Isotopic and Cosmic Chemistry,* edited by H. Craig and S. L. Miller, pp. 133–156. North Holland Publishing Co., Amsterdam.

Flemming, N. C.

1968 Holocene Earth Movements and Eustatic Sea Level Change in the Peloponnese. *Nature* 217:1031–1032.

Forbes, M. H. C.

1976a Farming and Foraging in Prehistoric Greece: A Cultural Ecological Perspective. In *Regional Variation in Modern Greece and Cyprus: Toward a Perspective on the Ethnography of Greece,* edited by M. Dimen and E. Friedl, pp. 127–142. Annals of the New York Academy of Science, vol. 268.

1976b Gathering in the Argolid: A Subsistence Subsystem in a Greek Agricultural Community. In *Regional Variation in Modern Greece and Cyprus: Toward a Perspective on the Ethnography of Greece,* edited by M. Dimen and E. Friedl, pp. 251–264. Annals of the New York Academy of Science, vol. 268.

Gejvall, N.-G.

1969 *Lerna, a Preclassical Site in the Argolid: The Fauna.* American School of Classical Studies at Athens, Princeton.

Ghisotti, E. (editor)

1964 *Schede malacologiche del Mediterraneo.* Società Malacologica Italiana, Milan.

Gifford, J. A.

1983 Core Sampling of a Holocene Marine Sedimentary Sequence and Underlying Neolithic Cultural Material off Franchthi Cave, Greece. In *Quaternary Coastlines and Marine Archaeology,* edited by P. M. Masters and N. C. Flemming, pp. 269–281. Academic Press, London.

Hansen, J. M.

1978 The Earliest Seed Remains from Greece: Palaeolithic through Neolithic at Franchthi Cave. *Berichte der Deutsches Botanisches Gesellschaft* 91:39–46.

1980 *The Palaeoethnobotany of Franchthi Cave, Greece.* Ph.D. dissertation, University of Minnesota. University Microfilms, Ann Arbor.

Imbrie, J., and Tj. H. van Andel

1964 Vector Analysis of Heavy Mineral Data. *Bulletin, Geological Society of America* 75: 1131–1156.

Ivell, R.
1979   The Biology and Ecology of a Brackish Lagoon Bivalve, *Cerastoderma glaucum* Bruguière, in Lago Lungo, Italy. *Journal of Molluscan Studies* 45:364–382.

Jacobsen, T. W.
1969   Excavations at Porto Cheli and Vicinity, Preliminary Report, II: The Franchthi Cave, 1967–1968. *Hesperia* 38:343–381.
1973   Excavations in the Franchthi Cave, 1969–1971, Part I and Part II. *Hesperia* 42:45–88, 253–283.
1976   17,000 Years of Greek Prehistory. *Scientific American* 234:76–87.
1979   Excavations at Franchthi Cave, 1973–1974. *Arkaiologikon Deltion (Khronika)* 29:268–282.
1981   Franchthi Cave and the Beginning of Settled Village Life in Greece. *Hesperia* 50:303–319.
1984   Investigations at Franchthi Cave. *Arkhaiologikon Deltion (Khronika)* 31 (1976): 75–78.

Jacobsen, T. W., and W. R. Farrand
1987   *Franchthi Cave and Paralia: Maps, Plans and Sections.* Excavations at Franchthi Cave, Greece, T. W. Jacobsen, general editor. Indiana University Press, Bloomington and Indianapolis.

Jameson, M. H., C. N. Runnels, and Tj. H. van Andel
Forthcoming   *The Southern Argolid, a Greek Countryside from Prehistory to the Present Day.* Stanford University Press, Stanford.

Klovan, J. E., and J. Imbrie
1971   An Algorithm and Fortran IV Program for Large-scale Q-mode Factor Analysis. *Journal of the Association for Mathematical Geology* 3:1–37.

Koike, H.
1979   Seasonal Dating and the Valve-pairing Technique in Shell Midden Analysis. *Journal of Archaeological Science* 6:63–64.
1980   *Seasonal Dating by Growth-line Counting of the Clam, Meretrix lusoria; Toward a Reconstruction of Prehistoric Shell Collecting Activities in Japan.* Bulletin of the University Museum, University of Tokyo, No. 18. University of Tokyo, Tokyo.

Kutzbach, J. E.
1981   Monsoon Climate of the Early Holocene: Climate Experiment With the Earth's Orbital Parameters for 9,000 Years Ago. *Science* 214:59–61.

Lange, M., and F. B. Hora
1965   *Mushrooms and Toadstools.* 2nd ed. Collins, London.

Meehan, B.
1977   Man Does Not Live by Calories Alone: The Role of Shellfish in a Coastal Cuisine. In *Sunda and Sahul: Prehistoric Studies in Southeast Asia, Melanesia and Australia,* edited by J. Allen, J. Golson, and R. Jones, pp. 493–531. Academic Press, London.
1982   *Shell Bed to Shell Midden.* Australian Institute of Aboriginal Studies, Canberra ACT.

Montero Agüera, I.
1971   *Moluscos bivalves españoles.* Anales de la Universidad Hispalense de Sevilla, Serie Veterinaria 5. University of Seville, Seville.

Morton, J. E.
1960   The Habits of *Cyclope neritea,* a Style-bearing Stenoglossan Gastropod. *Proceedings of the Malacological Society* 34:96–105.

Palombi, A., and M. Santarelli
1969   *Gli animali commestibili dei mari d'Italia.* Ulrico Hoepli, Milan.

Payne, S.
1972   Partial Recovery and Sample Bias: The Results of Some Sieving Experiments. In *Papers in Economic Archaeology,* edited by E. S. Higgs, pp. 49–64. Cambridge University Press, Cambridge.

Payne, S.

1975 Faunal Change at Franchthi Cave from 20,000 B.C. to 3,000 B.C. In *Archaeozoological Studies,* edited by A.T. Clason, pp. 120–131. Elsevier, New York and Amsterdam.

Perlès, C.

Forthcoming *Les industries lithiques taillées de Franchthi.* Tome II, *Les industries du Mésolithique et du Néolithique initial.* Excavations at Franchthi Cave, Greece, fasc. 5, T. W. Jacobsen, general editor. Indiana University Press, Bloomington and Indianapolis.

Reese, D. S.

1978 Molluscs from Archaeological Sites in Cyprus: "Kastros," Cape St. Andreas, Cyprus, and other Pre-Bronze Age Mediterranean Sites. *Fisheries Bulletin* 5:3–112. Nicosia: Department of Fisheries, Ministry of Agriculture and Natural Resources.

Régis, M.-B.

1972 Etude comparée de la croissance des Monodontes (Gastéropodes Prosobranches) en Manche et le long des côtes Atlantiques et Méditerranéennes Françaises. In *Proceedings of the Fifth European Marine Biological Symposium,* edited by B. Battaglia, pp. 259–267. Piccin Editore, Padova.

Rowley-Conwy, P.

1981 Mesolithic Danish Bacon: Permanent and Temporary Sites in the Danish Mesolithic. In *Economic Archaeology: Towards an Integration of Ecological and Social Approaches,* edited by A. Sheridan and G. Bailey, pp. 51–55. British Archaeological Reports, International Series 96, Oxford.

Russell, P. J. C.

1971 A Reappraisal of the Geographical Distributions of the Cockles, *Cardium edule* L. and *C. glaucum* Bruguière. *Journal of Conchology* 27:225–234.

Schaeffer, M. C.

1976 An Attribute Analysis of Franchthi Ornaments Designed for Data Bank Storage and Computer Utilization. *Journal of Field Archaeology* 3:118.

1977 *An Attribute Analysis and Formal Typology of the Ornaments from Franchthi Cave, Greece.* Unpublished M.A. thesis, Department of Anthropology, Indiana University, Bloomington.

Schifano, G., and P. Censi

1983 Oxygen Isotope Composition and Rate of Growth of *Patella coerulea, Monodonta turbinata* and *M. articulata* Shells from the Western Coast of Sicily. *Palaeogeography, Palaeoclimatology, Palaeoecology* 42:305–311.

Shackleton, J. C., and Tj. H. van Andel

1980 Prehistoric Shell Assemblages from Franchthi Cave and Evolution of the Adjacent Coastal Zone. *Nature* 288:357–359.

1986 Prehistoric Shore Environments, Shellfish Availability, and Shellfish Gathering at Franchthi Cave, Greece. *Geoarchaeology* 1:127–143.

Shackleton, N. J.

1968 Appendix IX. The Mollusca, the Crustacea, the Echinodermata. In *Excavations at Saliagos near Antiparos,* edited by J. D. Evans and Colin Renfrew, pp. 122–138. Thames and Hudson, London.

1969 Appendix I: Preliminary Observations on the Marine Shells. In Excavations at Porto Cheli and Vicinity, Preliminary Report, II: The Franchthi Cave, 1967–1968, by T. W. Jacobsen. *Hesperia* 38:379–380.

1973 Oxygen Isotope Analysis as a Means of Determining Season of Occupation of Prehistoric Midden Sites. *Archaeometry* 15:133–141.

1974 Oxygen Isotopic Demonstration of Winter Seasonal Occupation. In Results of Recent Investigations at Tamar Hat, by E. C. Saxon. *Libyca* 22:69–70.

Sordinas, A.

1969   Investigations of the Prehistory of Corfu during 1964–1966. *Balkan Studies* 10:393–424.

van Andel, Tj. H., T. W. Jacobsen, J. B. Jolly, and N. Lianos

1980   Late Quaternary History of the Coastal Zone near Franchthi Cave, Southern Argolid, Greece. *Journal of Field Archaeology* 7:389–402.

van Andel, Tj. H., and N. Lianos

1983   Prehistoric and Historic Shorelines of the Southern Argolid Peninsula: A Subbottom Profiler Study. *Journal of Nautical Archaeology and Underwater Exploration* 12:303–324.

1984   High Resolution Seismic Reflection Profiles for the Reconstruction of Post-glacial Transgressive Shorelines: An Example from Greece. *Quaternary Research* 22:31–45.

van Andel, Tj. H., and J. C. Shackleton

1982   Late Paleolithic and Mesolithic Coastlines of Greece and the Aegean. *Journal of Field Archaeology* 9:445–454.

van Andel, Tj. H., and S. B. Sutton

1987   *Landscape and People of the Franchthi Region.* Excavations at Franchthi Cave, Greece, fasc. 2, T. W. Jacobsen, general editor. Indiana University Press, Bloomington and Indianapolis.

Vencl, S.

1959   Spondylové Šperky v Podunajském Neolitu. *Archeologické Rozheldy* 11:699–742.

Vickery, K. F.

1936   *Food in Early Greece.* Illinois Studies in the Social Sciences, Vol. 20, No. 3. Urbana, Illinois.

Vitelli, K. D.

1974   *The Greek Neolithic Patterned Urfirnis Ware from the Franchthi Cave and Lerna.* Ph.D. dissertation, University of Pennsylvania. University Microfilms, Ann Arbor.

Voigt, E. A.

1982   The Molluscan Fauna. In *The Middle Stone Age at Klasies River Mouth in South Africa,* edited by Ronald Singer and John Wymer, pp. 155–186. University of Chicago Press, Chicago.

Wilkinson, T. J., and S. T. Duhon

Forthcoming   *Franchthi Paralia: The Archaeological Sediments and Stratigraphy.* Excavations at Franchthi Cave, Greece, T. W. Jacobsen, general editor. Indiana University Press, Bloomington and Indianapolis.

Identification of Molluscs

d'Angelo, G., and S. Gargiullo

1978   *Guida alle conchiglie mediterranee, conoscerle cercarle collezionarle.* Fabbri Editori, Milan.

Bucquoy, E., P. Dautzenberg, and G. Dolfus

1882   *Les mollusques marins du Rousillon.* J. B. Baillière et Fils, Paris. Vol. I and II. Reprinted 1975.

Davidson, A.

1972   *Mediterranean Seafood.* Penguin Books, London.

Faber, G. L.

1883   *The Fisheries of the Adriatic and the Fish Thereof.* Quaritch, London.

Fischer, W. (editor)

1973   *FAO Species Identification Sheets for Fishery Purposes: Mediterranean and Black Sea (Fishing Area 37),* vol. 2. FAO, Rome.

Fischer-Piette, E.

1977   *Révision des Cardiidae.* Mémoires du Muséum National d'Histoire Naturelle, Nouvelle Série Zoologie, Vol. 101. Paris.

Fischer-Piette, E., and B. Metivier

　1971　*Révision des Tapetinae.* Mémoires du Muséum National d'Histoire Naturelle, Nouvelle Série Zoologie, Vol. 71. Paris.

Ghisotti, E. (editor)

　1964　*Schede malacologiche del Mediterraneo.* Società Malacologica Italiana, Milan.

Koroneos, J.

　1979　*Les mollusques de la Grèce.* Papadakis, Athens.

Locard, A.

　1886　*Catalogue des mollusques vivants de France: mollusques marins.* H. Georg, Lyon.

　1892　*Les coquilles marines des côtes de France.* Annales Societé Linnéenne de Lyon, Vol. 37 (1891). J. B. Braillière et Fils, Paris.

Montero Agüera, I.

　1971　*Moluscos bivalves españoles.* Anales de la Universidad Hispalense, Serie Veterinaria 5. University of Seville, Seville.

Nordsieck, F.

　1968　*Die europäischen Meeres-Gehäuseschnecken (Prosobranchia).* G. Fischer, Stuttgart.

　1969　*Die europäischen Meeresmuscheln (Bivalvia).* G. Fischer, Stuttgart.

Parenzan, P.

　1970　*Carta d'identità delle conchiglie del Mediterraneo, 1: Gasteropodi.* Bios Taras, Milan.

　1976　*Carta d'identità delle conchiglie del Mediterraneo, 2: (i) & (ii) Bivalvi.* Bios Taras, Milan.

　1976　*Carta d'identità delle conchiglie del Mediterraneo, bibliografia.* Bios Taras, Milan.

Piani, P.

　1980　Catalogo dei molluschi conchiferi viventi nel Mediterraneo. *Bollettino Malacologico* 16: 113–224.

Radwin, G. E., and A. d'Attilio

　1976　*Murex Shells of the World.* Stanford University Press, Stanford.

Riedl, R.

　1963　*Fauna und Flora der Adria.* Paul Parey, Hamburg.

Rossi, P., and G. Prelle

　1971　*Conchiglie mediterranee, fam. Trochidae-Gibbula.* Studio con chiave analitica.

Sakellariou, E. G.

　1957　Les Mollusques vivants du Golfe de Thessaloniki et leurs contributions à la stratigraphie. *Annales Geologiques des Pays Helléniques* 8:135–221.

Plates

Plate 1. Principal species of marine shells from Franchthi Cave: **a.** *Monodonta* cf. *turbinata* (Born), **b.** *Gibbula* cf. *divaricata* (L.), and **c.** *Patella* sp. Scale 1:1.

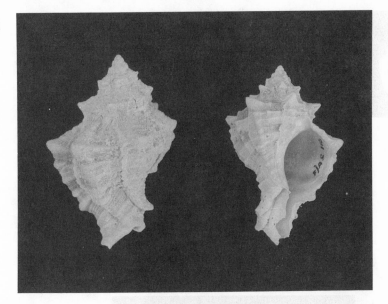

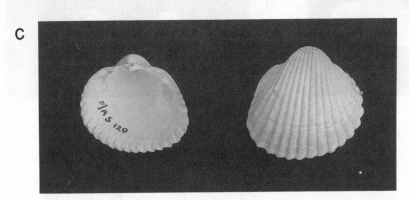

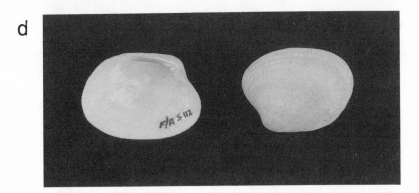

Plate 2. Principal species of marine shells from Franchthi Cave: **a.** *Murex trunculus* (L.), **b.** *Cerithium vulgatum* Bruguière, **c.** *Cerastoderma glaucum* Bruguière, and **d.** *Tapes decussatus* (L.). Scale 1:1.

Plate 3. Principal species of marine shells from Franchthi Cave: **a.** *Columbella rustica* (L.), **b.** *Donacilla cornea* (Poli), **c.** *Donax trunculus* L., and **d.** *Cyclope neritea* (L.). Scale 1:1.